WITH THE MASTER
AND
NOTHING ELSE

A Ladies' Bible Study of Colossians

By
Susan J. Heck

With the Master And Nothing Else
A Ladies' Bible Study of Colossians
By Susan J. Heck

©2022 Focus Publishing, Bemidji, Minnesota

Cover design by Amelia Schussman

ISBN 978-1-936141-64-7

Printed in the United States of America

Dedication

To Lois Burandt

who has exhibited a life of a godly woman

who needs nothing but the Master.

Endorsements

I love the book of Colossians and I love Susan Heck's book/Bible study on Colossians. She writes with such warmth and clarity, and weaves Scriptures together from all over the Bible. Her amazing depth of Scripture memory is also obvious throughout this study. Susan has a very high view of God, and she challenges the rest of us to have the same view. This study is deep but understandable. I personally will recommend it to individual ladies and for groups of ladies undertaking a Bible study. In Colossians, Paul wrote that in Christ are hidden all the treasurers of wisdom and knowledge. Do this study and you will know what that means.

Martha Peace
Biblical Counselor and author of *The Excellent Wife*

Truly there is nothing new under the sun. Just as Paul faced and confronted the threat of Gnosticism in the church at Colossae, we too face the very real and present danger of higher knowledge infiltrating the purity of the gospel in ours. With theological prowess, Christ-centered teaching, and heart penetrating application, my dear friend Susan's study of Colossians will arm you to guard against these destructive heresies infecting both the church and your personal devotion. Sit and study with Susan as you delve deeply into the word so that you may be a woman (as she is) who exemplifies what it is to live With the Master and Nothing Else.

Erin Coates, Pastor's Wife of James Coates,
Grace Life Church in Alberta, Canada

From the overflow of godly wisdom gained through decades of memorizing and studying the Scriptures, Susan Heck takes her students through methodical, detailed, and careful study of God's Word. Within the pages of this volume, Susan helps us to see with crystal clarity the absolute sufficiency of Christ for our salvation and our sanctification. Truly, we need the Master—and nothing else!

Andrea Heck, Pastor's Wife of Charles Heck, Wichita Bible Church in Wichita, Kansas

Table of Contents

Short Note of Introduction

The reality of With the Master and Nothing Else has been ever so true in light of the recent passing of my husband Douglas Heck. Do we as God's children really need anything else but Him alone? Is He truly enough? Paul, the apostle, sets forth Christ as pre-eminent. He is above all and by Him everything is held together. Because of this truth, we need nothing else; we avoid all false teaching, we put off sin and put on righteousness; and we share the good news with lost mankind.

Chapter 1

Introduction to Colossians

Colossians 1:1-2

More than 43 years ago I met a man who would become my husband. He was an unusual young man with a devotion to God unlike any man I'd ever met. I thought he was some kind of special—and he was! It wasn't too long after we met and began dating that he asked me if I was memorizing Scripture. I replied by telling him I had memorized a few verses here and there. He replied by asking me if I'd ever memorized a book of the Bible. "A *book* of the Bible?" I asked. (What I was really thinking was, "Are you *crazy*?!") But he challenged me by convincing me that it wasn't that hard. ("I bet!" I thought.) And because I was so crazy about him, and did not want to disappoint him, I agreed to give it a try. He suggested that I start by memorizing the Epistle to the Colossians. He convinced me that it was an easy book to memorize and that it would be a good place for me to begin. So, I began memorizing Colossians by using his memorization method—and I completed it. You can see why to this day the Epistle to the Colossians holds special memories for me. Not only is it the first book of the Bible that I memorized, but I've also had it in my mind and in my heart for all these years. It was the tool God used to whet my appetite to memorize His precious Word.

Colossians is a wonderful epistle with only four chapters, but they are four very powerful and very rich chapters! It is an epistle that was as relevant to the church at Colossae as it is relevant for the church of the 21st century. The heretical teaching that was going on in the church at Colossae is the same teaching going on in our churches today—the heretical teaching of Gnosticism. As I travel around and speak to various women, I am deeply saddened to see so much heretical teaching going on in our churches. We are hearing many of the same false teachings today that faced the church at Colossae, and we would do well to equip ourselves with the truth, so that we can face adversity, discern false teaching, be equipped to answer every man and woman, and arm our children and grandchildren with the truth. My friend, it is time for us to grow up and become women of The Book who reject the nonsense of Gnostic teaching. It is time for the churches in America to discern what is happening in the church of Jesus Christ.

Before we cover the first two verses of Paul's letter to the Colossians, it is essential that we understand the circumstances in which the book was written.

The first question we should ask as we approach the Epistle to the Colossians is this: *Who wrote the Epistle to the Colossians?* Colossians was written by the Holy Spirit through the Apostle Paul (see 1:1; 1:23; 4:18). It was delivered by Tychicus, as is evident from 4:7-8. The sister epistle of Colossians, Paul's Epistle to the Ephesians, was also sent by Tychicus, according to Ephesians 6:21-22.

The second question we need to ask is: *When did Paul write Colossians?* Paul wrote this epistle around A.D. 60-62.

Another question on our minds might be: *Where was Paul when he wrote Colossians?* He was the same place he was when he wrote Ephesians, Philemon, and Philippians; he was in Rome, but he was in prison. These four letters are known as the prison epistles. Within the book of Colossians, we find hints of Paul's imprisonment in 1:24, where he mentions rejoicing in his sufferings for the Colossians, and then again in 4:18, where he tells them to remember his bonds. Paul wrote Philemon about the same time as he wrote Colossians. According to 2:1, more than likely, Paul had never visited the church at Colossae. If this is indeed true, then the church may have been founded by Epaphras, who is mentioned in 1:7 and again in 4:12-13. Epaphras was likely converted during Paul's three-year ministry in Ephesus. Some scholars, however, think that Paul might have at some point been in Colossae and that the "many" mentioned in 2:1

is a reference to those who had not yet seen him. The reason for this is because Acts 19:10 says that "all who lived in the province of Asia heard the word of the Lord" and Asia would include the city of Colossae. If it is true that Paul spent some time in Colossae, then this would have occurred during Paul's third missionary journey.

Paul makes mention of two other cities, Hierapolis and Laodicea, in 4:13. Along with Colossae, these three were all originally Phrygian cities. If you can stop and locate Phrygia on a Bible map, it might help you in understanding the region at that time. When we consider how close these cities are to one another geographically, we can come to the conclusion that the dangerous heresy of Gnosticism had likely infiltrated all three of these cities.

Colossae was located about 100 miles east of Ephesus alongside the Lycus River. The city likely got its name from Colossus, a large statue of the sun god Helios. The region was rich in mineral deposits but also very beautiful and abundant in pine trees. For those of you who have lived in California, you'll be happy to know that Colossae was also known to have frequent earthquakes. (And, for us living in Oklahoma, we are now known for having more earthquakes than California!) In fact, soon after Paul wrote this epistle, Colossae, Laodicea, and Hierapolis were overwhelmed by a good size earthquake. Colossae was rebuilt at the time but was later destroyed in the 12th century, and only the remains of the city can be seen today.

Colossae was generally known as a pagan city. Its inhabitants were mainly Gentile, but a large group of Jews had settled there as well. Part of the reason the heresy of Gnosticism was able to creep into the church at Colossae was that both Jews and Gentiles had a significant presence in the city.

We've answered questions about who wrote the letter to the Colossians and where and when it was written, but we have not answered this question: *Why was it written?* Why did Paul feel compelled to write a letter to a church that he had perhaps never visited? Isn't that a little odd? Taking a look at Colossians 1:7-8, it appears that Epaphras had been to the church at Colossae and had come to visit Paul in prison, having brought word to him of how the church was faring. We will see in future lessons that Epaphras not only brought good news regarding the church, but also the bad news of a certain heresy that was creeping into the church. He was so concerned about this dangerous heresy threatening the church at Colossae that he traveled more than a thousand miles to Rome to visit Paul in prison. (There were no text messages, no social media, no cell phones, or even telegrams in those days!) More than likely, Epaphras would have traveled to Rome by foot since there were also no cars or planes or trains. The average traveler walked about 20 miles a day, so to travel 1000 miles at that pace would have taken about 50 days.

You might be wondering what kind of heresy could be so concerning that it would motivate Epaphras to travel that far under such challenging circumstances? Well, there were several heresies that had infected the church at Colossae, but each of them seemed to stem from one main heresy, the heresy of Gnosticism. You might be asking yourself, "What is *that*?" You may or may not be familiar with this term, but, my friend, we must understand the basics of this heresy because it is alive and well in the churches of our world today and we must be aware of it. (By the way, Gnosticism is also the heresy the apostle John deals with in 1 John.)

The word Gnosticism is derived from the Greek word gnosis, meaning knowledge. According to church history, the first Gnostic was Simon the Sorcerer, who is mentioned in Acts 8. It is said of him in Acts 8:9-11 that he claimed to be someone great, that he was someone "to whom they all gave heed, from the least to the greatest, saying 'This man is the great power of God.'" Simon claimed that he had some power that could reach up to God. This is where Gnosticism appears to have begun. The Gnostics were people who set themselves up above everyone else as those possessing superior knowledge. Gnosticism taught that only some people possessed special knowledge, who were "in the know" spiritually; that left others out of the loop, so to speak, as to these supposed secrets. If you ever did attain to this special knowledge, then you too could be among the special ones. These Gnostics thought they alone were in the know, and so they looked down upon others and led many astray. That's why Paul will clarify in Colossians 1:9-10 and 2:3 that knowledge comes from God and God alone, not from some special human who thinks they have secret revelation and understanding that the rest of us don't have.

It is important to understand that the Greeks loved knowledge. To them, the gospel message was too simplistic; Jesus was not enough, so they had to take Christ and add something to Him—Christ plus something else. To them it was not "With the Master and Nothing Else," but "With the Master and Something Else." They were in the know, they thought, so they had to come up with some strange ideas. They believed that anything created was evil and only what was spirit was good. They could not reconcile the idea of God being responsible for the creation of the world, because all that stuff was matter and it was evil. How could a holy God create a world that has sin in it? God was good, but matter, they said, was evil. Because the Gnostics claimed to have all that superior knowledge, they had to have an explanation for this. Are you ready for it? (I must tell you, these people in the know with their superior knowledge don't impress me at all with their great knowledge, but only reveal their ridiculous theology.) To reconcile these seemingly opposing concepts, the Gnostics argued that God's energy must have been limited and thwarted; in creation, God limited Himself. What they claimed happened was that there was a germination of God, and then another and another and so on. There were all these thousands of lesser gods, until there was one created so distant from Him that this god could touch evil and it was this god who created the world. Of course, this god was so far removed from "The God" that this little god became feebler; therefore, he could make contact with evil and then creation took place. Therefore, Paul corrects this idea in Colossians 1:15-17, when he says, "He is the image of the invisible God, the firstborn over all creation. For by Him all things were created that are in heaven and that are on earth, visible and invisible, whether thrones or dominions or principalities or powers. All things were created through Him and for Him."

This ridiculous thinking led the Gnostics into all sorts of other heresies. In their minds, Jesus, if He really was the Son of God, could not possibly have taken on a human body because the body, which is matter, is evil. To them, Jesus Christ, being human, was evil, because He was material. This is why Paul emphasizes in Colossians 1:21-22 that Jesus Christ reconciled us in the body of His flesh through death. The Gnostics denied that Jesus Christ was part of the Godhead; therefore, to them Jesus Christ died in appearance only, but not in reality. This is the reason Paul stresses in Colossians 2:9 that Jesus Christ dwelt in all the fullness of the Godhead bodily; He was God in the flesh. The Gnostics ignored the significance of the ministry, death, and resurrection of Jesus Christ as being real. They believed it was knowledge, not faith, that was necessary for salvation. This led them to deny the sufficiency of Christ. Paul confronts this error in 1:28, 2:3; 2:9-10 (do take time now to read these). Of course, when one denies the sufficiency of Christ, it leads one into all kinds of other heresy! The Gnostics were involved in much of the heresy we see in our day: legalism, mysticism, astrology, angel worship, and rigid asceticism (the doctrine that by abstinence and self-denial a person can train himself to be conformed to God's will). Paul confronts these ridiculous ideas in Colossians 2:16-23. This false belief fleshed itself out in things like abstaining from marriage and adhering to strict dietary restrictions. Some accepted marriage as necessary to preserve the race but regarded it as evil, and so they would adopt children. Other Gnostics thought that such a belief was too extreme because one simply cannot escape evil. So instead, they cultivated an indifference to the world of sense—they simply followed their impulses. This belief led to immoral living because, they claimed, the spirit was entirely separate from the body, therefore it was not responsible for the acts of the body. Because some did not believe in the resurrection of the body, they believed they could do whatever they wanted with their bodies. That's why when we get to Colossians 3, we'll see Paul's amazing list of put-offs and put-ons. It does matter how we live, even though some in

Colossae were teaching that it did not. My friend, some are teaching these same false ideas today! Let us not forget that without holiness no one will see the Lord!

In addition to all these errors, many Gnostics were involved in extreme forms of Judaism. They believed that circumcision was necessary for salvation, which is why Paul refutes this idea in Colossians 2:11 and 3:11. For many of them, their whole day was given over to religious exercises and exposition of the Scriptures. Next to God, Moses was held in highest esteem, and to blaspheme the name of Moses was punishable by death. But they went beyond the Mosaic Law. Marriage to them was an abomination; they drank no wine and ate no meat; they lived on bread and veggies; they refused to anoint their bodies with oil, and in many of those hot, arid countries this was necessary for life. Simply put, they condemned any natural cravings. Some Gnostics even worshiped the sun and even addressed their prayers to it, asking it to rise. They buried all polluting substances, so they would not insult the rays of the sun. Some even worshiped angels and got caught up in mystical experiences. Paul confronts these errors in Colossians 2:18-23.

Do you see now why Epaphras made the difficult journey from Colossae to Rome to inform the apostle Paul of the danger threatening the church? These weren't just minor issues; they were very serious errors, which had the potential to lead their souls to hell. I am sure, even as I've just given you a brief overview of the errors of Gnosticism, that you can see the many similarities to our own day. Oh, how I wish we had men and women in our day whose hearts, like Epaphras, burned for the errors in our churches! Clearly, the news Epaphras brought to Paul grieved Paul's heart, prompting him to write this little epistle to warn those who refused to recognize that Jesus Christ is supreme, that He is all-sufficient, and that we need nothing else. Paul reminds the Colossians, and us, that what we need is the Master and *nothing else*!

The last question we want to answer before we begin studying the first few verses of the Epistle to the Colossians is: *What is the theme of the book?* The theme of Colossians is the Preeminence of Christ, that is, the absolute supremacy and sufficiency of Jesus Christ as the Head of all creation and of all the Church. If there is a message that is needed in our day, it is the sufficiency of Christ. We are in trouble, my friend, and it is time for the church to awaken out of her complacency and get back to Christ alone, not Christ plus works, Christ plus knowledge, Christ plus philosophy, Christ plus dietary restrictions, Christ plus psychology, Christ plus a 12-step-program, Christ plus entertainment, Christ plus civil rights, or Christ plus political activism. We need the Master and nothing else! Oh, how I pray as we begin this study that you and I will awaken to the danger we are facing in our churches today, as well as the dangers we might be facing in our own personal lives. Is it possible that we have become Gnostic in our thinking and living? Is it possible that we have lost our distinctions from the world? Today, many churches are no longer teaching Christ as *the* answer, but Christ as *an* answer.

With this challenge in mind, let's begin our study by simply examining the first two verses of Colossians.

Colossians 1:1-2

> Paul, an apostle of Jesus Christ by the will of God, and Timothy our brother, ²To the saints and faithful brethren in Christ who are in Colossae: Grace to you and peace from God our Father and the Lord Jesus Christ.

Our brief outline for this introductory lesson will be two-fold; we'll learn about

> *The Author* (v 1)
> *The Audience* (v 2) of this brief letter

The Author

Colossians 1:1

> Paul, an apostle of Jesus Christ by the will of God, and Timothy
> our brother, (Colossians 1:1)

Paul begins writing by mentioning his name. By starting out with his own name, Paul is not a narcissist like so many in our day; rather, he is simply doing what most in the biblical world did when writing a letter. Most writers would begin a letter by letting their readers know who the letter was from. In the 21st century, we typically end our letters with our names. I'm inclined to think the biblical world had a better idea!

So, who is *Paul*? We don't have to read much further before we find out who he is. He is an *apostle*, but not just any apostle. Paul is *an apostle of Jesus Christ*, who was the very One the Gnostics were denying as deity. Paul wasn't one of the 12 disciples whom Jesus initially sent out as apostles, but he had seen the risen Christ, which was a qualification for being an apostle. Consider 1 Corinthians 9:1, where Paul writes: "Am I not an apostle? Am I not free? Have I not seen Jesus Christ our Lord? Are you not my work in the Lord?" And then again, in 1 Corinthians 15:3-9:

> For I delivered to you first of all that which I also received: that
> Christ died for our sins according to the Scriptures, and that
> He was buried, and that He rose again the third day according
> to the Scriptures, and that He was seen by Cephas, then by the
> twelve. After that He was seen by over five hundred brethren at
> once, of whom the greater part remain to the present, but some
> have fallen asleep. After that He was seen by James, then by
> all the apostles. Then last of all He was seen by me also, as by
> one born out of due time. For I am the least of the apostles, who
> am not worthy to be called an apostle, because I persecuted the
> church of God.

There are some today who try to tell us they are also apostles, but we should take them to these passages and ask them if they have personally seen the risen Christ—of course, some will tell you that they have! We once had a female visitor at one of our worship services who told me that she was an apostle; she even put a check in the offering, and it was inscribed on her check that she was an apostle. I remember the conversation I had with her, and she was definitely full of herself—Gnostic to the core!

The word *apostle* comes from the Greek word apostolos, and it means one sent with a message. Notice Paul says he is an apostle, not by his will, but *by the will of God*. God has a will and a purpose for each one of His children, and it was God's will that Paul be an apostle. I hope you know what God's will is for your life and the purpose for which He created you. Speaking of God, the word here for *God* is the Greek word Theos, which refers to Elohim, the one and only true God. This was not a lesser god or a little god, as the Gnostics taught, but the one and only true God!

Paul mentions one more person in his opening statement and that person is *Timothy*, whom Paul calls *our brother*. The word for *brother* is adelphos, which is a reference to a Christian brother. Timothy was either present with Paul or in the vicinity at the time this letter was written and wished to send his greetings along with Paul to the church at Colossae. Timothy was Paul's dear friend, his son in the faith. It was on Paul's second missionary journey that he had picked Timothy up and from that point on had spent much time training and discipling him. Two of Paul's last letters are addressed to Timothy, and in them Paul calls Timothy his own son in the faith and his dearly beloved son. In fact, in Philippians 2, Paul describes Timothy as the only one he found to be like-minded and the only one not seeking his own things. Timothy was a humble servant and Paul was fortunate to have such a one to serve alongside him in ministry. What a comfort Timothy must have been to Paul there in prison. In his hour of trial, Timothy was present with Paul, his dearly beloved friend. What a blessing for Paul! It's been said that friendship multiplies our joys and divides our grief—how especially true that is for the believer! May we all be Timothy to someone!

The Audience

Colossians 1:2

To the saints and faithful brethren in Christ who are in Colossae:
Grace to you and peace from God our Father and the Lord Jesus
Christ. (Colossians 1:2)

We have seen in verse 1 that Paul is the author of this letter, but
who is his audience? Verse 2 answers that question for us. Paul's
audience is *the saints and faithful brethren in Christ who are in
Colossae. Saints* is a term for holy ones, those who are set apart unto
God. *Faithful* describes *brethren* who are steadfast and unswerving
in their faith. It is not by chance that Paul uses these terms; there
were some in the Colossian church who were dangerously close to
becoming apostate, if not already, and Paul wants to make sure when
he speaks of saints that they understand that he is talking about the
true and steadfast saints. He is not writing to unbelievers caught
up in this heresy; he is writing to true believers, those who are, in
fact, *in Christ*. There is a warning to all of us here. It is important
that we get away from all heresy, keeping true to God's Word, lest
we become caught up in false teaching. We must be always on the
alert and not give false teachers an ear. Christ warns that in the last
days false Christs and prophets will increase and, if it were possible,
deceive even the elect (Matthew 24:24).

Paul then extends greetings of grace and peace. In fact, Paul opens
all 13 of his letters with this greeting. He knew that grace and
peace come only *from God our Father and the Lord Jesus Christ.
Grace* was a common Greek greeting, meaning God's unmerited
favor. *Peace* was a common Hebrew greeting, meaning a sense of
well-being which springs forth from the presence of God; it is a
promised rest, a ceasing from strife, which comes from knowing
God. Paul uses both greetings, the Greek and the Hebrew, in part
because Colossae was made up of both Greeks and Jews. But he
also did so because, as he states in 1 Corinthians 9:19-23, he made
himself servant unto all that he might gain the more. So, to the Jew

he became a Jew; to those under the law, as being himself under the law; to those without the law, as without law; to the weak, he became weak. And the reason for doing so, he says, was for the sake of the gospel, that he might save some. It was Paul's desire to reach all men with the gospel. To be clear, he isn't compromising when he says this; rather, he's demonstrating a willingness to defer to the preferences of others for the sake of the furtherance of the gospel.

It is also possible that Paul uses the Hebrew greeting here to reach those in the Colossian church who were caught up in Judaism. This again is another good principle for us to keep in mind as we are dealing with people. We need to connect with our audience—not compromise but connect. How best can we reach those caught up in heresy? As we continue in our study, we will see that Paul greets them warmly, thanks God for them, and prays for them. He praises them before he tries to help them see the danger of the heresy they're in. Some of us, by a wrong attitude, perhaps miss great opportunities to help those caught up in heresy; we rebuke before we patiently instruct those who oppose the truth. We must set a tone that is Christlike, that entails meekness, and that considers our own frailties!

Paul mentions that this grace and peace are *from God our Father and the Lord Jesus Christ*. Those at Colossae would need God's grace to help them turn from their error. And as they turned themselves back to Jesus Christ as the all-sufficient One, peace would be their happy result.

Summary

The Author (v 1) of the Epistle to the Colossians is Paul. *The Audience* (v 2) he intended this letter for was the saints and faithful brethren in Christ in the city of Colossae.

As we conclude this introductory lesson, I'd like to leave you with a challenge—a challenge to be faithful to do your lessons and to have a heart ready and eager to learn all that God has for you in this study. It will be quite a journey as we travel together through this little epistle. And perhaps you are like me; before I take a journey, I like to know what is going to take place. What are we going to see? What will we do? Let me take you on a sneak preview.

In chapter one of Colossians, we will consider Paul's prayer for the church at Colossae, which is one of the most beautiful prayers in all the Scriptures. I trust that as you study it, your prayer life will be deepened and enriched. We will also consider the blessing of having our sins forgiven, the deity of Jesus Christ, His redemptive work on the cross, and His preeminence. We also look at Paul's labor on behalf of the Colossian believers and answer the question: What does the work of the ministry look like?

In chapter two of Colossians, we will consider Paul's warnings about the dangers of philosophy, legalism, angel worship, asceticism, and general heresy. He will appeal to them because a believer is complete in Christ and Christ alone—He is all-sufficient.

In chapters one and two, Paul will lay a good doctrinal foundation for us; then, in chapters three and four, he will instruct us in how doctrine dictates our duty. He does this same thing in Ephesians, the sister epistle of Colossians; chapters 1-3 are focused on doctrine, while chapters 4-6 are focused on duty. Perhaps some of you would rather just skip over the doctrine in chapters 1 and 2 of Colossians and just get to the practical stuff. But, my friend, what you believe right now as you are reading this sentence will dictate how you live tomorrow when you get out of bed! What you believe dictates how you behave!

In chapter three of Colossians, Paul will instruct us to set our affections on things above and not on things of the earth, and he will give us ample motivation to do so. Chapter three is where we find the familiar put-off/put-on passage. We will ask and find answers to questions such as: What does the new man in Christ look like? What things should we be putting off and how do we do that? What characteristics should we be putting on? Understanding these things would be so needed for the church at Colossae, given that they were prone to legalism. Paul will remind them, and us, that it is not the outward stuff that manifests true Christianity, but the inward change of the heart—things like love, peace, meekness, longsuffering, and kindness. In this same chapter, we will also look at the wife's relationship to the husband, and the husband's relationship to the wife. We will see what the children's relationship to the parents should be and, likewise, the parents to the children. We will also study the master and slave relationship and what that should look like.

Finally, in chapter four of Colossians, we will again deal briefly with prayer; consider how our speech should be conducted, especially towards the lost; and consider Christian friendships as we look to those who were Paul's dearest friends.

It is going to be a great journey, and I am grateful to be able to travel it together with you as my traveling companions, and most of all with our great Guide, our Lord Jesus Christ. He is our Master and our friend—and we need nothing else!

Questions to Consider
Introduction to Colossians
Colossians 1:1-2

1. Locate the city of Colossae on a map, either online or in a Bible atlas or study Bible. (a) What cities and bodies of water are surrounding Colossae? (b) How far is Colossae from Rome?

2. What facts do you already know about Colossae?

3. Memorize Colossians 1:1.

4. (a) Read the entire book of Colossians. Write down at least one question that you have from each chapter. (b) Endeavor to try to find out the answer.

5. (a) Who wrote the book of Colossians? (b) What do you already know about the author?

6. (a) What is Gnosticism? (b) How do you see it manifested in our churches today? (c) Would you say you hold to any form of Gnosticism?

7. (a) What are you hoping to learn as you study the book of Colossians? (b) What areas of change would you like to see in your life as you study this book? (c) Come with a prayer request to share based on your answers in question 7.

Chapter 2

Commendations to the Church at Colossae
Colossians 1:3-8

Have you ever wondered what the churches of the New Testament looked like? Now, I don't mean have you ever wondered what kind of building they met in, or what the people looked like, or what kind of clothes they wore, but have you ever wondered what the church looked like in the sense of how they functioned as a body, or what were each of the churches' distinctives? In Revelation 2 and 3, we get a glimpse of what some of those churches were known for. The church of Ephesus was known for her patience; the church of Smyrna was known for her poverty and tribulation; the church of Pergamum was known for her faithfulness; the church of Thyatira was known for her love, service, faith, and patience; the church of Sardis was known for her believing remnant; the church of Philadelphia was known for her keeping of the Word and not denying the name of Christ; and the church of Laodicea was known for being lukewarm.

When we read Paul's letter to the Philippians, we see a warm, friendly church, one Paul says that he thanked God for every time he thought about them. He longed after them with an intense longing. The church at Thessalonica was a church Paul said he gave thanks for when he prayed to God for them. He said he remembered their work of faith, their labor of love, and their patience of hope in the Lord. But, like the church of Laodicea, not all the churches Paul ministered to were known for their good qualities. We can read the book of Galatians and barely get into the introduction and already notice that Paul was a little upset with them. He said that he marveled that they had so quickly left the grace of Christ for another gospel. He even called them "foolish Galatians"—a rather strong term—and asked them who had bewitched them. They had perverted the gospel and were in danger of being anathema, or accursed or destroyed. Also troubling, the church at Corinth was known for divisions, strife, and carnality among its members, even to the point of allowing incest to be tolerated. Paul told them that he stood in doubt of their souls and that they should examine themselves to see whether they were even in the faith!

But what about the church at Colossae? What were they known for? We already know from our introductory lesson that they were in danger of being led away by the heresy of Gnostism. But what good things were the Colossian believers known for? In the verses we'll study in this lesson, the apostle Paul has some commendations for the church at Colossae. What are they? Let's read and find out.

Colossians 1:3-8

> We give thanks to the God and Father of our Lord Jesus Christ, praying always for you, [4]since we heard of your faith in Christ Jesus and of your love for all the saints; [5]because of the hope which is laid up for you in heaven, of which you heard before in the word of the truth of the gospel, [6]which has come to you, as it has also in all the world, and is bringing forth fruit, as it is also among you since the day you heard and knew the grace of God in truth; [7]as you also learned from Epaphras, our dear fellow servant, who is a faithful minister of Christ on your behalf, [8]who also declared to us your love in the Spirit.

As we consider Paul's commendations of the church at Colossae, our outline for this lesson will include:

Paul's Thanks to Whom? (v 3)
Paul's Thanks for What? (vv 4-6)
Paul's Thanks for Whom? (vv 7-8)

In our introductory lesson, we discovered that the author of the book of Colossians was Paul and the audience of the book was the saints and faithful brethren in Christ in the ancient city of Colossae. We also considered some background information about the book, especially the heresy of Gnosticism.

As we move on to consider Paul's commendations of the church of Colossae, I think it merits pointing out that Paul commends the church at Colossae before he warns her. This is very much like what Jesus does in Revelation with the seven churches in Asia; He commends them before He rebukes them. I believe we can learn a principle from Christ and from Paul for when we are dealing with individuals or even churches—we, too, should commend before we rebuke. When we take time to do this it helps the rebuke to be received more readily. So, Paul begins by giving thanks for the good characteristics he sees in the church at Colossae. Who does he thank for these good things? Well, let's see in verse 3.

Paul's Thanks to Whom?

Colossians 1:3

> We give thanks to the God and Father of our Lord Jesus Christ, praying always for you (Colossians 1:3)

The first question we want to ask of this verse is: who does *we* refer to? We discovered in our last lesson, from verse 1, that Timothy was with Paul, either in prison or in the vicinity, as Paul was writing this letter, so this would be a reference to Paul and Timothy. Together as a ministry team they *give thanks*, and the person they give thanks to is *the God and Father of our Lord Jesus Christ*. Notice that Paul and Timothy don't thank the church at Colossae, nor do they commend themselves, but they thank the *Father*. They didn't high five each other and say, "Good job!" Neither did they try to build up the self-esteem of the church; rather, they gave the glory to *God*. Paul and Timothy knew that everything the Colossians had was because of God. They would not take the credit for any progress the church had made. Perhaps, lingering in their minds would be the awful judgment of God on Herod when he took glory that was not rightfully his (but the Lord's!) and was eaten by worms and died (Acts 12:20-23). We must remember, ladies, that all we have is because of what God has done and what He has given us.

The way Paul and Timothy express their thanks to God is through prayer. Do you also thank God for your church and for her qualities? Paul and Timothy did, and notice that they were also *praying always* for the church. What an encouragement that must have been to the church! I know I'm encouraged when others tell me that they thank God for me and pray for me. Now, when you first glance at this phrase, *praying always for you*, it may look if Paul and Timothy are always praying for them, but that would be impossible. In the Greek it reads like this: "We give thanks for you always and pray for you." In other words, when Paul and Timothy prayed for the Colossians, it was not without giving thanks. Ladies, once again, we can learn from these dear saints. When you pray for others, do you thank God for them as well? When I pray for others, I usually petition God on their behalf, and that is not a bad thing, but I confess that I do not thank God for others as much as I should. We would do well to get in the habit of being thankful people, especially in our prayers to God. Many times, we ask God to change this person and do such and such in that person's life, but we should have a heart of thanksgiving for those people God brings into our lives, even those we may find difficult. We might just find our attitudes changing toward those people as we thank God for them.

The word for *prayer* here has the idea of being definite and direct in prayer, with consciousness on the part of the one praying that he or she is talking face to face with God. I'm sure we all could testify to the fact that we often lack direction and clarity and exactness in our prayers. But we must also admit that many times we don't recognize that in our prayers we are face to face with the Almighty God. We will be talking more about prayer in the next few lessons, but for now, it might be a good idea for us to get on our knees and pray out loud to God in order to remind ourselves that we are indeed talking face to face with Almighty God. We easily become too casual in our praying. We easily treat God more like our "best bud" than the Almighty God who is to be revered. Paul and Timothy give thanks to God, and now we see what they give thanks for in verses 4-6.

Paul's Thanks for What?

Colossians 1:4-6

> since we heard of your faith in Christ Jesus and of your love for
> all the saints (Colossians 1:4)

We find in these verses Paul's commendations of the church at
Colossae and there are four of them.

1. *What is Paul's first commendation? The Colossian's faith!* Paul
and Timothy had *heard* of their *faith in Christ Jesus.* The Greek
word for *faith* is <u>pistis,</u> and it means to be persuaded that something
is true and to trust in it. But it involves more than intellectual assent;
it involves obedience as well, because at the root of the term pistis is
the term peitho, which means to obey. I may have faith that my desk
chair will hold me up—believing that it can hold me and trusting that
it will do so—but that does not mean I obey my desk chair. My dear
sister, the New Testament church, unlike the 21st century church,
knew nothing of a faith that came without obedience. Gnosticism
teaches that, but God certainly does not! Consider Acts 6:7: "Then
the word of God spread, and the number of the disciples multiplied
greatly in Jerusalem, and a great many of the priests were obedient
to the faith." Genuine faith is not spurious, as is seen in many of our
churches today. John is clear in 1 John 2:3 that one of the biggest
tests of genuine faith is obedience; we know we know Him if we
keep His commandments. It is not by chance that Paul commends
the Colossians for their faith first, because without faith there can
be no love, no hope, and no fruit-bearing, all which Paul goes on to
commend them for.

2. *Paul's second commendation is for their love for the saints.* In
other words, their love that was manifested toward all the saints.
The *love* Paul speaks of here is agape, which is not only a giving
to one who has desires but giving to one who has needs, like God
who sent His Son to die for us because we needed a Savior. It is a
love which impels a person to sacrifice oneself for the object of that

person's love. Notice their love was for *all the saints*, not a select few. The Gnostics were an elite group and certainly did not agape those who were not in the know. They were enamored with the elite who were in the know.

The preposition *for* (or *to* in KJV) is the Greek term eis, which means into; it communicates that the love the Colossians had reached into the very hearts of other saints. Ladies, that is an awesome kind of love that only God can give, one that can reach down into the very hearts of others. I hope that describes the love you have toward others. We would do well to remind ourselves often of what Jesus says in John 13:35, "By this all will know that you are My disciples, if you have love for one another," and of what John says in 1 John 3:14, "We know that we have passed from death to life, because we love the brethren. He who does not love his brother abides in death." There is yet another commendation of the church of Colossae in verse 5. Paul and Timothy were thankful for this one as well.

> because of the hope which is laid up for you in heaven, of which you heard before in the word of the truth of the gospel (Colossians 1:5)

3. *Paul's third commendation of the Colossians is for their hope.* This hope which was *laid up for them in heaven. Hope* is not a word that means wishful thinking; rather, it is a firm assurance. It is a fervent yearning and confident expectation and patient waiting for the fulfillment of God's promises; it is the desire of some good with the expectation of obtaining it. Paul describes this hope in Romans 8:24-25; he says, "For we were saved in this hope, but hope that is seen is not hope; for why does one still hope for what he sees? But if we hope for what we do not see, we eagerly wait for it with perseverance." The day I was writing this lesson, I was having lunch with a friend, and we were talking about this blessed hope. She looked at her watch and remarked that right now would be a good time for the rapture. The glory to come is our blessed hope! The Colossians were known for looking forward to this glory—are you?

This hope we possess is active, as is evident in the preposition *for*, which in this case comes from the Greek term dia. It is active; it is working in the believers at Colossae, energizing their faith and love to a greater intensity. It is a hope that is *laid up* for them or reserved for them *in heaven*. And, ladies, it is reserved for us as well; it awaits us. The idea of being stored up or laid up gives us the picture of being put out of the reach of all enemies and sorrows. Hallelujah! Peter reminds us of this in 1 Peter 1:3-4, where he writes, "Blessed be the God and Father of our Lord Jesus Christ, who according to His abundant mercy has begotten us again to a living hope through the resurrection of Jesus Christ from the dead to an inheritance incorruptible and undefiled and that does not fade away, reserved in heaven for you." Jesus reminds us in the Sermon on the Mount, in Mathew 6:20, to lay up treasure in heaven where nothing will corrupt it and no one will steal it.

How did the Colossians hear of such an incredible hope? The very same way you and I heard of the hope of heaven! They heard it *in the word of the truth of the gospel*. The Greek term for *word* is logos, and it refers to the spoken word. *Gospel* is euaggelizo, which means to evangelize. Notice that Paul says the *truth* of the gospel. This would be in contrast with the *false* gospel of the Gnostics. Paul seems to be reminding them here of the gospel, as though he's saying to them, "Don't you remember the change that occurred in you? The gospel needs nothing added to it! It is sufficient in itself—Christ plus nothing else!" Paul will remind them later, in Colossians 2:8-10, "Beware lest anyone cheat you through philosophy and empty deceit, according to the tradition of men, according to the basic principles of the world, and not according to Christ. For in Him dwells all the fullness of the Godhead bodily; and you are complete in Him, who is the head of all principality and power." There is yet one more commendation for the church mentioned in verse 6.

> which has come to you, as it has also in all the world, and is bringing forth fruit, as it is also among you since the day you heard and knew the grace of God in truth; (Colossians 1:6)

Paul begins this verse with an interesting phrase about the gospel. He says *which has come to you*, which means "is being alongside you." The idea is that the gospel has snuggled close to the Colossian believers, and they have taken it into their hearts. Isn't that what the gospel does in each of our lives? It gets right up in our heart and changes us. Praise be to God! And Paul adds *as it has in all the world*. Now, does this mean that the whole world had heard the gospel? No, because Jesus said in Matthew 24:14 that the "gospel of the kingdom will be preached in all the world as a witness to all the nations, and then the end will come." This obviously has not happened yet because we are all still here. What Paul is doing here is using hyperbole, as he often does in his epistles. The phrase *in all the world* is hyperbole. It is like Romans 1:8, where Paul says to the church at Rome that their faith is spoken of throughout the whole world. It would have been impossible in Paul's day for that to have happened. In our day, not so impossible with social media! Here in Colossians, Paul is using hyperbole to celebrate the gospel's dynamic power and its universality. Unlike the Gnostic foolishness, which was reserved for only a select few, Christ's good news is for all—the gospel is offered to the whole world.

4. Now, what happens when one hears the gospel, and it snuggles deep into his or her heart? Paul says it *brings forth fruit. This is his fourth commendation of the church at Colossae. They were known for fruit-bearing.* In fact, the Greek indicates that the gospel is a reproductive organism. It is not like a seed that grows a plant that in turn exhausts itself bearing fruit and then withers away. On the contrary, the external growth keeps pace with the reproductive energy. That fruit had been producing among the Colossian believers *since the day they heard* the gospel preached—and it was still being productive. This is a mark of genuine salvation. Jesus says in John 15:16, "You did not choose Me, but I chose you and appointed you that you should go and bear fruit, and that your fruit should remain, that whatever you ask the Father in My name He may give you." He also says in John 15:8, "By this My Father is glorified, that you bear much fruit; so you will be My disciples." God is glorified when we bear much fruit. According to Psalm 1, it is the godly man

that brings forth fruit, his leaf never withers and whatever he does prospers. Just like faith without obedience is not genuine faith, so faith without fruit—or works, as James would say—is dead (James 2:26).

Paul ends with a little phrase in verse 6: *and knew the grace of God in truth*. The Colossian believers had come to know the grace of God in all its truth in comparison to the false teaching of Gnosticism. *Grace* is God freely giving us the forgiveness of sin and eternal life that we do not deserve and cannot earn. God's grace is the only way that we are redeemed. Paul is clear about this in the sister epistle to this letter to the Colossians, the epistle to the Ephesians. Ephesians 2:8-9 states, "For by grace you have been saved through faith, and that not of yourselves; it is the gift of God, not of works, lest anyone should boast." So how did the Colossian's hear about this grace of God? Does one hear without a preacher? No, one doesn't, and that's why Paul and Timothy give thanks for a certain individual in verses 7 and 8.

Paul's Thanks for Whom?

Colossians 1:7-8

> as you also learned from Epaphras, our dear fellow servant, who is a faithful minister of Christ on your behalf (Colossians 1:7)

We learned in our last lesson that Epaphras was a native of the church in Colossae and probably the founder of the church, as well as being its pastor. Epaphras had taken the gospel of the grace of God to the Colossians. And Paul speaks well of him; in fact, he specifically mentions two things about him. First, Paul says that Epaphras was a *dear fellow servant*. I kind of like that term, dear fellow servant. (Maybe we should start calling each other that?) This would indicate that Paul and Timothy had a strong friendship with Epaphras. Second, Paul says that Epaphras was also a *faithful minister*. *Faithful* means he was worthy to be believed. *Minister* is the Greek word diakonos, which simply means a servant, a deacon, a minister. It comes from a Greek word which means in the dust laboring or running through dust. That's kind of interesting because Epaphras traveled through lots of dust from Colossae to Rome to get to Paul—1000 miles to be exact! Epaphras was not a lazy guy; he labored hard. He was faithful in his labor for the Lord. Paul makes that clear when he says Epaphras' labor was *of Christ*. That should be a motive for each of us when we are tempted to give up. We do what we do for the Lord. We are to be steadfast in it, always abounding in His work (1 Corinthians 15:58). Paul also writes in 1 Corinthians 4:1-2, "Let a man so consider us, as servants of Christ and stewards of the mysteries of God. Moreover, it is required in stewards that one be found faithful." One day, Lord willing, we will hear those words, "Well done, good and faithful servant; you have been faithful over a few things, I will make you ruler over many things. Enter into the joy of your lord" (Matthew 25:23).

Epaphras is also mentioned in Philemon 1:23 as Paul's fellow prisoner in Christ Jesus. Evidently, he spent some time in prison with Paul for the sake of the gospel. Many believe that Epaphras was martyred at Colossae. This is a man we don't hear much about, but what a legacy he left for us. He was faithful servant. And verse 8 gives us a glimpse into his faithful service by telling us what news Epaphras brought to Paul and Timothy regarding the church at Colossae.

who also declared to us your love in the Spirit. (Colossians 1:8)

Epaphras must have been impressed with the love the Colossians had for one another because this is the second time Paul mentions this about them (here, and in verse 4). The word here for *love* is the same as in verse four; it is agape. Again, that kind of love can only be produced supernaturally, by the Holy *Spirit*. Paul is clear in Galatians 5:22-23, "But the fruit of the Spirit is love, joy, peace, longsuffering, kindness, goodness, faithfulness, gentleness, self-control. Against such there is no law." Paul begins with love because it is the heading for the rest of the fruits. Love is preeminent and under it falls joy, peace, longsuffering, gentleness, goodness, faith, meekness, and self-control. Love from the Spirit manifests itself by loving the brethren. Apart from the Holy Spirit, there can be no genuine love. It is amazing that I love you and you love me. Apart from God, it could not be. (A side note: Did you notice that Paul mentions each part of the Trinity in his opening remarks? The Father is mentioned in verses 1, 2, 3, and 6. Jesus Christ is mentioned in verses 1, 2, 3, 4, and 7. And the Holy Spirit is mentioned in verse 8.)

We can learn from Epaphras that a true servant of Jesus Christ will focus on the good qualities of others, not the bad qualities. Love does not keep a record of things done wrong, according to 1 Corinthians 13, and it does not rejoice in iniquity. It might have been tempting for Epaphras to say something to Paul and Timothy like, "I am just not sure about these Colossian guys; they're getting caught up in all kinds of errors. Joseph is an unbelievable legalist, and you won't believe it, but Sarah thinks by denying her body certain things, she can gain favor with God. And then there's Steven, he has accepted that old doctrine that he has got to be circumcised to get to heaven, and now even though he's 50, he's going to be circumcised?! Can you believe it?!" But Epaphras doesn't do that. He first focuses on the things they were doing right. He commends them for the great faith they had, the incredible love they showed one other, the hope of heaven in their hearts, and their continual fruit-bearing.

Summary

To whom do Paul and Timothy give thanks regarding the Colossians (v 3)? They give thanks to God! When you think of your church family or other fellow believers, do you find yourself being thankful to God for them? Do you look for the good in them? Do you find things to be thankful for, especially regarding your local church? Our temptation is to complain and murmur, but God's people should be a thankful people and we should look for the good in others and in our churches.

For what do Paul and Timothy give thanks (vv 4-6)? They give thanks for four things they see in the Colossian believers: their faith, their hope, their love, and their fruit-bearing. If I were to ask you what four things you could commend your church for, what would they be?

For whom do Paul and Timothy give thanks (vv 7-8)? They give thanks to God for their dear friend and fellow minister Epaphras. What a testimony of a man who delivered the good news to the Colossians and was a faithful servant of God! Are you a faithful servant of God? Who are you reaching out to with the good news of the gospel?

As we think about the church of Colossae and the things for which they were commended, let's think about the churches we attend and the things for which our churches would be commended. What would Paul and Timothy and Epaphras say about the church you attend? If Paul were writing a letter to the church you attend, what would he commend it for? What do others say about the church you attend? What is the reputation of your church among those who are outside your church? Or, perhaps even more thought-provoking, what would Jesus say about the church you attend? For what would He commend it? What are its strengths? Its weaknesses? What dangers is it facing? In what ways is it being led astray?

The church at Colossae had some strengths and some weaknesses.

In this lesson we have seen their strengths, the things they were known for: their faith, their hope, their love, and their fruit-bearing. Their focus was upward, outward, forward, and onward. Their faith was demonstrated in their souls looking upward to God. Their love was shown in looking outward to the needs of others. Their hope was displayed in their looking forward to the future in heaven. Their fruit-bearing was manifested in moving onward in service to God and others. May God grant each of us the grace as individuals and as churches to be known for these four wonderful evidences of children who know the Master!

Questions to Consider

Colossians 1:3-8
Commendations of the Church at Colossae

1. (a) Read Colossians 1:1-8. What does the term *we* refer to in verses 3-8? (b) According to these verses what should happen when the gospel is proclaimed?

2. Memorize Colossians 1:3.

3. (a) Notice the beginnings of all of Paul's writings: Romans, 1 and 2 Corinthians, Galatians, Ephesians, Philippians, Colossians, 1 and 2 Thessalonians, 1 and 2 Timothy, Titus, Philemon and Hebrews. (There is debate among scholars as to who wrote Hebrews; I am of the persuasion that Paul wrote it, so I am including it here with his other letters.) (b) How many of these letters mention that Paul either prays for those he is writing to or that he is thankful for them? Which books are they? (c) How many of these letters do not mention these things? Which books are those? (d) What does this tell you about Paul? (e) What might it tell you about those churches, especially the churches that are not commended?

4. (a) According to Colossians 1:4-5, what things had Paul heard about the Colossian believers that convinced him that they were believers? (b) What similar New Testament passages come to mind when you read these verses?

5. (a) How does love manifest itself, according to John 13? (b) What are some practical ways that we as Christians should be showing love to the brethren?

6. (a) What are some of the things you are looking forward to in heaven? (b) How do these things give you hope as you walk through this life?

7. If Paul were writing a letter to the church you attend, for what things do you think he would commend your church?

8. Does your life truly demonstrate the love of Christ? How could it improve? Please write a prayer request that reflects your need in this area.

Chapter 3

Paul's Petitions for the Church at Colossae

Colossians 9-11

Almost 70 years ago a young missionary named Raymond
Edman staggered in from an Ecuadorian jungle, desperately
ill. "He'll be dead by morning," the doctor predicted. Edman's
wife dyed her wedding dress black, so it would be ready for
the funeral. (In the tropics funerals must be held immediately.)
However, thousands of miles away in Boston, Edman's friend,
Dr. Joseph Evans, interrupted a prayer meeting, saying, "I feel
we must pray for Ray Edman in Ecuador." The group prayed
earnestly, until finally Evans called out, "Praise the Lord! The
victory is won!" The rest is oft-repeated history: Raymond
Edman recovered, his wife's dress did not, and Dr. Edman went
on to become president of Wheaton College and to minister for
40 years![1]

This true and beautiful story affirms the power of intercessory
prayer. Do you believe in the power of prayer? Paul did! He prayed
often for the churches for whom he was burdened. How did he
pray for them? What elements were included in his prayers? Paul's
prayers for each one of the churches were rich, not mundane and
rote, like some of ours. (I remember one from a book I used to read
to my children when they were little that went something like this:
"God sees the moon and God sees me, God bless the moon and God
bless me! Amen!") Paul's prayers contained requests that pertained
to each of the churches' specific needs. What was his prayer for the
church at Colossae? Let's read it together and find out!

Colossians 1:9-14

For this reason we also, since the day we heard it, do not cease to
pray for you, and to ask that you may be filled with the knowledge
of His will in all wisdom and spiritual understanding; [10]that

---

1 R. Kent Hughes, *Colossians and Philemon: The Supremacy of Christ (Westchester:
Crossway Books, 1989)*, 21.

you may walk worthy of the Lord, fully pleasing Him, being fruitful in every good work and increasing in the knowledge of God; [11]strengthened with all might, according to His glorious power, for all patience and longsuffering with joy; [12]giving thanks to the Father who has qualified us to be partakers of the inheritance of the saints in the light. [13]He has delivered us from the power of darkness and conveyed us into the kingdom of the Son of His love, [14]in whom we have redemption through His blood, the forgiveness of sins.

As we turn to Paul's prayer, found in verses 9-14, we find that it isn't one we should rush through, since it is so rich with meaning. Because of this, we will take up the first three verses of this prayer in this lesson and will cover the remaining verses in our next lesson. There are two parts to this prayer, which makes for a simple outline:

Paul's Petitions (vv 9-11)
Paul's Praise (vv 12-14)

We will study the first portion of the prayer, the petitions, in this lesson, and the praise portion of the prayer in our next lesson.

For many of us, this order is the opposite of what we've been taught about prayer. We're often told that praise must come first and petition last. Yet, as I've mentioned already, Paul's prayer requests are specific to each church; in the case of the church at Colossae, it may be that Paul was using this prayer as a means of introducing his warning regarding the traditions of men. In chapter 2, verse 8, he issues this warning: "Beware lest anyone cheat you through philosophy and empty deceit, according to the tradition of men, according to the basic principles of the world, and not according to Christ." Whatever Paul's reason may be for beginning with petition, I will say that both elements, petition and praise, are important in our prayers. Paul begins the prayer before us now by praying,

For this reason we also, since the day we heard it, do not cease to pray for you, and to ask that you may be filled with the knowledge of His will in all wisdom and spiritual understanding; (Colossians 1:9)

Paul begins by saying *for this reason* we pray. This phrase begs us to ask the question, "For what reason?" What is Paul talking about? If we look back at verses 3-8 of chapter 1 and consider 2:1-10 and even chapter 3—which is the well-known "put off, put on" chapter—we will understand the reason Paul and Timothy are praying this specific prayer for these specific believers. The reason is as we have mentioned before: Epaphras, who was the pastor of the church, had traveled more than 1000 miles, from Colossae to where Paul was in prison, to bring Paul a report of how the church was doing. Epaphras brought not only the good report of the Colossian believers' faith and love but also the bad report of the dangerous heresy of Gnosticism that had crept into the church.

Paul says that for this reason *since the day we heard it*, we *do not cease to pray for you*. This does not mean that Paul prayed for the Colossians 24 hours a day, but it does mean that he never forgot to pray for them. Some people are just naturally on our mind, and so our natural inclination is to pray for them. That's what Paul is saying here. He's motivated to pray because of the good report he's received. But he's also motivated to pray because of the bad report he's received. The good report motivates him to pray that these believers will continue to grow. The bad report of heresy motivates him to pray that they will get away from this dangerous heresy. Many times, when we hear someone is doing well spiritually, we don't pray as much or as often for them, but that is when we need to pray for them the most, because the enemy would like nothing more than to thwart what is being done for God. We are more prone to pray when we hear bad news about someone's spiritual walk; perhaps we ought to be just as fervent when they are doing well spiritually.

Notice that Paul says he and Timothy started praying *since the day we heard* about it. The *we* here refers to both Paul and Timothy (see verse 1). Isn't it a blessing to have a like-minded friend with whom you can pray? Timothy was Paul's son in the faith, and I just imagine that the two of them had a grand time praying for all the churches. I find it encouraging that they began to pray the day they heard the report from Epaphras. When they heard the news, they began their intercession. They didn't put it off until a better time, because there was no time like the present to pray for those Colossian believers. Often, people ask me to pray about something, and I usually find there is no time like the present to pray. I usually either pray with them right then on the phone or in person, if I am with them, or as soon as I have a moment to utter a prayer to God.

Paul goes on to say that he and Timothy also *did not cease* to pray for the Colossians. This has the idea of praying without ceasing, as Paul mentions to the church at Thessalonica (1 Thessalonians 5:17). The word for *prayer* in this verse embraces all that is included in the idea of prayer. It includes thanksgiving, as well as asking for and requesting special things. What things do Paul and Timothy pray for here? There are seven rich prayer requests. We'll look at six of them in this lesson and then the seventh one in our next lesson, as it leads right into the praise portion of this prayer.

1. The first request in Paul and Timothy's prayer is that the Colossian believers *might be filled with the knowledge of His will in all wisdom and spiritual understanding*. What is the difference between *wisdom* and *spiritual understanding*? *Wisdom* is the Greek word sophia; it is practical knowledge that comes from God that gives us the ability to gather and organize principles from Scripture. It is spiritual, and it is practical. It is not the wisdom of the false teachers, the Gnostics who were influencing the Colossian church, but it is the wisdom from above that James speaks of in James 3:17: "But the wisdom that is from above is first pure, then peaceable, gentle, willing to yield, full of mercy and good fruits, without partiality and without hypocrisy." *Spiritual understanding* is the Greek word sunesis, and it is the special ability to discriminate between the false and the true. Spiritual understanding speaks of clear analysis and decision making in applying this knowledge to various problems. Paul speaks of this in 1 Corinthians 2:12-16; he says,

> Now we have received, not the spirit of the world, but the Spirit who is from God, that we might know the things that have been freely given to us by God. These things we also speak,

> not in words which man's wisdom teaches but which the Holy Spirit teaches, comparing spiritual things with spiritual. But the natural man does not receive the things of the Spirit of God, for they are foolishness to him; nor can he know them, because they are spiritually discerned. But he who is spiritual judges all things, yet he himself is rightly judged by no one. For "who has known the mind of the Lord that he may instruct Him?" But we have the mind of Christ.

But Paul doesn't only ask for wisdom and spiritual understanding for the Colossians; he goes a step further and asks that they be *filled with the knowledge of his will* in all wisdom and spiritual understanding, which suggests a filling to completeness, being totally controlled. This would include one's thoughts, actions, and motives. Paul's desire is that they be totally controlled by wisdom and spiritual understanding.

There's a word Paul uses here that would have caused the Colossian readers to perk up, and that word is *knowledge*. This knowledge is not gnosis, which means to know experientially. That is what the Gnostics taught and practiced. They were looking for experiences, the novel, and the new stuff. Rather, the word Paul uses here for knowledge is epignosis, which is heart-transforming and life-renewing knowledge. It is a larger and more thorough knowledge; it grasps and penetrates an object. It indicates that there is a knowing of the subject, which, in this case, is God. This was in stark contrast to the false teachers who offered an appearance of wisdom (see 2:23, where Paul speaks of the "appearance of wisdom"). The false teachers were teaching the Colossian believers that they needed a better knowledge, a gnosis. They said, "Hey, Christ is a good place to begin, but that's not enough. You need Christ plus other stuff and then you will be in the know." Today, this kind of teaching might manifest itself by claiming that you need Christ plus experience, Christ plus psychology, Christ plus psychotropic drugs, Christ plus New Age philosophies, Christ plus Karma, Christ plus—you fill in the blank! Paul confronts this heresy by praying that the Colossian believers would have knowledge that is different than what the Gnostics taught. And we know that he's referring to a heart-transforming knowledge because he prays for the knowledge of

His will, that is, God's will. My friend, the only way we will know God's will is if we are in His Word! Paul knew the importance of knowledge. Most of his writings, in fact, deal with doctrine. In his epistle to the Romans, Paul writes 11 chapters about doctrine, which is knowledge, before he turns to practical godly living in chapters 12-16. In his epistle to the Galatians, Paul writes in the first four chapters about knowledge, or doctrine, before he writes chapters five and six, dealing with the practical. In his letter to the Ephesians, Paul's first three chapters deal with doctrine, and the last three show us how to live. Even here in Colossians, we have two chapters that deal with doctrine and two that deal with duty. I once heard of a man who said he was sick of doctrine. Such thinking is extremely dangerous, my friend! Hosea 4:6 says "My people are destroyed for lack of knowledge. Because you have rejected knowledge, I also will reject you from being priest for Me; because you have forgotten the law of your God, I also will forget your children." We also would do well to remember Proverbs 1:7, which states, "The fear of the Lord is the beginning of knowledge, but fools despise wisdom and instruction."

Now, if all we ever do is possess biblical knowledge, we'll find ourselves in just as much danger because, as Paul wisely says in 1 Corinthians 8:1, "knowledge puffs up." Knowledge is important, to be sure, but so is applying the knowledge we've been given. Some of us want knowledge without any duty. There must be a balance of knowledge and spiritual understanding, knowledge and duty. We should take the truths we learn from our own study of the Word of God and from the preaching and teaching we listen to and apply them to our everyday lives. This is what Paul is praying.

Notice before we go on that Paul prays for all the saints here and not just for a limited few. This is in clear contrast to what the Gnostics taught. They taught that knowledge was reserved for only a selected few. Now, why does Paul pray that these believers might be filled with all wisdom and spiritual understanding? There is a reason, and the reason is found in verse 10, and in it we find Paul's second petition for the Colossians.

> that you may walk worthy of the Lord, fully pleasing Him, being fruitful in every good work and increasing in the knowledge of God; (Colossians 1:10)

2. This second prayer request is a good one to follow the first one because we cannot walk worthy of the Lord if we do not first have knowledge of God and wisdom in how to live for Him. *Paul's second prayer request for the Colossians is that they would walk worthy of the Lord.* The word *worthy* means equal weight. It communicates the idea that believers are to be equal to the Lord's standard, to be holy as He is holy. We are to conduct ourselves in harmony with the responsibilities of our relationship to God. One's *walk* refers to the order of one's behavior or conduct. What Paul is saying here is this: "Walk your talk!" It is one thing for a believer to possess knowledge, but it is another thing entirely—and it is essential—that we act out the knowledge we possess. There is nothing more heartbreaking than one who talks Christianity but doesn't walk Christianity.

This prayer here in Colossians is not the only place Paul calls believers to walk in a manner *worthy of the Lord.* In Ephesians 4:1, he writes, "I, therefore, the prisoner of the Lord, beseech you to walk worthy of the calling with which you were called." In 1 Thessalonians 2:12, he relates how he had exhorted the Thessalonians to "walk worthy of God who calls you into His own kingdom and glory." And to the church at Philippi, he writes in Philippians 1:27, "Only let your conduct be worthy of the gospel of Christ, so that whether I come and see you or am absent, I may hear of your affairs, that you stand fast in one spirit, with one mind striving together for the faith of the gospel." Joni Eareckson Tada put it well, "To walk with God, we must make it a practice to talk with God." And when we consider the word *walk*, we realize that it indicates progress; to be walking worthy of our Lord, we should be progressing in our relationship with God and not remaining stagnant.

Paul adds that as they walk worthy of the Lord, they should also be *fully pleasing Him.* In other words, as they walk with the Lord, they should do so with a desire to please Him. We should desire to be a delight to our Father, just as a child delights to please his earthly father. In Hebrews 11:5, we read of Enoch that "before he was taken [up into heaven], he had this testimony, that he pleased God." This is interesting because we know from Genesis 5:24 that Enoch walked with God. To the Gnostics this would be nonsense! They taught that the body was evil and the spirit was good, therefore it did not make any difference what one did in the body. And this belief gave them all kinds of license to sin! This is exactly why Paul prays that these believers would walk worthy of the Lord with a view to please Him. To the Gnostics, it didn't matter what they did in the body, because to them it was evil and that excused their sin. "Walk worthy?! Nonsense!" they said. But for those who are filled with the knowledge of God's will and spiritual understanding, this is not nonsense but good sense!

Under this heading of pleasing God fall all the rest of Paul's petitions for the Colossians. If we are pleasing God, we will be fruitful in every good work, we will be increasing in the knowledge of God, we will be practicing patience and longsuffering with joy, and we will be giving thanks.

3. Continuing to pray, Paul moves on to his third prayer request for the Colossians: *that they would be fruitful in every good work.* He's already mentioned in verse 6 that the gospel brings forth fruit, so it would only be natural that God's children would produce fruit. The participle *being fruitful* is present and continuous, meaning that Paul's prayer is that the Colossians would bear fruit constantly. That should be the norm for all believers. Fruit has different shapes and colors, but all of us should be producing some fruit. Sometimes that fruit is visible in the sense that we can see outward manifestations of the Spirit's work in a person's life in the form of works or deeds. Jesus said in Matthew 7:20 that "by their fruits you will know them." But fruit also can be invisible in the sense that there is an inward working of God's Spirit to help us be more at peace in our hearts or less judgmental in our thoughts towards others. Paul prays that they would be fruitful in *every good work*. This means that their fruit would be profitable or useful in all that they do.

As the Colossian believers would walk worthy of the Lord with a view to please Him, and as they were being fruitful in every good work, it would only be natural they would then be increasing in the knowledge of God.

4. Therefore, Paul's fourth prayer request for them is *that they would be increasing in their knowledge of God.* The word for *knowledge* here is the same one Paul used in verse 9. Given that this is the second time Paul prays regarding their knowledge, we must assume that the heresy of these false teachers and the implications of their false teaching of Gnosticism were grave. They were creeping into the church and the problem was real and it was serious. As we read Paul's words, we see that he isn't content for these believers to simply be filled with knowledge; he wants them to be *increasing* in that knowledge. I can relate to what he's saying because of my own experience. I've been a believer for 31 years and yet I feel like I lack so much as it pertains to knowledge of the Word of God—I need to keep growing and learning! Peter understood this need just like Paul did; he writes in 2 Peter 3:17-18, "You therefore, beloved, since you know this beforehand, beware lest you also fall from your own steadfastness, being led away with the error of the wicked; but grow in the grace and knowledge of our Lord and Savior Jesus Christ." It's possible that some of the Colossian believers were like many 21st century Christians—content with the status quo. But Paul prays that they would be *growing* in their knowledge of God. Oh, how we need to pray that for one another! I fear that many think John 3:16 is all that they need to know!

You might be thinking to yourself, "Why should I be increasing in the knowledge of God? I'm too busy raising these kids and enjoying my best life now!" In his book, *Growing Deep in the Christian Life*, Charles Swindoll gives us five reasons why we should be growing in knowledge.[2] Allow me to paraphrase them here for you; perhaps they will help you to understand the necessity of growing in our knowledge of God. Pastor Swindoll says that growing in our knowledge of God:

---

2 Charles Swindoll, *Growing Deep in the Christian Life* (New York: Harper Collins, 1995) 25-26.

- *Stabilizes our faith.* Second Peter 3:17-18 says, "You therefore, beloved, since you know this beforehand, beware lest you also fall from your own steadfastness, being led away with the error of the wicked; but grow in the grace and knowledge of our Lord and Savior Jesus Christ."

- *Stabilizes us during our time of testing.* James 1:2-4 tells us, "My brethren, count it all joy when you fall into various trials, knowing that the testing of your faith produces patience. But let patience have its perfect work, that you may be perfect and complete, lacking nothing."

- *Enables us to handle Scripture accurately.* Paul writes Timothy in 2 Timothy 2:15, "Be diligent to present yourself approved to God, a worker who does not need to be ashamed, rightly dividing the word of truth." In that same epistle, in 2 Timothy 3:16-17, Paul goes on to state that "All Scripture is given by inspiration of God, and is profitable for doctrine, for reproof, for correction, for instruction in righteousness, that the man of God may be complete, thoroughly equipped for every good work."

- *Equips us to detect error.* First John 4:1 warns us: "Beloved, do not believe every spirit, but test the spirits, whether they are of God; because many false prophets have gone out into the world."

- *Makes us confident in our daily walk.* First Peter 3:15 tells us: "But sanctify the Lord God in your hearts, and always be ready to give a defense to everyone who asks you a reason for the hope that is in you, with meekness and fear."

Building on this fourth request, Paul's fifth request for the Colossian Christians is found in verse 11.

> strengthened with all might, according to His glorious power, for all patience and longsuffering with joy; (Colossians 1:11)

5. Paul's fifth prayer request is for the Colossians is *that they be strengthened with all might, according to God's glorious power.* The words *strengthened with all might* mean to be invigorated with all vigor. And this strengthening is continuous as we are continually being strengthened with the power of God. The words *according to His glorious power* mean according to the might of His glory, which would be power that is characteristic of His glory. Our strength cannot come without His power. The word *might* is the Greek word dunamoo, from which we get our English word dynamite. In fact, might and strength come from the same Greek root word; both words speak of inherent power that gives one the ability to do something. Now, ladies, that is power! And how are you and I strengthened? *According to His glorious power. Glorious* refers to God's attributes and power and strength in action. The power available to us is continuous and limitless because it is God's power; He is the source of this power. The Colossian believers would need this inner power to withstand the heresy that was creeping into their midst, but they would also need it for the ability to maintain patience and longsuffering, which is Paul's sixth request for them. This God-given strength produces great endurance and patience. His strength in action in us. Then and only then can we be patient and longsuffering with joy.

6. Number six on Paul's prayer request list for the church at Colossae is *that they would be patient and long-suffering with joy. Patience* is endurance to remain under and hold your position. It is the grace to bear up under, despite every hardship and trial. Included in that would be the refusal to succumb to despair or cowardice. Patience enables us to deal with circumstances in which we might find ourselves—things like affliction, suffering, and persecution. *Longsuffering*, however, has more to do with being long-tempered. This is possessed by someone who practices self-restraint and does not hastily retaliate. Longsuffering characterizes the person who refuses to yield to passion or to outbursts of anger. This would be one who does not allow himself to be provoked by people or to become angry. It is, as one has said, "a long holding out of the mind before it gives room to action or passions." If you want it stated

more simply, patience is more in respect to circumstances or events in one's life, whereas longsuffering is more in respect to difficult people in one's life. A lack of patience often results in desponding or losing heart. A lack of longsuffering toward others often leads to wrath or revenge. Is being patient and longsuffering always easy for the believer? No! It is attainable, though, because we have that dynamite power working within us to produce those virtues in us. The Lord never gives us more than we can bear, and He is our supreme example, having been patient in the most difficult of circumstances and longsuffering with the most trying of people. His promises are true, and He will not give us more than we can bear!

As Paul ends his petition for the Colossians, he leaves them with an attitude that should accompany all this patience and longsuffering. What is this attitude he desired that they would have through all this? *Joy!* And this word means exuberant joy, good cheer, gladness of heart. That's where the rubber meets the road, isn't it? You know, with some Christians, you can clearly tell when they are under a heavy burden because their disposition is gloomy and sour. And yet, for all of us—every believer—we should be so filled with a sense of joy that we are confident that God is able to help us in all our circumstances and with all our difficult people. We can be sorrowful but always rejoicing, as Paul says in 2 Corinthians 6:10. It is possible, praise be to God!

Summary

Let's review Paul's six petitions for the church at Colossae.

1. *Be filled with the knowledge of God's will in all wisdom and spiritual understanding.* Would you say your life is filled with the knowledge of His will? Are you taking in a steady diet of the Word of God so that you will understand doctrine? Does your life manifest that you live out the biblical principles that you know?

2. *Walk worthy of the Lord with a view to please Him.* If I were to ask your closest family members or friends if you walk in a manner that pleases the Lord, what would they tell me? Is your life equal with the standards that God has asked of you?

3. *Bear fruit in every good work.* What is some of the fruit you have seen manifested in your life this week, invisible and visible? Are you producing more fruit this year than last year?

4. *Increase in the knowledge of God.* How have you grown in your knowledge of God this past year? What new facts about God and His Word have you learned? Has it changed the way you live?

5. *Be strengthened with all might according to His glorious power.* Do you pray for God to strengthen you with His mighty power for situations or people you need help with? How has God strengthened you in the past?

6. *Be patient and longsuffering with joyfulness.* What difficult situations do you find yourself in today? Is there anyone in your life that is testing your ability to be longsuffering? Do you find yourself more patient and more longsuffering as the years go by? Do you find that inner joy in all circumstances and all people, knowing that God is the blessed controller of every event and every person in your life? Do you really trust God with those irregular people and those difficult trials?

Perhaps you can't answer some of these questions the way you would like to. Could it be that the problem is you haven't prayed about these things? Do you believe in the power of prayer? If so, does your life manifest it by time spent in prayer, not only for yourself, but for those God has placed in your life? If you have not already done so, I hope you will take some time right now to pray Paul's prayer for yourself or for someone else. There is power in intercessory prayer, and the Apostle Paul knew it. What a priceless gift Paul gave to the Colossian believers right there from prison—he gave them the gift of prayer. What a priceless gift we can leave to our children, our grandchildren, our family, and our friends by giving them the gift of intercessory prayer. May God help us to be women of prayer!

Questions to Consider
Colossians 1:9-11
Paul's Petitions for the Church at Colossae

1. (a) Read Colossians 1:9-14. What does Paul pray for the Colossian believers? (b) Do you see any significance in this prayer, especially as it relates to the heresy that had crept into the church?

2. Memorize Colossians 1:10.

3. Compare and contrast Paul's prayer for the Colossians with his prayer for the Ephesians. (See Colossians 1:9-14 and Ephesians 1:15-21.) (a) What things do you see that are similar? (b) What things are different?

4. (a) Paul prays that the Colossian believers would be "fruitful in every good work." What are the conditions of a fruitful life, according to John 15:3, 4, and 10? (b) Is it necessary that a believer bear fruit? See Matthew 7:16-20. (c) How much fruit should we bear? See John 15:8. (d) What causes one to be unfruitful? See Matthew 13:22.

5. (a) According to the following verses, what are some types of fruit we should be producing? See Proverbs 12:14; 31:31; Isaiah 57:19; Jeremiah 6:19; 17:10; Matthew 3:8; Romans 1:13; Galatians 5:22-23; and Hebrews 13:15. (b) Are you producing these fruits?

6. Paul prays that the Colossian believers "might walk worthy of the Lord." (a) According to the following verses, in what ways are we as believers to walk? Romans 13:13; 1 Corinthians 7:17; 2 Corinthians 5:7; Ephesians 2:10; 4:1-3; 4:17-32; 5:2, 8, 15; and 3 John 3-4. (b) Why are we to walk in these ways? (c) What attitudes should accompany our walk?

7. (a) How do you think we as believers are "filled with knowledge"?
   (b) What is our responsibility in this?

8. What are the benefits of praying Scripture for yourself and others? Spend some time this week praying Paul's prayer for someone.

9. Choose one element of Paul's prayer that you would like to be more evident in your own life. Write it down in the form of a prayer request.

Chapter 4

Thanks for What?

(Part 2 of Paul's Prayer for the Church at Colossae)
Colossians 1:12-14

The following is a true and shocking story:

> On September 8, 1860, the Lady Elgin, a crowded
> passenger steamer, floundered off the shore of Lake
> Michigan just above Evanston. One of the students
> gathered on the shore, Edward W. Spencer, a student
> in Garrett Biblical Institute, saw a woman clinging
> to some wreckage far out in the breakers. He threw
> off his coat and swam out through the heavy waves,
> succeeding in getting her back to the land in safety.
> Sixteen times during that day did young Spencer
> brave those fierce waves, rescuing seventeen people.
> Then he collapsed in a delirium of exhaustion. Ed
> Spencer slowly recovered from the exposure and
> exertion of that day, but never completely. With
> broken health he lived quietly, unable to enter upon
> his chosen lifework of the ministry but exemplifying
> the teachings of Jesus Christ in his secluded life. He
> died in California at the age of 81. In a notice of his
> death, one paper said not one of these 17 persons
> ever came to thank him. This true story illustrates a
> grave problem in our society—unthankfulness![3]

For the Christian, an attitude of thankfulness should be the norm.
Paul exhorts us in 1 Thessalonians 5:17, "in everything give thanks!"
If today you do not have an attitude of gratitude, I trust that after we
have finished examining Paul's prayer to the church at Colossae, you
will find yourself filled with gratitude. Let's read it in its entirety.

---

3 R. Kent Hughes, *Colossians and Philemon: The Supremacy of Christ (Westchester:*
Crossway Books, 1989), 27.

Colossians 1:9-14

For this reason we also, since the day we heard it, do not cease to pray for you, and to ask that you may be filled with the knowledge of His will in all wisdom and spiritual understanding; ¹⁰that you may walk worthy of the Lord, fully pleasing Him, being fruitful in every good work and increasing in the knowledge of God; ¹¹strengthened with all might, according to His glorious power, for all patience and longsuffering with joy; ¹²giving thanks to the Father who has qualified us to be partakers of the inheritance of the saints in the light. ¹³He has delivered us from the power of darkness and conveyed us into the kingdom of the Son of His love, ¹⁴in whom we have redemption through His blood, the forgiveness of sins.

We began looking at Paul's prayer in our last lesson and we learned that in this prayer for the Colossians Paul prayed seven specific prayer requests for the church. We covered the first six of those requests in our last lesson. We come now to Paul's seventh petition for the Colossians, which is yet another way that you and I can walk worthy of the Lord: by being a thankful people. This is the second part of Paul's prayer for the Colossians. You will remember that the first part of Paul's prayer contains petitions, in verses 9-11, and the second part contains praises, in verses 12-14. Again, I want to bring out that Paul does it opposite of how some of us have been taught to pray. I remember as a new believer someone sharing with me that I needed to use the ACTS method when praying—Adoration, Confession, Thanksgiving, and Supplication. I've often wondered where that method came from, as it has the potential to make prayer a legalistic ritual instead of natural and genuine talking to God. The ACTS method is certainly a valid method of praying, but there are many others. I would encourage you to not get caught up in a method but do get caught up in prayer! With that in mind, let's look at this seventh petition more closely.

giving thanks to the Father who has qualified us to be partakers of the inheritance of the saints in the light. (Colossians 1:12)

7. Here we find the seventh petition Paul prays for the Colossians: that they would be giving thanks to the Father. Because of our desire to please the Lord, and because we have that dynamite strength imparted to us, we should be able to give thanks to the Father, right? We have been made supernaturally different! It is always a puzzle to me when believers murmur and complain continually. As God's daughters, we can always find something to be thankful for! Some think that this phrase is actually translated, "joyously giving thanks to the Father," meaning that the joy is associated with the thanksgiving, not with the patience and longsuffering, as seen in verse 11. Take whichever interpretation you want because both are true biblically. Paul's desire is that the Colossians would be a thankful people, and so he prays that for them. This is not, however, the only time Paul reminds them in this letter to be thankful, but he reminds them three other times in this letter alone that they need to be thankful—in 3:15 and 17, and again in 4:2.

These believers were not any different from you and me. How many times do we need to be reminded to be thankful? In fact, what are some of the first things a parent usually teaches a child is to say? Please and *thank you*! Have you ever noticed in your own life how being thankful can change everything about your attitude? One of my mentors has said to me often, "Susan, it's amazing what praising can do!" This was illustrated to me when my husband and I were out to eat with another couple, and I asked the man how his job was going. He replied to me that it was going great since he had learned to be thankful. He went on to share with us that he had realized his discontent with his job was a real affront to God and that he was sinning against Him. He said God had dealt with him, and he had confessed and forsaken that sin, and now all was well. My husband and I were so encouraged! What changes a thankful attitude can produce in each of us. Paul prays for the Colossian believers to be thankful, and my friend, I think it would wise of us to pray that for ourselves and for others, as well.

You might be thinking to yourself, "Susan, I don't have anything to be thankful for. You aren't walking in my shoes this week! Why should I be giving thanks to the Father?" This passage alone gives us five reasons to give thanks.

1. *We must be thankful and give God praise is because He has qualified us to be partakers of the inheritance of the saints in the light.* The word *qualified* means to be made fit, to enable us to be qualified. The word has the idea of having sufficient means or enough to accomplish anything. And notice that it is God who has made us fit to be partakers of the inheritance of the saints in the light. It is not of our own works that we are qualified. This would contrast with what the Gnostics taught. They taught that it was only a special few who merited this inheritance. The phrase *has qualified* is also a present tense participle, which indicates that we possess it now. We are right now qualified to be partakers of the inheritance. We have already been transferred from the darkness to the light. In fact, later in this epistle, Paul will admonish the Colossians—and us—to live in light of that reality. He states in Colossians 3:1-3, "If then you were raised with Christ, seek those things which are above, where Christ is, sitting at the right hand of God. Set your mind on things above, not on things on the earth. For you died, and your life is hidden with Christ in God." Paul also says in Ephesians 2:19 something very similar: "Now, therefore, you are no longer strangers and foreigners but fellow citizens with the saints, and members of the household of God."

Paul says we are qualified *to be partakers of the inheritance*. The *inheritance* here means the portion of the lot. This has the idea of each of us receiving our own individual allotment or portion of the total inheritance. Remember in the book of Joshua when they went into the Promised Land and conquered it, that the Lord gave each of the tribes certain portions of the land for their inheritance, their lot? Joshua 14:2 tells us, "Their inheritance was by lot, as the Lord commanded by the hand of Moses." Just as in the Old Testament, when the Lord provided for Israel an earthly inheritance that was distributed to the tribes by lot, so He has provided for the Colossians and for us an allotment or a share in a better inheritance. Jesus gives a foretaste of this in John 14:1-4, where He says, "Let not your heart be troubled; you believe in God, believe also in Me. In My Father's house are many mansions; if it were not so, I would have told you. I go to prepare a place for you. And if I go and prepare a place for you, I will come again and receive you to Myself; that where I am, there you may be also. And where I go you know, and the way you know." Evidently, we each have our own place, our own mansion, our own lot, so to speak. Perhaps you are wondering what our inheritance consists of. Paul says in Ephesians 1:3 that it includes all spiritual blessings: "Blessed be the God and Father of our Lord Jesus Christ, who has blessed us with every spiritual blessing in the heavenly places in Christ." We can only imagine what that looks like, but Paul tells us in 1 Corinthians 2:9 that, "Eye has not seen, nor ear heard, nor have entered into the heart of man the things which God has prepared for those who love Him." And keep in mind that this inheritance is a gift, just like our salvation is a gift. This inheritance is not deserved but is given to us from a loving Father. Now, that is something to indeed be thankful for, right?! Isn't that something you can praise God for?!

Paul says that we will share this inheritance with *the saints in the light*. *Saints* is a common word for the apostle Paul—he uses it about 40 times in his letters—and it always refers to redeemed ones. Saints *in the light* would refers to believers who live in the light; that is the character or quality of their life, and it is the character and quality of our inheritance. *Light* is a picture of purity and truth. I don't know about you, but I am happy that I will be in glory with the saints in light. I would not be too fond of sharing that inheritance with partakers of darkness! Now, just to make this clear, we are presently in the light, but it is also a future reality. This inheritance is already ours, but the full possession of it pertains to the future. It is that hope which is laid up for us in heaven, as Paul says in verse 5. Having said that, the second reason we are to give thanks is found in verse 13.

> He has delivered us from the power of darkness and conveyed us into the kingdom of the Son of His love, (Colossians 1:13)

2. *We must praise God because we have been delivered from the power of darkness. Delivered* means to be drawn out of danger or calamity and to be liberated. God rescued us while we were grasping in darkness, delivering us from our condition of wretchedness. Paul writes of this power of darkness in Titus 3:3; he says there, "For we ourselves were also once foolish, disobedient, deceived, serving various lusts and pleasures, living in malice and envy, hateful and hating one another." *The power of darkness* refers to the rule of Satan and his demons over the unsaved world. The word *darkness*, or scotia in the Greek, is not a figurative term for sin, but refers rather to the consequences of sin. Darkness would speak of Satan and his angels, sin, disobedience, rebellion, ignorance, blindness, falsehood, hatred, wrath, shame, strife, and gloom. Ladies, this was your life before Christ—you were living in darkness, but now you have been delivered. Now, when you were delivered out of darkness, God did not just leave you out in the open, but He put you somewhere else.

3. *The third reason we should be giving praise to God is because He has conveyed us into the kingdom of the Son of His love.* This phrase, *the kingdom of the Son of His love* could also be translated as the kingdom of His dear son. *Conveyed*, or translated, is the idea of removing something from its place and putting it in another place. The biblical world would understand this concept, because in the times of the Old Testament this kind of transferring would be used to describe a king who would take an entire population and deport them to another realm. We find a couple examples of this in 2 Kings. Second Kings 15:29 reads, "In the days of Pekah king of Israel, Tiglath-Pileser king of Assyria came and took Ijon, Abel Beth Maachah, Janoah, Kedesh, Hazor, Gilead, and Galilee, all the land of Naphtali; and he carried them captive to Assyria." And 2 Kings 17:6 says, "In the ninth year of Hoshea, the king of Assyria took Samaria and carried Israel away to Assyria, and placed them in Halah and by the Habor, the River of Gozan, and in the cities of the Medes." Earthly rulers would, at times, transplant a conquered people from one country to another. We might find it hard to understand this illustration in our day and age, but the audience to whom Paul originally wrote would have understood it quite well.

The Colossian believers, like us, had been lifted out of the realm of darkness, which was their depraved state prior to salvation, and had been carried into the Kingdom of God's Son. Paul mentions this very idea when he writes to the Ephesians in Ephesians 2:1-6,

> And you He made alive, who were dead in trespasses and sins, in which you once walked according to the course of this world, according to the prince of the power of the air, the spirit who now works in the sons of disobedience, among whom also we all once conducted ourselves in the lusts of our flesh, fulfilling the desires of the flesh and of the mind, and were by nature children of wrath, just as the others. But God, who is rich in mercy, because of His great love with which He loved us, even when we were dead in trespasses, made us alive together with Christ (by grace you have been saved), and raised us up together, and made us sit together in the heavenly places in Christ Jesus.

Praise be to God! As the songwriter put so well, in a song we don't sing all that often anymore:

> Out of my bondage, sorrow and night,
> Jesus, I come; Jesus, I come.
> Into thy freedom, gladness, and light,
> Jesus, I come to Thee.
> Out of my sickness into Thy health,
> Out of my want and into Thy wealth,
> Out of my sin and into Thyself,
> Jesus, I come to Thee.
>
> Out of the fear and dread of the tomb,
> Jesus, I come; Jesus, I come.
> Into the joy and light of Thy home,
> Jesus, I come to thee.
> Out of the depths of ruin untold,
> Into the peace of Thy sheltering fold,
> Ever Thy glorious face to behold,
> Jesus, I come to thee.[4]

Having delivered us from the power of darkness, God carries us *into the kingdom of the Son of His love*, or the Son that He loves. This

---

4 *Jesus, I Come, by William True Sleeper (1819-1904), hymnbook.igracemusic.com.*

is a royal kingdom. And this kingdom that we are translated into is the same one mentioned in verse 12, which is the inheritance of the saints in the light. Now, the question might come to your mind, "Is this inheritance present or is it future?" In principle, we have already been transferred into the kingdom of God's Son. However, the full possession of that kingdom remains for us in the future. It is like Paul states in Ephesians 2:6, where he says that God has "raised us up together and made us sit together in the heavenly places in Christ Jesus." We have been completely delivered from darkness, and we have a complete inheritance with the saints in light. It is the hope that is laid up for them in heaven, that Paul mentions in verse 5.

Paul not only was blessed to receive this transformation from darkness to light but was also given the commission to share this great news with others who were in darkness. In Acts 26, Paul rehearses his salvation experience on the Damascus Road, giving a masterful defense of the gospel to King Agrippa. In Acts 26:14-18, Paul says,

> And when we all had fallen to the ground, I heard a voice speaking to me and saying in the Hebrew language, "Saul, Saul, why are you persecuting Me? It is hard for you to kick against the goads." So I said, "Who are You, Lord?" And He said, "I am Jesus, whom you are persecuting. But rise and stand on your feet; for I have appeared to you for this purpose, to make you a minister and a witness both of the things which you have seen and of the things which I will yet reveal to you. I will deliver you from the Jewish people, as well as from the Gentiles, to whom I now send you, to open their eyes, in order to turn them from darkness to light, and from the power of Satan to God, that they may receive forgiveness of sins and an inheritance among those who are sanctified by faith in Me."

(By the way, verse 18 is a wonderful prayer to pray for those who are still wandering in darkness.) Now, the fourth and fifth praises Paul gives in his prayer for the church at Colossae are found in verse 14.

> in whom we have redemption through His blood, the forgiveness of sins. (Colossians 1:14)

4. *The fourth part of Paul's praise is for the redemption we have through Christ's blood.* Notice that Paul has shifted the pronoun in his prayer from *you* in verses 9-11 to *we* in verses 12-14. Paul's heart is so evident in this praise portion of his prayer; he seems to be overcome with the blessings that we have in Christ. He appears to be deeply conscious of the fact that he was completely unworthy, and yet the Lord in His mercy had delivered him and translated him and purchased him and granted him forgiveness of sins. Paul expresses this well in 1 Timothy 1:12-17; he says,

> And I thank Christ Jesus our Lord who has enabled me, because He counted me faithful, putting me into the ministry, although I was formerly a blasphemer, a persecutor, and an insolent man; but I obtained mercy because I did it ignorantly in unbelief. And the grace of our Lord was exceedingly abundant, with faith and love which are in Christ Jesus. This is a faithful saying and worthy of all acceptance, that Christ Jesus came into the world to save sinners, of whom I am chief. However, for this reason I obtained mercy, that in me first Jesus Christ might show all longsuffering, as a pattern to those who are going to believe on Him for everlasting life. Now to the King eternal, immortal, invisible, to God who alone is wise, be honor and glory forever and ever. Amen

Paul breaks out in a doxology of praise to God at the end of this section in 1 Timothy; he seems to have never gotten over the fact that he had been redeemed through the blood of Christ—and he desired that the Colossian believers never get over it either. Have you gotten over the fact that you have been redeemed by the precious blood of Jesus? Perhaps we should pray that we never get over that fact. Even as I was preparing to write this lesson, I was given a sobering reminder of this wonderful grace of Jesus as my oldest brother died and went to a Christless eternity!

Now, what is *redemption*? What does it mean to be redeemed? It means to be delivered by payment of a ransom, and it was used to speak of slaves who were freed from bondage. In the biblical world, slaves were set free by the payment of a ransom. In fact, when the Colossians would have heard this Greek word mentioned (lutron), it would have been natural for them to think of the purchase money for slaves. They had been delivered and set free by the payment of a ransom just like the slaves of their day, only they had been delivered and set free from the penalty of sin by the payment of a much more costly ransom—Christ's death! As Galatians 3:13 states, "Christ has redeemed us from the curse of the law, having become a curse for us." And how do you and I have redemption? With what have we been bought? It was a high price, that's for sure. The price was not money, as with slaves, but with the precious blood of Christ. Peter puts it well in 1 Peter 1:18-19 when he writes that, "you were not redeemed with corruptible things, like silver or gold, from your aimless conduct received by tradition from your fathers, but with the precious blood of Christ, as of a lamb without blemish and without spot."

5. *Through Christ's payment of our ransom with His own blood, you and I have obtained forgiveness of sins. This is the fifth reason Paul prays for the Colossian believers to give thanks and praise to God—we have forgiveness of sins!* Forgiveness is the Greek word aphesis, and it means release from bondage or imprisonment. It also comes from another Greek word which means to send from oneself, to send away, to bid to go away or depart. It speaks of Christ paying the penalty for our sin at Calvary and putting away our sin by sending it away. In the Old Testament, this was symbolized by the goat which was laden with the sins of Israel by the hand of the priest and was then sent away into the wilderness and lost. Israel never saw that scapegoat again and, therefore, never saw their sins again. Psalm 103:12 puts it so well. "As far as the east is from the west, so far has He removed our transgressions from us." And in Hebrews 8:12, we are reminded of God's promise: "For I will be merciful to their unrighteousness, and their sins and their lawless deeds I will remember no more." The sinner's sins have been released! The Colossian believers' sins have been released! Your sins have been released! My sins have been released! My friend, if you cannot praise and thank God for that in your prayers, then something is certainly amiss!

It's possible that some of us don't realize the depth of the darkness that we were once in and so we need to be reminded of what sin really is. What is it? What is sin? Is it just the ten commandments? No. Sin is missing the true end and scope of our lives, which is God. It is an offense in relation to God with emphasis on guilt. That includes not only our actions which are offensive, but also our words and, yes, even our thoughts. And even if you and I only committed three sins a day, in a year's time we'd have committed 1095 sins. Now multiply that by living to the ripe old age of 70 and it amounts to 76,650 sins. That's a big burden to carry around! But not for those of us who have been granted forgiveness. We do not have to carry those sins around. Should we not give thanks for all eternity that our sins have been taken away?! All the power, the guilt, and the infectious results of all our sin have been forgiven! All sin of every kind has been sent away, just like the scapegoat that Israel never saw again. Is that a reason to be thankful or what?! Not only because we have forgiveness of sins, but also because we have redemption through His blood, we have an inheritance in glory, we have been delivered from darkness, and we have been translated into the kingdom of the Son of His love. How can we not give praise and thanks for these things?!

Summary

The following is a true and shocking story:

Centuries ago, there was a man named Jesus. He went to a certain village and met ten men who stood far away from him. They were lepers. They asked Jesus for mercy, for cleansing from their leprosy. He gave it to them. They were all healed, but as they went to the priest to be inspected, only one came back and fell on his face to give thanks. Jesus was a little surprised and said to the man, "Were there not ten cleansed? Where are the other nine?" This same Jesus, a few years later, gave His life on a cross to save mankind from death and sin. Have you come back to thank Him for your salvation? Maybe for you it is not an issue of being thankful, but of even possessing salvation at all. Perhaps you do not know the joy of having your sins forgiven and being freed from the bondage of sin. Sin is often referred to as leprosy in the sense that it needs complete cleansing. My friend, if that is your need, don't put it off. You do not know when your life on earth will end, just as I'm sure my brother did not know his life would end. Today may be the day of your salvation.

For those of you who have been translated from the darkness to the light, are you thankful? Have you thanked Jesus lately that one day you be a partaker in that mansion He is building for you and for all who have been redeemed by the blood of the Lamb? Have you shown your gratitude for the fact that He delivered you from the power of darkness and has transferred you into the kingdom of His son whom He loves? How are you showing your gratitude? We should praise God for the redemption we have because of the blood of His Son Jesus Christ. And we should constantly say thank you for the fact that every one of our ugly, awful transgressions has been forgiven. Will you by God's grace, with me, endeavor to cultivate that spirit of thankfulness, and therefore show that you are indeed walking worthy? Even now, would you sing this chorus of thanksgiving and praise to God?

> Thank you, Lord, for saving my soul,
> Thank you, Lord, for making me whole;
> Thank you, Lord, for giving to me
> Thy great salvation so rich and free.[5]

---

5 Words and music by Mr. and Mrs. Seth Sykes, 1940.

Questions to Consider

Colossians 1:12-14

Thanks for What?
(Part 2 of Paul's Prayer for the Church at Colossae)

1. Read Colossians 1:9-14, and then rewrite Paul's prayer for the Colossians in your own words.

2. Memorize Colossians 1:12, 13, or 14.

3. (a) Compare and contrast Paul's prayer for the Colossians (1:9-14) with Paul's prayer for the Philippians (1:9-11). What things do you notice that are the same? (b) What things are different?

4. (a) According to the following verses, what was your life like before you became a Christian? See Romans 1:18; 3:10-18; Ephesians 2:1; 1 John 5:19. (b) What happened at the moment you were saved, according to Romans 6:22; 2 Corinthians 5:17; and Ephesians 2:5? (c) What do you now possess, according to Romans 8:16-17 and 2 Corinthians 5:21? (d) What is your response to all of this?

5. (a) Read Leviticus 16. What preparations were required to be made for the Day of Atonement? (b) What animals were used? (c) What was done to those animals? (d) What specifically would happen to the scapegoat? (e) What did this represent? (See Hebrews 9 for additional help.) (f) How does this help you understand Colossians 1:14?

6. (a) What does having your sins forgiven mean to you? (b) How has it changed the way you live?

7. Ask God for an opportunity this week to share with somcone how they can know the blessings of having their sins forgiven. Come prepared to share the results of that conversation.

8. Write a prayer of thanksgiving to God for the new life you have in Christ.

Chapter 5

Who is the Lord?

Colossians 1:15-19

There is a portion of the Old Testament that reveals a question on the heart of many men and women. The scene is when Moses is setting out to lead the children of Israel out of their bondage in Egypt. God tells Moses that he is to go and tell Pharaoh, the one who was holding the Israelites captive, that he is to let God's people go. Moses and Aaron go and speak to Pharaoh, giving him this message from God, and Pharaoh responds by saying, in Exodus 5:1-2, "Who is the Lord that I should obey His voice to let Israel go? I do not know the Lord, nor will I let Israel go." What interests me about that dialogue is Pharaoh's question, "Who is the Lord?" as well as his statement, "I do not know the Lord." In those two sentences, Pharaoh represents the vast majority of mankind today in their lost condition. They do not know the Lord and, therefore, they do not obey Him. Had Pharaoh known who the Lord is, perhaps he would not have sinned so greatly against Him. And if Paul's letter to the Colossians had already been written, Moses could have taken Pharaoh to the verses we are covering in this lesson. He could have said to Pharaoh, "I'm so glad you asked that question; I have the answer for you in Colossians 1:15-19." Let's read it.

Colossians 1:15-19

> He is the image of the invisible God, the firstborn over all creation. [16]For by Him all things were created that are in heaven and that are on earth, visible and invisible, whether thrones or dominions or principalities or powers. All things were created through Him and for Him. [17]And He is before all things, and in Him all things consist. [18]And He is the head of the body, the church, who is the beginning, the firstborn from the dead, that in all things He may have the preeminence. [19]For it pleased the Father that in Him all the fullness should dwell.

In these few short verses Paul gives us eight descriptions of who Jesus is. There is no other portion of the Word of God which contains so many descriptions of the supremacy of Jesus Christ. We've just finished two lessons on Paul's prayer for the church at Colossae, first looking at his petitions, and then looking at his praises. Paul ended that prayer by praising God for delivering us from the power of darkness and transferring us to the kingdom of the Son He loves. Just who is this Son, anyway? Who is Jesus? This is an important question and it's one that Paul answers because the Gnostics, the false teachers who had invaded the church at Colossae, were teaching that Jesus Christ was not the only way, but that He was only the beginning of many gods who would lead up the ladder to the true God. Many in Colossae were giving heed to this false doctrine, which essentially taught that Jesus was not God and denied that Christ was enough for salvation. Paul confronts these heresies in the verses we'll look at in this lesson.

There is also a very interesting fact about these verses. It is said that verses 15-20, which deal with the supremacy of Christ, were an early Christian hymn sung by the saints of Paul's day. These certainly would be wonderful truths to put to music! Let's consider the first answer to the question that Pharaoh asked, "Who is the Lord?"

> He is the image of the invisible God, the firstborn over all creation. (Colossians 1:15)

1. *Jesus is the image of the invisible God.* To understand what Paul is saying we must define what he means by an image. The Greek word for *image* is eikon, from which we get our English word icon, which means a resemblance, a likeness. An example of this can be found in our coinage, on which we see a direct imitation of the head of a president. This is the same word used in Matthew 22:20 to describe the image of Caesar depicted on a coin. In that passage, the Pharisees had been trying to trip up Jesus with their questions and in this instance they had asked Him whether or not it was lawful to give tribute to Caesar. He instructs the Pharisee to show Him the money, and they bring it to Him. He asks, "Whose image and inscription

is this?" and they reply by telling Him that it is Caesar's. Just like the impression of Caesar's head or a president's head on a coin or a dollar bill is the exact representation of that person, so Christ is the exact representation of God. In 2 Corinthians 4:4, when Paul is talking about the blindness of the unbeliever, he states this very principle. He says, "Whose minds the god of this age has blinded, who do not believe, lest the light of the gospel of the glory of Christ, *who is the image of God,* should shine on them" (emphasis mine). Christ reflects and reveals God.

Paul is, of course, referring to the true God in contrast to the god the false teachers were declaring. Hebrews 1:3 also adds weight to this truth; it says of Jesus, "who being the brightness of His glory and the *express image of His person,* and upholding all things by the word of His power, when He had by Himself purged our sins, sat down at the right hand of the Majesty on high" (emphasis mine). These words here in Hebrews mean that He is the exact impression of the essence of God, just like the impression left by a die on a coin or a seal on wax. My friend, Jesus Christ is the exact representation of the essence of God. And Jesus Himself, while He was on earth, stated this very thing to Philip, in John 14, when Philip asked to see the Father so that the disciples would be satisfied. Jesus replied to Philip in verse 9, "Have I been with you so long, and yet you have not known Me, Philip? He who has seen Me has seen the Father; so how can you say, 'Show us the Father'?" In other words, "Philip, I am the exact representation of God."

Now friends, this truth has very sobering implications for us because we know from Genesis 1:26 that man was made in the image of God. And according to Romans 8:29, we have been predestined to be conformed to the image of His Son. Our Lord is the exact representation of God, and we too have been made in that same image. That is a profound and sobering truth which should motivate us to put Him first in our lives. We are to represent Him, and we are to put Him on display. Are you?

2. *Jesus is the firstborn over all creation. Firstborn* is a word in the Greek, prototokos, which means absolutely first. It implies two things. First, it implies that Jesus preceded all creation; second, it implies that He is sovereign over all creation. Jesus was there before Creation ever took place. Psalm 89:27, speaking of Christ, says, "Also I will make him My firstborn, the highest of the kings of the earth." And in Revelation 1:17, John relates to us the words of Christ Himself, "Do not be afraid; I am the First and the Last." Jesus is the firstborn of all creation because He is before all things, an indication that He is first in rank or honor.

This truth is also in direct contrast to what the Gnostics taught. They did not believe that Jesus was first in anything. Rather, they taught that God limited Himself in the act of creation. That there was a germination of God, and then another and another and so on, all these thousands of lesser gods, until there was one created so distant from Him, that this god could touch evil, and it was this lesser god who created the world. Of course, this god was so far removed from The One True God that this lesser god became feebler and could, therefore, make contact with evil, and so then creation took place. To the Gnostics, Jesus Christ was simply one of these lesser gods. Only one of these lesser gods, who was less holy and less sovereign, could create matter, which was evil. (This is also what the Jehovah's Witnesses teach.) Yet Paul is saying, "This is not true at all—Jesus is the firstborn of all creation! Do not let this error creep into the church!" And, my friend, you and I must not let it creep into our churches either! Paul goes on in verse 16 with yet a third description of our Lord, and it follows beautifully after the truth that He is firstborn over all creation.

> For by Him all things were created that are in heaven and that are on earth, visible and invisible, whether thrones or dominions or principalities or powers. All things were created through Him and for Him. (Colossians 1:16)

3. *Paul is clear that all things were created by Christ and for Christ. This is the third thing we learn from Paul about the Lord.* The things *that are in heaven* would include the heavenly bodies, as well as all

those invisible things that you and I cannot see. The things created *on earth* refers to the visible things: animals, plants, and anything that you and I can see with the human eye. *All things* have been *created* by God. John 1:3 says, "All things were made through Him, and without Him nothing was made that was made."

Paul goes on to elaborate a bit more on what things were created by Christ. He says that thrones, dominions, principalities, and powers were all created by Christ. *Thrones* and *dominions* refer to the spirits and angels around God's throne. *Principalities* and *powers* refer to earthly rulers or authorities. These four classifications of powers refer to both holy and fallen angels, demons, and man; some of these are even the chariots on which He rides, displaying His glory. Consider Psalm 68:17, "The chariots of God are twenty thousand, even thousands of thousands; The Lord is among them as in Sinai, in the Holy Place."

Paul makes it clear, as he ends this verse, that *all things were created through [Christ] and for [Christ]*, reiterating what he said in the first part of this verse. Twice Paul emphasizes this so that the Colossian believers would understand the facts about Christ's creation of all things. The false teachers denied this fact, and so Paul combats their claim with the repetition of this phrase. Paul makes it clear that Christ created all things and that He and He alone is the only true God.

The Gnostics also believed in angel worship, as Paul mentions in Colossians 2:18. They taught that Jesus Christ was basically one of many angels to be worshiped. But Paul makes it clear that Jesus Christ is supreme even over all the angels; He created the angelic beings and therefore has authority over them. He *created* the angels; He is not an angel to be worshiped. Rather, He is the only One who is to be worshiped. Perhaps, like me, you've noticed in the past few years an increasing preoccupation with angels among many in our culture. There are even some who encourage you to get in touch with your personal angel. Sister, this is a dangerous form of Gnosticism, and certainly, as Christians, we should be avoiding such nonsense.

Jesus is above the angels. We would do well to remind ourselves, and any who get caught up in angel worship, of Hebrews 1:1-6:

> God, who at various times and in various ways spoke in time past to the fathers by the prophets, has in these last days spoken to us by His Son, whom He has appointed heir of all things, through whom also He made the worlds; who being the brightness of His glory and the express image of His person, and upholding all things by the word of His power, when He had by Himself purged our sins, sat down at the right hand of the Majesty on high, having become so much better than the angels, as He has by inheritance obtained a more excellent name than they. For to which of the angels did He ever say: "You are My Son, today I have begotten You"? And again: "I will be to Him a Father, And He shall be to Me a Son"? But when He again brings the firstborn into the world, He says: "Let all the angels of God worship Him."

The false teachers, I'm sure, would not have liked Paul writing that not only did Christ create all things but that all things were *for Him*, meaning that everything began with Him and will end with Him. We have come to some false notion in our churches today that God is somehow enamored with us and that He is for us in the sense that He is all about us! We were made for Him and, my friend, it's all about Him! We are made to glorify Him, now and forever. Consider Romans 11:33-36, "Oh, the depth of the riches both of the wisdom and knowledge of God! How unsearchable are His judgments and His ways past finding out! 'For who has known the mind of the Lord? Or who has become His counselor?' 'Or who has first given to Him and it shall be repaid to Him?' For of Him and through Him and to Him are all things, to whom be glory forever. Amen." The fourth and fifth answers to the question, "Who is Jesus?" are found in verse 17.

> And He is before all things, and in Him all things consist. (Colossians 1:17)

4. *Jesus is before all things.* Our Lord put it well in John 8:58, to some skeptic Jews, "Most assuredly, I say to you, before Abraham was, I AM." (This, by the way, prompted them to try to stone Him!)

In Revelation 22:13, Jesus says, "I am the Alpha and the Omega, the Beginning and the End, the First and the Last." Christ is eternal; He always has been, and He always will be.

5. *Not only is He before all things, but in Him all things consist.* By the way, the words *all things* are mentioned five times in verses 15-19 and 6 times in verses 16-20. Paul seems to emphasize this so that his readers will clearly recognize that Christ is above all things. When Paul writes here that *in Him all things consist*, it refers to the fact that by Christ all things hold together. He is the sustainer of the universe. It is only because of Him that the world continues and stands together. This phrase is in the present tense, which would indicate that Christ is presently holding everything together. "It is the Son of God's love that holds in His almighty hands the reins of the universe and never even for a moment lets them slip out of His grasp."[6] Can you imagine what would happen if only for a second Jesus would relinquish His power, that power which holds all things together? The world would be in upheaval! "If He suspended the laws of gravity only for a moment, we would lose all points of reference. If any of the physical laws varied slightly, we could not exist. Our food could turn to poison; we ourselves could drift out into space or get flooded by the ocean tides. Countless other horrible things could happen."[7]

Take a glass ornament and drop it on a tile floor and you'll have an idea of what would happen if God let go of the universe. It's funny to me that people are all upset about climate change, and how the world is going to be destroyed because our former president pulled out of the Paris climate agreement. At the same time, no one is talking about how the world will be destroyed when God says it will be, as Peter states in 2 Peter 3:10. The writer to the Hebrews says that Christ "upholds all things by the word of His power" (Hebrews 1:3). I am so grateful He is holding all things together; aren't you? And, since He is the Creator who holds all things together, He also

6 William Hendriksen, *New Testament Commentary: Exposition of Colossians and Philemon (Grand Rapids: Baker, 2002),* 76.

7 John MacArthur, *Drawing Near (Wheaton: Crossway, 1993), December 9*[th.]

knows how to order the events of our lives. If He can hold the world together by the word of His power, then He can surely hold my life together—and He can hold your life together, too. My friend, what comfort and security this truth should give us. We come to the sixth and seventh qualities of our blessed Lord, in verse 18.

> And He is the head of the body, the church, who is the beginning, the firstborn from the dead, that in all things He may have the preeminence. (Colossians 1:18)

6. *The sixth answer to the question, "Who is the Lord?" is that He is the head of the body, the church.* Christ is the *head of the body*, which is the church. *The church* is the invisible or universal *body* of Christ, consisting of all believers. To say that He is *the head* means that He is the sustaining power of the church. We know that the head is an imperative part of any living being. Just as a human head, that is, the brain of a human body, controls everything about that body, so Christ controls the body of believers, that is, the church. He supplies the church's spiritual life and motion. This is a very interesting analogy Paul uses here, especially as we consider the functions of the human head. They tell me that it is in the head we find the pituitary gland, which promotes our growth, including the health and growth of tissues, cartilage and bones. Also, from the head we receive guidance. The brain, they tell me, receives impulses from the outside world as well as from inside the body. Then it organizes and interprets those impulses. It thinks and reacts, both voluntarily and involuntarily. Because of that, it guides and directs one's actions. From these things, we can clearly see Paul's analogy as we think of Christ being the head of the church; it is through Him that we grow and through Him that we receive guidance. Ephesians 1:22-23 is such a precious passage in this regard: "And He put all things under His feet and gave Him to be head over all things to the church, which is His body, the fullness of Him who fills all in all." Ephesians 4:15-16 also states, "but, speaking the truth in love, may grow up in all things into Him who is the head—Christ—from whom the whole body, joined and knit together by what every joint supplies, according to the effective working by which every part does its share, causes growth of the body for the edifying of itself

in love." I am so thankful that we have a head over the church who is holy, undefiled, and separate from sinners; aren't you? He is the only One whom we can trust to lead us, guide us, and lead us to all truth. He is the only one that equips us to serve Him and His body. What joy!

7. *Jesus is the beginning; the firstborn from the dead.* This does not mean that Christ was the first to rise from the dead with a resurrected body, as Lazarus was resurrected before Jesus was, but it does mean that Christ is preeminent among those who have been raised. He is head of all who have been raised from the dead. Lazarus is not above Jesus. It also means that Christ was the only one raised who did not die again. He was immortal. Though Lazarus had been raised from the dead, he did eventually die again. First Corinthians 15:20 puts it so well: "But now Christ is risen from the dead and has become the firstfruits of those who have fallen asleep." Why is this needful? So *that in all things He might have the preeminence.* In other words, so that He will stand above all others, superior to others. He is to have the supremacy. He has preeminence over the universe as Creator, as chief among those who have risen from the dead, as head of the church and of our lives. He has first place in all things. This truth would have been a rebuke to the Gnostics and a challenge for the church at Colossae—just as it is for us. It means that Christ must have first place in our families, our marriages, our professions, our ministry, time, love, conversation, pleasure, eating, playing, athletics, what we watch, art, music, money, worship, and anything else you can think of to add to that list. Christ must have first place in all of it! Does He have first place in your life? Is there anything that you have placed before Him? It should go without saying that the One who is firstborn, the Creator and Sustainer of the Universe, the Head of the Body, and firstborn from the dead should have the right to preeminence in our lives as well. Paul now gives us the eighth and final answer to our question, "Who is Jesus?" in verse 19.

> For it pleased the Father that in Him all the fullness should dwell (Colossians 1:19)

8. *The eighth quality of our Lord is that in Him all fullness dwells.* This means that in Christ is the totality of God with all His powers and attributes. There is no deficiency in Him. He is complete in His being. Paul says later, in Colossians 2:9, "For in Him dwells all the fullness of the Godhead bodily."

The word *pleased* means that God thought it good that in Jesus all fullness would dwell. He was well-pleased, in fact. The word *fullness* means completion, and, interesting enough, Paul uses a Greek term here for fullness which was used by the Gnostics to refer to the totality of all those lesser gods. They believed that fullness dwelt in all these lesser gods and was divided among them, but Paul is saying there is no way that these gods possess the fullness of God—Christ alone possesses the fullness of God. His power was not distributed to any other gods. Jesus was fully God and fully man with a fully human body. God the Father found pleasure in having all His fullness dwell in His Son Jesus Christ. And this dwelling was not fleeting; the word *dwell* means to be at home permanently, in a certain place. The idea here is that the fullness of God is at home permanently in Jesus Christ; it was not something that was added but was always a part of His being.

How would the Gnostics have received this? Not too well. To the Gnostics, Jesus was only a lesser god, and there would be no way in their minds that God could have always dwelt in Christ. That would have been absurd to them. But to the Colossian believers, these few short verses should have been an encouragement to them. And they should be an encouragement to you and me, as well. To think that this type of honor was ascribed to Jesus! Jesus, the one who some 30 years before Paul wrote this, had died on the cross. Paul encourages the Colossians—and us—that this Jesus, who is preeminent in all things, who is the creator and sustainer of the universe, is able to answer all those requests that Paul had just prayed for them in verses 9-14. This same Jesus is all-sufficient, regardless of what the Gnostics taught about Him. What hope! What joy!

Summary

Is there any other portion of the Word of God that is more detailed in its descriptions of the person of Jesus Christ? When you and I truly understand what Paul is saying in these few verses, there should be absolutely no reason for us to look anywhere else but to Jesus for purpose and meaning in our lives.

1. *He is God in the flesh.* Therefore, He deserves our worship and adoration and trust. Does He have your worship, your adoration, and your trust? If not, who do you worship, and who do you trust?

2. *He is the firstborn.* Therefore, He should have the highest place in your life. Does Christ have the highest place in your life? If not, who or what does?

3. *He is the Creator.* Therefore, He has the right to command your life. Do you obey the commands that Christ has set forth for you in His Word? Are there some commandments that you avoid?

4. *He is before all things.* Therefore, as you place Him first in your life, there is no reason for you to worry about the past or the future. Are you anxious or worried about anything this day?

5. *He is the Sustainer of the entire Universe.* Therefore, He can hold your life together. Does your life seem out of control this day? Oh, dear friend, if God can hold the entire universe together, He can hold your life together. Are you letting Him hold your life together?

6. *He is the head of the church.* Therefore, you should let Him guide you and you should submit to His headship as you grow in His grace and knowledge. Is He your guide? If not, whose counsel do you follow? How have you grown in His grace and knowledge this past year?

7. *He is the beginning, the firstborn from the dead.* Therefore, He must have preeminence and you must put away all idols. Is there

anyone or anything that you love more than God? What do you think about the most? What is your heart set on?

8. *He and He alone is complete; in Him all fullness dwells.* Therefore, dear friends, there is nothing you need to add to Jesus Christ! It is not Christ plus something else in your life that will make you happy or complete. Is there anything or anyone that you are looking toward to make your life complete or happy?

When we consider the ramifications of these eight essential characteristics of our Lord and when we consider that the heresy of Gnosticism has crept into our churches even today, we must pause and soberly reconsider just whom this One is that we call Lord. Is He really our Lord? For some of you, it is possible that there is some repentance that needs to take place after you've finished reading this lesson. For those of you who have grasped these truths, the next time someone says to you, "Hey, just who is the Lord anyway? I don't know the Lord," take them to Colossians chapter one and introduce them to Jesus, the Lord. It will be the most life-changing introduction they'll ever have.

Questions to Consider

Colossians 1:15-19
Who is the Lord?

1. (a) Read Colossians 1:15-19. What appears to be the theme of these verses? (b) List 5 questions an unbeliever might ask when reading this passage for the first time. (You do not need to answer the questions; just list them.)

2. Memorize Colossians 1:16.

3. (a) We know from Colossians 1:18 that Christ is the head of the body, the church. What does that mean, according to Ephesians 1:22-23 and Ephesians 4:15-16? (b) What does Christ do as the Head of the church? (See 1 Corinthians 12 for more help.)

4. (a) Read Job 38 and 39. Write down at least 10 observations that you find in Job 38-39 that are especially meaningful to you concerning God as Creator and Sustainer of the universe. (b) What is Job's response to all that God says? See Job 40:3-5. (c) How do these verses help you to understand more clearly what Paul says in Colossians 1:15-19? (d) Is your response like Job's? Why or why not?

5. (a) In the following passages, who is being raised from the dead, and by whom are they being raised? 2 Kings 4:18-37; Luke 7:11-15; John 11:41-44; John 20:1-10; Acts 9:36-42; and Acts 20:7-12. (b) What is different about the Lord's resurrection in contrast to these others? (c) What is the significance of Christ's resurrection, according to 1 Corinthians 15:12-28? (d) How does 1 Corinthians 15:20 help you better understand Colossians 1:18?

6. (a) How could you use Colossians 1:15-19 in presenting the gospel to someone? (b) How could you use Colossians 1:15-19 to help those who are caught up in Gnosticism?

7. What does it mean to you personally that Christ is the Creator of all things?

8. (a) In what ways can Jesus Christ be given first place in our lives? (b) What things might we put before Him?

9. After meditating on Colossians 1:15-19 this week, what encouragement does it give you for any difficulties you are now facing? Write down your petitions and pray with faith that the Lord of all Creation, who upholds the world by His power, will answer your prayers. Bring a petition to share.

Chapter 6

From Rotten to Reconciled

Colossians 1:20-23

The hymn *Amazing Grace* is not only sung often in our churches, but is also known and sung by many unbelievers at a variety of events. I've often wondered if we who are God's children really understand the depths of what we're singing when we utter the words, "Amazing grace, how sweet the sound, that saved a wretch like me!" But John Newton, who wrote this beloved hymn, understood the depths of what he wrote. He knew he'd been lost and blind, and indeed, a wretch. He had lived a life of sin, and according to his own accounts, starting at the age of 11 his life began to grow more and more evil. He spent his life capturing natives from West Africa and selling them into slavery. But through various providential acts of God, John Newton bowed his knee to Christ at the age of 23, and from that day until he died at the age of 82, he never ceased to marvel at the grace of God that had saved a wretch like him. He never got over the fact that God had taken him from being rotten to being reconciled to Christ. My dear friend, have you marveled at the precious fact of your own reconciliation to Christ? I trust that after we study this portion of God's Word, we will realize the amazing grace that has saved wretches like us!

We have come to a portion of God's Word that should not only be a spiritual B12 shot to all of us but should leave us with an attitude of gratitude and joy. When we contemplate the incredible fact that we have been reconciled to a Holy God, it should astonish us! None of us deserve this great gift of transformation, but all of us should humbly bow in grateful adoration and thank our Lord for His tremendous gift. We have come from rags to riches, from being rotten to being reconciled! Let's read the text together.

Colossians 1:20-23

and by Him to reconcile all things to Himself, by Him, whether things on earth or things in heaven, having made peace through the blood of His cross. [21]And you, who once were alienated and enemies in your mind by wicked works, yet now He has reconciled [22]in the body of His flesh through death, to present you holy, and blameless, and above reproach in His sight—[23]if indeed you continue in the faith, grounded and steadfast, and are not moved away from the hope of the gospel which you heard, which was preached to every creature under heaven, of which I, Paul, became a minister.

As we consider this wonderful act of the reconciling work of Christ, we'll consider the following questions:

> *How are We Reconciled?* (vv 20, 22a)
> *Who is Reconciled?* (v 21)
> *Why are We Reconciled?* (v 22b)
> *What is the Result of Being Reconciled?* (v 23)

Paul has just written regarding the supremacy of Christ and really answered the question of just who Jesus is by giving us eight descriptions of Him. Paul now shifts his thoughts to the work of reconciliation. This One whom Paul has just described is quite able to reconcile us to God. He does indeed reconcile us and, my friend, that is a humbling fact! So, the first question we want to consider in this lesson is: How are we reconciled? Paul writes,

How are We Reconciled?

Colossians 1:20

and by Him to reconcile all things to Himself, by Him, whether things on earth or things in heaven, having made peace through the blood of His cross. (Colossians 1:20)

Since we are going to be studying the act of reconciliation, we should begin by defining it. The term *reconcile* means to change or exchange, and this changing is a thorough changing from one condition to another. When we are reconciled to God, we are completely altered and adjusted to a required standard. Paul puts it well in Romans 5:1-2: "Therefore, having been justified by faith, we have peace with God through our Lord Jesus Christ, through whom also we have access by faith into this grace in which we stand, and rejoice in hope of the glory of God." And again, in Romans 5:10-11: "For if when we were enemies we were reconciled to God through the death of His Son, much more, having been reconciled, we shall be saved by His life. And not only that, but we also rejoice in God through our Lord Jesus Christ, through whom we have now received the reconciliation." Paul writes of this same concept in Ephesians 2:14-18, as well. There, he says,

> For He Himself is our peace, who has made both one, and has broken down the middle wall of separation, having abolished in His flesh the enmity, that is, the law of commandments contained in ordinances, so as to create in Himself one new man from the two, thus making peace, and that He might reconcile them both to God in one body through the cross, thereby putting to death the enmity. And He came and preached peace to you who were afar off and to those who were near. For through Him we both have access by one Spirit to the Father.

This amazing story of reconciliation was foretold by the prophet Isaiah in Isaiah 53:5. "But He was wounded for our transgressions, He was bruised for our iniquities; the chastisement for our peace was upon Him, and by His stripes we are healed." When two human beings are at odds with each other, we say that they need to be reconciled, that they need to be at peace with each other. Even though God does not need to be reconciled to us, we do need to be reconciled to Him. God is not the offender; we are. And so, Paul says that God reconciled us *to Himself,* because it is man who needs to be brought into a proper relationship with God, not God with man. One man put it well: "In reconciliation, the sinner stands before God as an enemy, but becomes His friend."[8]

Paul makes it clear from this verse that we are reconciled by Christ *through the blood of His cross*, and then in verse 22a Paul mentions

---

8 John MacArthur, *The MacArthur New Testament Commentary: Colossians and Philemon* (Chicago: Moody Press, 1992), 56.

that this reconciliation is through the body of Christ's flesh through His death, which we'll get to in a moment. These two truths go together. We are reconciled through the blood of the cross, and that blood was shed from Jesus' body by His death. A price had to be paid for your reconciliation, and that price had to be a blood sacrifice. The mention of *blood* in this verse indicates that Christ's death was a violent death. In the Old Testament, the blood would have come from an animal as the sacrifice required for the atonement for sins. Those animals were not beaten to death or starved to death but were sacrificed, their throats slit and their blood poured out for the atonement of the people's sins. This act served as a symbol of what was to come in Christ, the Passover Lamb, who would shed His blood once for all on the cross. This reality is elaborated on in Hebrews 13:11-12:

> For the bodies of those animals, whose blood is brought into the sanctuary by the high priest for sin, are burned outside the camp. Therefore Jesus also, that He might sanctify the people with His own blood, suffered outside the gate." Hebrews 9:12 also states, "Not with the blood of goats and calves, but with His own blood He entered the Most Holy Place once for all, having obtained eternal redemption.

And Hebrews 9:22, "And according to the law almost all things are purified with blood, and without shedding of blood there is no remission." Those Old Testament sacrifices could never reconcile you and me to a Holy God, but Jesus shed His own blood so that you and I could be reconciled to Him. That is indeed a humbling fact!

This precious truth was not taught by the false teachers invading the Colossian church. The Gnostics taught that reconciliation was made to God through angelic mediators, not by Jesus. To them, Jesus' blood was not enough; Christ was not sufficient for reconciliation. That reminds me of some religions today which require the performance of certain works to attain heaven. Of course, they throw Christ into the picture, but to them Christ alone is never enough. This is teaching what Paul condemns in Galatians and calls anathema— cursed by God! (See Galatians 1:8-9.) It is not by chance that Paul mentions that we have *peace* through this reconciliation because it is such a contrast to the turmoil that false teaching brings to one's life. When we try to attain reconciliation to God by works, we are left with nothing but frustration because we can never do enough works to attain heaven! This idea of peace means to bind together, to harmonize. The Lord Jesus by His death on the cross bound we who are sinful women to a Holy God. Christ was the bridge that closed that gap! We now have peace with our Creator! Incredible!

So then, what does Paul mean when he says that God did this to reconcile *all things* unto Himself? Does this mean everyone will be saved? Some have taken this passage out of context, claiming that it proves that everyone will be saved, but that is contrary to what the rest of Scripture teaches. A passage that helps us understand this is Philippians 2:10-11, in which Paul writes to the church at Philippi, "that at the name of Jesus every knee should bow, of those in heaven, and of those on earth, and of those under the earth, and that every tongue should confess that Jesus Christ is Lord, to the glory of God the Father." Paul is saying in Philippians the same thing he is saying in Colossians—whether it be things in earth or things in heaven, one day *all* will acknowledge Christ's Lordship. One day all will bow to His Lordship, but that does not mean all will be saved. We can either bow the knee in this life or we can bow the knee when we stand before the judgment seat before being cast into the lake of fire! I don't know about you, but I prefer to bow my knee in this life!

It is interesting to note that twice in this verse this reconciliation is said to be *by Him*, that is, by Christ. Paul does this for emphasis, so that his readers will clearly understand that this reconciliation is only through Jesus Christ, and is not accomplished by anything or anyone else, contrary to what the Gnostics were teaching.

Who is Reconciled?

Colossians 1:21

> And you, who once were alienated and enemies in your mind
> by wicked works, yet now He has reconciled (Colossians 1:21)

The second question we want to consider is: Who is reconciled? And the answer is found in verse 21. Those who are reconciled are those *who once were alienated and enemies in your minds by wicked works*. First, Paul says they *were alienated*. *Alienated* means to be estranged, cut off, or separated; it is a powerful word which indicates a persistent and permanent condition. My friend, that describes you and me prior to our salvation. I was estranged from God, and I was persistent in my separation from Him. But in addition to being alienated, Paul also says we were *enemies*, that is, hateful or hostile, *in your mind by wicked works*. This means we were hostile at heart in our evil deeds. And notice that the enmity and alienation from God begins in the mind and manifests itself by wicked works. As the Psalmist put well in Psalm 10:4: "The wicked in his proud countenance does not seek God; God is in none of his thoughts." Titus 1:15-16 is also clear: "To the pure all things are pure, but to those who are defiled and unbelieving nothing is pure; but even their mind and conscience are defiled. They profess to know God, but in works they deny Him, being abominable, disobedient, and disqualified for every good work." Paul put it well in Ephesians 2:1-3:

> And you He made alive, who were dead in trespasses and sins, in which you once walked according to the course of this world, according to the prince of the power of the air, the spirit who now works in the sons of disobedience, among whom also we all once conducted ourselves in the lusts of our flesh, fulfilling the desires of the flesh and of the mind, and were by nature children of wrath, just as the others.

But thanks be to God, the Colossian believers and you and I were not left in that state! Paul says of us *yet now He has reconciled*. Second Corinthians 5:17 puts it so beautifully: "Therefore, if anyone is in Christ, he is a new creation; old things have passed away; behold, all things have become new." Ephesians 2:13 also gives us this hope: "But now in Christ Jesus you who once were far off have been brought near by the blood of Christ."

How are We Reconciled?

Colossians 1:22a

in the body of His flesh through death, (Colossians 1:22a)

Paul again reiterates how God reconciled us along with explaining why He reconciled us. We are reconciled *by the body of His flesh through death*. This is similar terminology to that found in verse 20, where Paul wrote that we were reconciled through the blood of the cross. Here, Paul combines two words, *body* and *flesh*, to emphasize that the actual human body of Jesus was involved. This would be in direct contrast to the teachings of the Gnostics, who denied Christ's humanity. They taught that reconciliation could be accomplished by other spiritual beings like angels, but Paul emphasizes here that one can only be reconciled by the physical death of Christ, the blood of the Lamb. Gnosticism was also the heresy the aged old apostle John wrote about to the church at Ephesus. In 1 John 4:1-3, he warns the Ephesian believers,

> Beloved, do not believe every spirit, but test the spirits, whether they are of God; because many false prophets have gone out into the world. By this you know the Spirit of God: Every spirit that confesses that Jesus Christ has come in the flesh is of God, and every spirit that does not confess that Jesus Christ has come in the flesh is not of God. And this is the spirit of the Antichrist, which you have heard was coming, and is now already in the world.

The people that teach this stuff are antichrist—they are not for our Lord but against Him! There are many cults and many false teachings going around today that are teaching this same thing. Please beware, my friend. The morning before I sat down to write this lesson, I listened to a message by a popular speaker. A lady I had recently counseled wanted my opinion on what this particular teacher was saying. I got through about 15 minutes of it and turned it off. The things he was saying were heretical, were not backed up by Scripture, and were delivered in an angry tone. My friend, please,

please measure what you hear with Scripture! In fact, Jesus even warns us in Mark 4:24 to take heed what we hear! Do you?

Why are We Reconciled?

Colossians 1:22b

> to present you holy, and blameless, and above reproach in His sight— (Colossians 1:22b)

We now come to the third question we find answered in this text, which is the why question: Why are we reconciled, or why have we been reconciled? There are three answers to this why question in this verse. First, we have been reconciled so that we might be *holy*. The word holy means to be cleansed from all sin and worldly defilement and separated entirely to God and His service. You and I have been saved, we have been reconciled to God, so that we would be presented before God free from worldliness and dedicated to Him and His service. The apostle Peter is clear about this in 1 Peter 1:15-16: "but as He who called you is holy, you also be holy in all your conduct, because it is written, 'Be holy, for I am holy.'" (Interestingly, in Titus 2, older women are called to have behavior that is holy, that which pertains to a priest.)

The second reason we have been saved is so that we might be *blameless*, or unblameable, as the King James Version says. This word means to be without blemish of any kind. When an animal in the Old Testament was sacrificed, it had to be without any blemish. Any animal with a blemish or defect could not be offered on the altar as an atonement for sins. This same word is also used in the New Testament in a passage we would do well to heed, especially for all you murmurers! In Philippians 2:14-15, Paul writes, "Do all things without complaining and disputing, that you may become blameless and harmless, children of God without fault in the midst of a crooked and perverse generation, among whom you shine as lights in the world." When we are not blameless, whether it's in our speech or actions or even our thoughts, we fail to shine as lights in a dark world, and we certainly do not please the One who reconciled us with His blood.

The third reason for our reconciliation is that we would be *above reproach*, or unreprovable. This means to be completely above reproach, to be free from accusation. Satan, who is the accuser of the brethren, cannot even make a charge against those who have truly been reconciled by God. This is the same word that is found in 1 Timothy 3:10 and Titus 1:6-7 to describe the qualifications of leaders in the church, that is, they are to be above reproach. Lest any of you think this word only pertains to leaders in the church, Paul makes it clear that this is for all of God's reconciled ones. He makes it clear by the last words in this verse, *in His sight* or in His presence. The idea is that we are directly in front of God's sight, His searching, penetrating gaze. God is right now at this moment in our presence, and He knows if we are living in a manner that is holy, blameless, and without reproach.

All these qualities are required of us as reconciled believers, and they are proof that we are saved. We are to continue to grow in them as we are continually being sanctified. However, right now, we possess what we call positional righteousness because of Christ's finished work on the cross. Right now, God is viewing you as robed in the righteousness of Jesus Christ. Because of Jesus' shed blood, God sees you as holy, blameless, and above reproach. My friend, this is an amazing and humbling thought! The songwriter put it well: "When He shall come with trumpet sound, oh, may I then in Him be found, clothed in His righteousness alone, faultless to stand before the throne!"[9] We can join our brother Jude in his doxology in Jude 24-25: "Now to Him who is able to keep you from stumbling, and to present you faultless before the presence of His glory with exceeding joy, to God our Savior, who alone is wise, be glory and majesty, dominion and power, both now and forever. Amen." Is this not an amazing truth, that God would take us, who were once His enemies, and present us to Himself as unblameable and unreprovable in His sight?!

---

9 Words by Edward Mote, 1797-1874.

What is the Result of Being Reconciled?

Colossians 1:23

> if indeed you continue in the faith, grounded and steadfast, and are not moved away from the hope of the gospel which you heard, which was preached to every creature under heaven, of which I, Paul, became a minister. (Colossians 1:23)

We come now to the last question Paul answers for us and that is: What is the result of being reconciled? Maybe you've wondered, "How do I know I've been redeemed?" The answer is found in verse 23. (To be clear, Scripture gives several validations of our salvation; here, Paul gives us one such validation—and it is vitally important.)

Paul is clear that those who are reconciled will persevere to the end. He describes it as continuing in the faith, being grounded, steadfast, and not moving away from the gospel. If there is ever a message for our age, it is this: genuine believers do not apostatize. We are living in the age of apostasy; there is an alarming increase in those who once professed Christ but are now denying the very Christ they professed. My friend, those who do so were never actually redeemed by the blood of the Lamb. Paul says we are reconciled *if* we *continue in the faith*. The word *continue* means to abide, to persist in, to stay with, and to adhere to. And the word *if* here communicates the idea of assuming; it's as though Paul is saying, "assuming that you continue in the faith." The apostle John, as we already mentioned, was fighting this same heresy when he wrote in 1 John 2:19, "They went out from us, but they were not of us; for if they had been of us, they would have continued with us; but they went out that they might be made manifest, that none of them were of us."

Genuine believers persevere in the faith, and they do it by being *grounded and steadfast*. *Grounded* means to be firmly established upon a true foundation, like a building that is built on a strong foundation, like the man in Matthew 7 who was wise and built his house upon a rock. When the rains and winds came, that man's house stood firm. Likewise, those who are grounded in the faith don't abandon the faith; they stand firm in it. They also are *steadfast*, Paul says, which means they are established, immovable, and settled. These people don't constantly shift in their beliefs about God; they're not like the double-minded man in James 1, who is unstable in all his ways. In fact, the context of James 1 indicates that the double-minded and unstable man is not even redeemed. My friend, genuine believers can echo "Amen" to Paul's words in 1 Corinthians 15:58: "Therefore, my beloved brethren, be steadfast, immovable, always abounding in the work of the Lord, knowing that your labor is not in vain in the Lord." (An interesting side note is that the word *grounded* implies a firm foundation by which we are supported, and the word *settled* suggests an inward strength which we possess. The writer to the Hebrews has quite a bit to say about this truth. Hebrews 3:6 states, "But Christ as a Son over His own house, whose house we are if we hold fast the confidence and the rejoicing of the hope firm to the end." And then in verse 14 of that same chapter, we read, "For we have become partakers of Christ if we hold the beginning of our confidence steadfast to the end.")

Not only are we grounded and settled, but Paul describes those who are reconciled as *not* being *moved away from the hope of the gospel*. The idea is that we do not move away from the hope of the gospel to some other place. This is a very important point Paul makes because of the dangerous heresy that was creeping into the Colossian church. If the Colossians accepted the heresy of Gnosticism, they would certainly move away from the hope of the gospel. They would slip away. There is a warning here for all of us. We ought to always be examining the things we hear in light of what God's Word says. So many ideas are creeping into our churches today, and they may look good and sound good, but they are damaging to God's people. I would encourage you to be like the Berean believers, to always be searching and studying to be certain that the things you read and hear match up with the Word of God.

Paul also makes it clear in this verse that the gospel was something that the Colossian believers had *heard*. We learned in verses 5 and

6 that Epaphras had more than likely brought the gospel message to them. The gospel was preached to them just as it was preached to us. Paul makes clear in Romans 10:14 that we will not hear without a preacher! Someone had to herald the gospel message to the Colossians, and someone had to preach that gospel message to us, as well. And it was *the hope of the gospel* that they heard, a message of hope to them and a message of hope to you and me and to all those we evangelize. *Hope* is a word which means to anticipate with pleasure. Paul mentions this in verses 5 and 27 as well. Ladies, if you and I don't have a holy anticipation, a holy and pleasurable longing for heaven now, then something is amiss in our hearts.

Paul ends this verse by saying this gospel *was preached to every creature under heaven*. This is similar to what we read back in verse 6, which indicated the universality of the gospel. Paul is emphasizing here that the gospel is offered to all, another stark contrast to what the Gnostics taught. They taught that the good news was only for a select few, those who were in the know. But Paul says it is offered to *every creature* that is *under heaven*, of which Paul *became a minister*. We know that when God reconciled Paul on the Damascus Road, He saved Paul to be a minister of the gospel. When Paul is rehearsing his salvation experience before King Agrippa, he quotes what Christ said to him on the Damascus Road, "But rise and stand on your feet; for I have appeared to you for this purpose, to make you a minister and a witness both of the things which you have seen and of the things which I will yet reveal to you" (Acts 26:16). A minister is not a glamorous position, even though it is an honor to serve the Lord. *Minister* just means to be an attendant, to run errands, to be a table waiter. Paul was not ignorant about his position, as many ministers are today. The truth is that there are no Christian celebrities, even though so many ministers think of themselves that way. Paul referred to himself in 1 Corinthians 15:9 as the least of the apostles, and in Ephesians 3:8 he said that he was less than the least of all the saints, and in 1 Timothy 1:15 he described himself as the chief of sinners. Paul did not have a puffed-up view of himself. He saw himself as a table waiter for Christ, the one who had reconciled his soul to God.

Summary

How are We Reconciled? (vv 20, 22a) Through the blood of the cross and through the death of Christ. Have you been reconciled by the redeeming blood of the lamb?

Who has been Reconciled? (v 21) Those who were once alienated from Christ, enemies of the Lord, and involved in all kinds of wickedness. What was your life like before you came to Christ? In what wickedness were you engrossed? Have you thanked God that He brought you from being rotten to being reconciled?

Why are We Reconciled? (v 22b) So that we might be holy, blameless, and above reproach. To be clear, we stand positionally before God even now and are seen by Him as holy, blameless, and above reproach because of Christ's finished work on the cross, but we also are to be striving to flesh out these qualities in a practical way in our daily lives. Do these three qualities describe your life and your pursuits in life?

What is the Result of Being Reconciled? (v 23) That we will be grounded and settled and not move away from the gospel; we will persevere to the end. Are you more and more settled in your faith as the years go by? Or have you considered following the popular crowd in our day which is denying even the existence of God?

Have you made peace with God? Do you know for certain that if you were to die today you would stand before Him as reconciled? Does your life manifest that certainty by holy living and by being steadfast? Are you grounded and settled and unmovable? If you are unsure that such a change has taken place in your life, I want to beg you, as though Christ Himself were here pleading with you, receive the love He offers you—be reconciled to God!

For those of you who know for certain that you are reconciled to God, don't ever forget this blessed work of Christ. John Newton died at the age of 82 and right before his death, he was heard saying this "My memory is nearly gone, but I remember two things: That I am a great sinner, and that Christ is a great Savior!" Dear child of God, whatever age you are, never, ever get over the fact that you are a great sinner, and that Christ is a great Savior!

Questions to Consider
Colossians 1:20-23
From Rotten to Reconciled

1. (a) Read Colossians 1 and list all the words or phrases that are repeated. (b) What significance do these repeated words and phrases seem to have?

2. Memorize Colossians 1:21.

3. (a) How is one reconciled to God, according to Romans 5:10-11; 2 Corinthians 5:17-21; and Ephesians 2:14-17? (b) Why is it necessary that one be reconciled to God? (c) How would you explain reconciliation to a non-believer?

4. (a) According to the following passages, in what ways was the apostle Paul once alienated from God and an enemy of God? Acts 9:1-18; 22:1-21; 26:1-23. (b) What were the events that took place when Paul was reconciled to God?

5. (a) What does John say in 1 John 2:19 about those who have not continued in the faith? (b) Were they ever in the faith? (c) With these things in mind, read Jesus' parable in Matthew 13:1-23. Which of these were truly saved? (d) How do you know? (e) What does this teach you about the perseverance of the saints? (f) What other verses come to mind when you think of what Scripture says about true believers persevering in the faith?

6. (a) Why did Jesus have to die? (b) Why was it necessary that a body be offered as well as a blood sacrifice? See Hebrews 10 to help you with these answers.

7. (a) Have you been reconciled to God? (b) If so, what changes have you seen in your life, especially this past year, that give evidence of that reconciliation? (c) Have you thanked the Lord lately that He has reconciled you to Himself?

8. (a) What does it mean to you to "continue in the faith"? (b) How does a believer's life manifest being "grounded and steadfast"? (c) In what ways would you like to be more steadfast in your faith?

9. Write a prayer of thanks to God for your reconciliation to Him.

Chapter 7

The Call and Cost of Ministry

Colossians 1:24-29

Well-known author and radio speaker, R.C. Sproul, tells of the following exchange with one of his students: "I remember a starry-eyed college student who looked at me and said in wonderment, 'What was it like for you when you were *just* a minister?' I lost it! 'What do you mean *just* a minister? Don't you realize that the parish ministry is the highest calling on earth? God had only one Son and He made him a preacher!'"[10]

Perhaps some of you feel that way when you fill out those information forms at the doctor's office or some other place and you come to that line which asks, "What is your occupation?" and you write down that you're a housewife or a home-school mom. "Oh, you're *just* a housewife? You *just* stay at home and school your kids?" Maybe you want to "lose it" like RC did. Maybe you've been tempted to say, "What do you mean *just* a housewife?! Don't you know the highest calling God gave to women was to be a homemaker?" Or "Homeschooling my children is a blessing and a privilege!"

You might be wondering what all this has to do with this lesson. Well, the apostle Paul was called to the ministry, and he certainly wasn't "just a minister." He was divinely called to the work of the ministry. In this lesson, we are going to learn a lot about this man who was "just in the ministry." I trust it will be encouraging to you as you contemplate the ministry to which God has divinely called you.

We considered in our last lesson that we have been reconciled to God through the blood of the cross and the death of Christ. Paul

10 R. Kent Hughes, *Preaching the Word: Colossians and Philemon, The Supremacy of Christ (Westchester: Crossway Books, 1989), 43.*

ended his thoughts in those verses with a reminder that this gospel has been preached everywhere and that he is a minister of it. But Paul doesn't only write about his call to ministry; as we will see in this lesson, he also writes about the cost of ministry.

Colossians 1:24-29

> I now rejoice in my sufferings for you, and fill up in my flesh what is lacking in the afflictions of Christ, for the sake of His body, which is the church, ²⁵of which I became a minister according to the stewardship from God which was given to me for you, to fulfill the word of God, ²⁶the mystery which has been hidden from ages and from generations, but now has been revealed to His saints. ²⁷To them God willed to make known what are the riches of the glory of this mystery among the Gentiles: which is Christ in you, the hope of glory. ²⁸Him we preach, warning every man and teaching every man in all wisdom, that we may present every man perfect in Christ Jesus. ²⁹To this end I also labor, striving according to His working which works in me mightily.

In these verses, we will learn of

> *Paul's Rejoicing in Ministry* (v 24)
> *Paul's Responsibility in Ministry* (vv 25-27)
> *Paul's Reason for Ministry* (v 28)
> *Paul's Resource in Ministry* (v 29)

Paul's Rejoicing in Ministry

Colossians 1:24

> I now rejoice in my sufferings for you, and fill up in my flesh what is lacking in the afflictions of Christ, for the sake of His body, which is the church. (Colossians 1:24)

Paul's attitude in ministry is one of rejoicing. As you read verse 24, did you notice that he was rejoicing in the sufferings of ministry and not just in the happy times of ministry? When Paul says *I now rejoice*, it means he is calmly cheerful or happy. And the *sufferings*

he says he's rejoicing in would indicate hardships or pain. This is an incredible statement that Paul is writing! How could he say such a thing? One man answers it quite well for us: "People lose their joy when they become self-centered, thinking they deserve better circumstances or treatment than they are getting."11 Paul didn't allow the difficulties of ministry to rob him of his joy and make him want to abandon the ministry.

As a speaker, I have had some experiences that have been tests for me, for sure—though none quite like Paul. (Some might think that traveling and speaking is a glamorous vocation. It is most certainly a privilege, and I do love it, but it is not without some adversity.) During one event, a woman asked to speak with me during one of the breaks. She was angry, shaking her finger at me, and grabbing my shoulders! I genuinely thought, "I think she might slug me!" She began to spew out the offenses she had with me, and it was one of those I-can't-believe-this-is-happening-to-me moments! (By the way, that was not the first time something like this had happened.) I was thankful for the calm spirit the Lord gave me, along with self-control to handle the situation. I certainly have not gone through the sufferings Paul endured, but we all should know, just as Paul did, that these sufferings are only temporary inconveniences.

Paul describes his sufferings as afflictions in his *flesh*, or his body, we might say. We know that at the time Paul composed this letter, he was writing from prison, and that would certainly have been suffering in the flesh. Imprisonment in the biblical world was not like it is in our day. Paul was not only chained to a Roman soldier but also received very little food or water. Few toilets were available, which led to sickening stench. Sexual immorality was rampant, and many prisoners committed suicide in prison or begged for a speedy death. And Paul spent 25% of his life in prison! In the Questions to Consider for this lesson, you will look up a number of Scriptures and learn of the many other things Paul suffered. And you will notice in those passages how Paul repeatedly mentions rejoicing in those sufferings. Here in this verse, he says he is *now* rejoicing! Amid

11 John MacArthur, *The MacArthur New Commentary: Colossians and Philemon* (Chicago: Moody Press, 1992), 78.

the trial that he's currently in, he's rejoicing—a mindset certainly echoed by his words in 2 Corinthians 6:10: "sorrowful but always rejoicing."

Paul writes also that this suffering was for the Colossian believers. It was not for recognition, or so that people would feel sorry for him. Rather, it was *for you*, he says. This means that it was for the sake of his readers, for their behalf, for their account. He states something very similar in 2 Timothy 2:9-10 when he writes to the church at Ephesus. There, he says, "for which I suffer trouble as an evildoer, even to the point of chains; but the word of God is not chained. Therefore I endure all things for the sake of the elect, that they also may obtain the salvation which is in Christ Jesus with eternal glory." This should cause you and me to ponder and ask ourselves why we serve the Lord. Is it for Him and for those we serve? Or is it for ourselves? What really are our motives?

Paul ends this verse with a mysterious phrase that has puzzled scholars for many years. In fact, it is one of the most debated verses in the entire Bible, to the point that in the last 2000 years entire books have been written on this one verse alone. I'll give you some possible interpretations of this verse and then I'll leave you with the one I think is correct. Paul says, *I ... fill up in my flesh what is lacking in the afflictions of Christ.*

Some interpret this verse to mean that Christ's atonement was lacking or insufficient and that Paul's sufferings were necessary to fill up what was missing in Christ's sufferings. I say that is ludicrous! Paul did not help with the atonement because Christ's atonement was sufficient in and of itself and not lacking anything. Colossians 1:12-14 is clear about this. And Hebrews 10:14 unashamedly states, "For by one offering He has perfected forever those who are being sanctified."

Another view is that Paul's sufferings benefitted others in that he presented Christ to them through his suffering. In so doing, others would watch how Paul responded to suffering and be encouraged by it. These things are certainly true, but they do not constitute the proper interpretation, in my opinion.

The interpretation which I believe to be correct is this: that which was lacking was not Christ's sufferings, but Paul's. Paul wanted to fill up through suffering what was lacking in his own life, so that he could be more like Christ. Paul desired to be more like Christ, and in order for that to be accomplished, he desired to suffer more. One man helps us understand this: "Having this strong wish he had been led to pursue a course of life which conducted him through trial strongly resembling those which Christ Himself endured, and as fast as possible, he was filling up that in which he fell short."[12] Isn't that what Paul writes about to the church at Philippi in Philippians 3:10? "That I may know Him and the power of His resurrection, and the fellowship of His sufferings, being conformed to His death." Paul wanted to be so much like His Savior that he not only wanted to live as Christ did but also to suffer as Christ did. Albert Barnes says, "Many are willing to reign with Christ, but they would not be willing to suffer with Him; many would be willing to wear a crown of glory like Him, but not the crown of thorns; many would be willing to put on the robes of splendor which will be worn in heaven, but not the scarlet robe of contempt and mockery."[13]

There are certainly other thoughts on this verse, but I'll leave you to study those on your own. We will move from learning of Paul's rejoicing in ministry to learning of his responsibility in ministry, in verses 25-27.

Paul's Responsibility in Ministry

Colossians 1:25-27

> of which I became a minister according to the stewardship from God which was given to me for you, to fulfill the word of God. (Colossians 1:25)

---

12 Albert Barnes, *Barnes Notes: Ephesians – Philemon (Grand Rapids: Baker Book House, 1962), 254.*
13 Ibid, 197.

Paul mentions here that he *became a minister according to the stewardship from God*. We saw in our last lesson that a *minister* is one who runs errands, an attendant, a table waiter. How did Paul get this job of a table waiter? Did he just wake up one morning, and say, "I think I will be a minister"? No, it was given by *the stewardship from God*, which means it was commissioned by God. It was a divinely appointed *stewardship*, a word which speaks of a house-steward, a person who was given the responsibility of administering the rules of a house. A steward would handle the financial affairs of the house and oversee its' servants. It was a position that would free up the owner of the house to travel and do other things. A steward was a trusted position.

And Paul says to the Colossians that he was given the responsibility of stewardship *for you*. Just as he was suffering for them, he also was ministering for them. This call on Paul's life was not for him or his own self-esteem, but for their benefit. God gave Paul these abilities for the benefit of others, just as He gives you and me spiritual gifts for the benefit of others and for the glory of Christ. Ladies, serving the Lord is not about us—it is about Him and others. Paul writes of this truth, again to the church at Ephesus, in Ephesians 4:11-12. He says, "And He Himself gave some to be apostles, some prophets, some evangelists, and some pastors and teachers, for the equipping of the saints for the work of ministry, for the edifying of the body of Christ." Our spiritual gifts are given for the benefit of others. We would be wise women to evaluate why we do the things we do. If it is for recognition or selfish ambition, we should repent and ask God to help us do it for His glory and the service of others. Remember, even Jesus came not to be ministered to but to minister and to give His life a ransom for many (Matthew 20:28).

Paul ends this verse by writing that this charge to be a minister was given *to fulfill the word of God*. The word *fulfill* means to satisfy, complete, or perfect. Paul desired to preach so that the Word of God would be proclaimed. Paul says something very similar in Romans 15:19, "in mighty signs and wonders, by the power of the Spirit of God, so that from Jerusalem and round about to Illyricum I have fully preached the gospel of Christ." His desire was to preach the gospel faithfully and completely, and to be true to that calling. We are living in an age where there are few who are fully carrying out the preaching of God's Word. They might have a lot of cute stories and jokes to tell and perhaps even some amusing video clips or skits, but there is a famine in their churches—and in our land—for the Word of The Lord! It is the Word of God that changes lives, not philosophy, not man's ideas. I am often puzzled by churches that do not preach the Word of God and even many women's ministries which gravitate toward fuzzy devotional material but have no interest in genuine Bible study. Paul's message to young Timothy needs to be heeded in our day; he writes to Timothy in 2 Timothy 4:2-5: "Preach the word! Be ready in season and out of season. Convince, rebuke, exhort, with all longsuffering and teaching. For the time will come when they will not endure sound doctrine, but according to their own desires, because they have itching ears, they will heap up for themselves teachers; and they will turn their ears away from the truth and be turned aside to fables. But you be watchful in all things, endure afflictions, do the work of an evangelist, fulfill your ministry." There is that word again—fulfill your ministry, complete the ministry, satisfy the ministry. That's what Paul has just said here in Colossians, that he was a minister to fulfill the Word of God. We need ministers like Paul and Timothy who will faithfully preach the Word of God! And Paul goes on to give a description of this Word in verse 26.

> the mystery which has been hidden from ages and from generations, but now has been revealed to His saints. (Colossians 1:26)

Paul writes that the word is a *mystery which has been hidden*. The word *mystery* simply means a truth that was once hidden but now is revealed. Paul elaborates on this more in the sister epistle to Colossians, his letter to the Ephesians. Consider Ephesians 3:1-7.

> For this reason I, Paul, the prisoner of Christ Jesus for you Gentiles—if indeed you have heard of the dispensation of the grace of God which was given to me for you, how that by

revelation He made known to me the mystery (as I have briefly written already, by which, when you read, you may understand my knowledge in the mystery of Christ), which in other ages was not made known to the sons of men, as it has now been revealed by the Spirit to His holy apostles and prophets: that the Gentiles should be fellow heirs, of the same body, and partakers of His promise in Christ through the gospel, of which I became a minister according to the gift of the grace of God given to me by the effective working of His power.

The mystery is the gospel, as Paul so clearly explains. The Christian mystery is not secret knowledge for a select few, as the Gnostics claimed. It had been hidden *from ages and from generations*, which simply refers to those who lived in former times. They did not understand the mystery of which Paul is writing.

But now, Paul says, indicating a contrast, that mystery *has been revealed to His saints*. The word *reveal* means to make manifest or to render apparent. It is as clear as daylight now, so to speak. And *saint* refers to those who are called of God. This mystery, this gospel, which was once hidden, has now been offered. And, according to verse 27, it has been offered even to the Gentiles.

To them God willed to make known what are the riches of the glory of this mystery among the Gentiles: which is Christ in you, the hope of glory. (Colossians 1:27)

To them God willed to make known the riches of the glory of this mystery. The Gnostics did not do this, contrary to what they taught. What did God *make known*? The *riches* or the abundance of *this mystery*. And amazingly enough, it is offered to *the Gentiles*. Remember Paul had been called to minister to the Gentiles. When rehearsing his Damascus Road experience before King Agrippa, Paul relates what God said to him on the Damascus Road, in Acts 26:17-18: "I will deliver you from the Jewish people, as well as from the Gentiles, to whom I now send you, to open their eyes, in order to turn them from darkness to light, and from the power of Satan to God, that they may receive forgiveness of sins and an inheritance among those who are sanctified by faith in Me."

This mystery Paul says is *Christ in you, the hope of glory*! *Christ in you* means that He is in a fixed position. Once He's there, it is a done deal. We are sealed until the day of redemption and no man can pluck us out of the Father's hand—praise be to God! This is our *hope*, which means that this is our anticipated pleasure. My friend, I hope we are overcome with gratitude at the thought of Christ being in us—Gentiles, who were once considered to be cut off from Christ and without hope! When Paul was struck on the Damascus Road, Jesus explained to Paul that he was to take the gospel to the Gentiles, something that had not been offered before. Judaism was only for a select few, but salvation through Christ is offered to all, even the Gentiles. What a mystery, now revealed, for which we should all thank God!

Did you notice the many interesting facts about this mystery that are nestled in this text? This mystery is made known by God; it is rich; it is glorious; it is available to the Gentiles; it is Christ in me; and it is the hope of glory. It certainly was not a mystery that was for the Gnostics, but it certainly was made known to those whom God elected to be His children!

Paul's responsibility in ministry was to minister the Word of God. We now turn from his responsibility in ministry to his reason for being in the ministry. And, my friend, it wasn't for money or to promote himself, as so many do today. It was for something much different. Let's peer into verse 28.

Paul's Reason for Ministry

Colossians 1:28

> Him we preach, warning every man and teaching every man in all wisdom, that we may present every man perfect in Christ Jesus. (Colossians 1:28)

Notice that Paul changes the pronoun from *my* to *we*, indicating that Paul and Timothy were both preaching the gospel, they were both preaching Christ. In our day, we have some who preach politics, some who preach religious rights, some who preach the rights of those who identify as LGBTQ, some who preach the rights of women, but for Paul and Timothy, and for us as Christians, *we preach* Christ, we declare or proclaim *Him*.

According to what Paul says in this verse, there are two elements to preaching. The first, he says, is *warning every man*. To warn means to caution or reprove gently, to admonish. This is something that is sorely lacking not only in the pulpit but in our daily living. We shy away from lovingly reproving others. We fear men more than we fear God. But, my dear sister, we must out of love for God and others reprove those who need to be reproved. Paul, however, warns often in his letters. In Acts 20:17-38, he warns the elders at Ephesus that some of them are going to fall away after he leaves them; and in verse 31, he says, "Therefore watch, and remember that for three years I did not cease to warn everyone night and day with tears." He was so concerned for them that he warned them, and he did so with tears; his warning was not without compassion. To the church at Corinth, which was living carnally, he writes in 1 Corinthians 4:14, "I do not write these things to shame you, but as my beloved children I warn you." We could give numerous examples from the apostles' preaching and our Lord's preaching in which they warned others of the need to repent. There is a judgment to come, and we should not let fear keep us from doing the right thing.

Of course, such warning is to be done in a spirit of meekness, considering ourselves, lest we be tempted, as Paul says in Galatians 6:1. Perhaps you have the misconception that confronting sin or error is only for those in leadership, but that is so far from truth. When we get to chapter 3 of Paul's letter to the Colossians, we will see in verse 16 that he writes, "Let the word of Christ dwell in you richly in all wisdom, teaching and admonishing one another in psalms and hymns and spiritual songs, singing with grace in your hearts to the Lord." This is an admonition for all of God's children to admonish others. And, even in Romans 15:14, Paul writes, "Now I myself am confident concerning you, my brethren, that you also are full of goodness, filled with all knowledge, able also to admonish one another." If we really want to be conformed to the image of our Lord, then we will welcome those who love us enough to warn us that we are not representing Him. I am grateful for those who are willing to help me see the blind spots in my life.

The second way Paul says he and Timothy proclaim Christ is by *teaching every man in all wisdom. Teaching* means to instruct or to impart truth, and it is to be done *in all wisdom*, which means that the teaching is to be done in a practical manner. A preacher of God's Word is to warn and teach and to follow up that warning and teaching with practical admonition. This is where instruction is given on how to take what is learned and put it into practice. I know some women who come to Bible study and shy away from the hard study, which is not good. Others shy away from the application of what they've learned, which isn't good either. Both are equally important. Some preachers only teach and warn, some only give practical application, but a good steward of God's Word will do all.

There is a reason Paul and Timothy preach by warning and teaching, and it is so that they can *present every man perfect in Christ Jesus.* The words *may present* mean to stand beside or to recommend. And to present as *perfect* means to present as full grown or complete. Paul and Timothy's desire is to preach so that they can recommend those believers at Colossae as full-grown and mature. One day, the shepherds of our churches will give an account to the Chief Shepherd, and any shepherd that is worth his salt will desire to present those he has shepherded as perfect and complete. Paul reiterates this very thing in 1 Thessalonians 2:19-20, when he says, "For what is our hope, or joy, or crown of rejoicing? Is it not even you in the presence of our Lord Jesus Christ at His coming? For you are our glory and joy." The writer to the Hebrews also warns us of this in Hebrews 13:17, "Obey those who rule over you, and be submissive, for they watch out for your souls, as those who must give account. Let them do so with joy and not with grief, for that would be unprofitable for you." Did you notice how much of what Paul does is for those to whom he's ministering? He isn't doing these things for himself or even for the rewards he might receive but for their benefit. (It's also interesting to note that it is Christ who presents them in verse 22 and it is Paul who presents them in verse 28.)

Paul makes it clear to the Colossians that this completion or perfection is *in Christ*, not in themselves. Our perfection or completion is not accomplished by our own works, least we should boast. This is an important distinction Paul is making because the Gnostics taught a works-oriented system. We should also note that Paul uses the words *every man* three times here. He does so for the purpose of giving emphasis because he is acknowledging that the gospel is for everyone, not just for a select few, as the Gnostics claimed. Paul believed Christ could save anyone, and he saw that potential in everyone! Do you? Do you look on others and see them as those whom God may choose to save? Sometimes, we look at people and think that they will never change, that they will never come to Christ, and yet the gospel is offered to all, and it can change the most unlikely of individuals. What is Paul's reason for ministry? To present every man perfect in Christ Jesus.

So, we have seen Paul's rejoicing in ministry, his responsibility in ministry, and his reason for ministry. We come now to Paul's resource in ministry. I find myself reading about the apostle Paul and all that he did, and I think to myself, "Paul, how did you do all this? Did they have coffee in your day? Weren't you tired?" I get tired just thinking about it! But from what Paul tells us in verse 29, it's clear that Paul did not do all this in his own strength. Here we see where his resource in ministry comes from.

Paul's Resource in Ministry

Colossians 1:29

> To this end I also labor, striving according to His working which works in me mightily. (Colossians 1:29)

Paul says *to this end I labor*. The word *labor* means to work to the point that one is left so weary that it was if the person had taken a beaten. Paul says he not only labors but *strives*, which is a stronger term that means to agonize. It was used of one struggling in an athletic event or a fight. Paul didn't shrink from the hard labor of the ministry, nor was he afraid of hard work. In 1 Thessalonians 2:9, he writes, "For you remember, brethren, our labor and toil; for laboring night and day, that we might not be a burden to any of you, we preached to you the gospel of God."

Paul isn't the only one who has labored to the point of exhaustion in ministry. It was said of Martin Luther that he worked so hard that many times he just fell into bed at night. D. L. Moody's bedtime prayer on one occasion was "Lord, I'm tired! Amen." John Wesley rode 60-70 miles each day and would preach an average of 3 sermons a day. Serving the Lord, many times, is exhausting, but it is a good exhaustion. There truly is no better life. But we do not do the work of the ministry in our own strength—praise God! If we did, we would all throw up our hands and eventually give up! Paul did not do his work in his own strength, but in the Lord's. Paul says he does this *according to His working which works in me mightily*. *Working* refers to power or energy; and *works in me* means to be mighty in me, to be active in me. *Mightily* is a reference to dynamite power. Paul knew that without the power of God working in him he could not do the work of the ministry; it would simply be impossible. In 1 Corinthians 15:10, he says, "But by the grace of God I am what I am, and His grace toward me was not in vain; but I labored more abundantly than they all, yet not I, but the grace of God which was with me." And in Ephesians 3:7, he writes, "… I became a minister according to the gift of the grace of God given to me by the effective working of His power." Jesus is very clear in John 15:5 that without Him we can do nothing! Paul's resource in ministry was the mighty power of God—and it is yours and mine, as well!

Summary

Paul's rejoicing in ministry was evidenced by his rejoicing in his sufferings. What sufferings have you endured recently, especially as it pertains to your service to God? Did you find yourself rejoicing or murmuring in it? Do you serve Him with joy, even when things aren't going so well?

Paul's responsibility was to minister the Word of God—not man's ideas, but God's pure and sufficient Word. When you minister to others—your family, your friends, your church—do you minister the truth of the Word or do you gravitate to all the novel advice out there? Do you know the Word so well that you can minister it to others?

Paul's reason for ministry was to present those he ministered to as perfect and complete before the Lord on that day. What is your reason for serving the Lord? Is it fame? Fortune? The boosting of your own self-esteem? To impress others? We must carefully examine why we do what we do in ministry and repent of any motivation other than the glory of God and the desire to help others.

Paul's resource in ministry was the mighty power of God. Do you endeavor to serve the Lord in your own strength or in His strength? Do you ask God to enable you to accomplish His will?

As we meditate on these truths, we can praise God, because none of us are just housewives, just mothers, just employees, or just Americans. We are chosen by God before the foundation of the world to be used for His glory and for His kingdom.

Questions to Consider

Colossians 1:24-29
The Call and Cost to Ministry

1. Read Colossians chapter one, especially noting verses 24-29. (a) What do you think is the "mystery" Paul mentions? (b) What things do you observe about this mystery?

2. Memorize Colossians 1:28.

3. (a) What are Paul's motives for being in the ministry, according to Colossians 1:24-29? (b) What other things was Paul willing to endure for the sake of others, according to 2 Corinthians 4:8-15; 6:1-10; 11:23-28; and 1 Thessalonians 2? (c) Why do you think some are not willing to labor to the point of exhaustion for the brethren? (d) How can we change that?

4. (a) What was prophesied in Isaiah 49:6? (b) When was this fulfilled? See Acts 10. (c) Who was told to take the gospel to the Gentiles? (d) How was he told? (e) What happened after this, according to the rest of Acts 10? (f) According to Romans 15:9, how should we as Gentiles respond to this amazing truth?

5. (a) Paul says in Colossians 1:28 that in his preaching he both warns and teaches. Why do you think both are important? (b) Read over Colossians and make two columns. In one column list the verses in which Paul is warning the Colossian believers, and in the other column list the verses in which he is teaching them.

6. (a) According to the following verses, what are some of the reasons that Christians suffer? John 15:18-21; 2 Corinthians 1:3-7; 2 Corinthians 4:8-11; Philippians 3:10; 2 Timothy 1:8; 2 Timothy 2:9-10. (b) How do these personally help you face present sufferings?

7. What does it mean to you personally that "Christ is in you"?

8. (a) In what ways have you seen the Lord working mightily in your life, especially in the past year? (b) What things have happened in your life that can only be explained because of Christ working in you?

9. How could you be more effective in what God has called you to do? Please write your need in the form of a prayer request.

Chapter 8

Requests and Recommendations for Those Caught Up in Heresy

Colossians 2:1-7

The week before I wrote this lesson, I received an email from one of the ladies I disciple. She works in a job where she meets many different people and usually tries, when able, to bring the gospel to bear on their minds. She recently sent me an email in which she told of a pastor in our local town with whom she struck up a strange conversation. She recounted how she had asked him if he shared the gospel very much and he replied that he did when he could. But then she said, "Then we got onto the subject of sinners and he told me adamantly that we are not sinners anymore. We are not to even consider ourselves as sinners." She elaborated more about the conversation and then ended with this, "It was the strangest conversation, and I left him so thankful for my church, for truth, and for a pastor who understands the truth.

I imagine many of you have had similar conversations with family members, co-workers, neighbors, or even church-going people who are caught up in some sort of heretical doctrine. Perhaps you've tried diligently to point them to the truth, as my friend did, but have been unsuccessful. You may have become frustrated over the years and have reached a point of not knowing what to do next, or even if you should do anything more. It is heartbreaking to see those we love caught up in false teaching. This is exactly where we find the apostle Paul as we begin chapter two of his epistle to the Colossians. What makes Paul's situation different from ours is that he is in prison, 1000 miles away from those he loves so dearly, who are caught up in heresy. Is Paul hindered because of being chained to a soldier? Is he helpless to do anything? No! And neither are we, even if those we're concerned about are far away, and even if we've never met them, as was the case for Paul. Let's read together the first seven verses of Colossians chapter 2.

Colossians 2:1-7

> For I want you to know what a great conflict I have for you and those in Laodicea, and for as many as have not seen my face in the flesh, ²that their hearts may be encouraged, being knit together in love, and attaining to all riches of the full assurance of understanding, to the knowledge of the mystery of God, both of the Father and of Christ, ³in whom are hidden all the treasures of wisdom and knowledge. ⁴Now this I say lest anyone should deceive you with persuasive words. ⁵For though I am absent in the flesh, yet I am with you in spirit, rejoicing to see your good order and the steadfastness of your faith in Christ. ⁶As you therefore have received Christ Jesus the Lord, so walk in Him, ⁷rooted and built up in Him and established in the faith, as you have been taught, abounding in it with thanksgiving.

Our outline for this text will be as follows:

Four Prayer Requests for Those Caught Up in Heresy (vv 1-5)

Four Recommendations to Avoid Being Caught Up in Heresy (vv 6-7)

As we ended chapter 1 of Colossians, we saw Paul's rejoicing in ministry, even though it brought suffering; Paul's responsibility in ministry, to minister the Word of God; Paul's reason for ministry, to present the Colossians perfect and complete; and lastly, Paul's resource in ministry, God's mighty power. Now, there's an unfortunate chapter division here as we begin this second chapter of Colossians. Remember, Paul wrote the Colossians a letter, not four individual chapters; it was man who later divided our Bible into chapters and verses, not God. In these verses, Paul is still agonizing over these dear saints, and we know that because he wrote in the last verse of chapter 1 that he was laboring and agonizing over them. It was a labor to the point of exhaustion, and he continued with the metaphor in 1:29 of agonizing or struggling for them as he continued on in chapter two. He writes,

Four Prayer Requests for
Those Caught Up in Heresy

Colossians 2:1-5

> For I want you to know what a great conflict I have for you and those in Laodicea, and for as many as have not seen my face in the flesh (Colossians 2:1)

Paul wanted them *to know*, he wanted them to fully understand, this *great conflict* he was having for them. *Conflict* means an agonizing effort. It is a word which probably refers to the mental conflict he was having because of the heresy that was threatening these believers. It's as if Paul is in constant distress over them and the possibility that they would adopt the Gnostic heresy. This, perhaps, is the same distress that some of you feel over those you love who are caught up in false teaching. It is distressing, and it can be mentally exhausting as you agonize over them in prayer.

But Paul is not only distressed for the Colossians but also for two other groups of people. The first group is *those in Laodicea.* Laodicea was about 11 miles from Colossae and this letter was also to be read to them, according to Colossians 4:16. There, Paul writes, "Now when this epistle is read among you, see that it is read also in the church of the Laodiceans, and that you likewise read the epistle from Laodicea." Because Laodicea was close geographically to the church at Colossae, its people would have been exposed to the same heretical teachings. I would like to pause here to give a word of caution to those of us who are living in my hometown of Tulsa, because we are in much the same danger as the churches of Colossae and Laodicea: Beware! Our city is infiltrated with heretical teaching, mainly the prosperity gospel. We would be wise to arm ourselves with the truth of the Word, and with clear understanding of heresy. It sounds good, as that pastor told my friend— "we are not sinners"—

but we must shun those things that are in direct contradiction to what God's Word teaches. It is both interesting and sobering that the church of Laodicea is mentioned in Revelation 3:16 as being lukewarm.

But Paul's concern isn't only for the Laodiceans; he also says, *for as many as have not seen my face in the flesh.* Who is Paul talking about here? This would include those at Hierapolis, which he mentions in Colossians 4:13, "For I bear him witness that he has a great zeal for you, and those who are in Laodicea, and those in Hierapolis." Hierapolis was located about 11 miles from Laodicea. There were others also in surrounding areas whom Paul had never met. He agonized for them even though he'd never met some of them. Does that characterize you and me? Do we agonize over those in our city or even around the world whom we don't know, yet who are caught up in heresy? Is our agonizing limited to only those we know? Paul was in agony for people he had never met, brothers and sisters in Christ who were caught up in dangerous heresy. When I see a false teacher and the massive crowds they're speaking to, I am grieved and burdened for them. Paul speaks about this in 2 Corinthians 11:29, "Who is weak, and I am not weak? Who is made to stumble, and I do not burn with indignation?" Things like false teaching caused Paul to burn with indignation and to agonize for those affected by it.

Now, Paul did something about this distress. He didn't just sit around in prison, chained to some guard, worrying, "Oh my! What am I going to do about the saints at Colossae?" He turned his inward agonizing upward to God in prayer for them. What did Paul pray for them? What was his desire? The answer is found in verse two, in a four-fold prayer. Paul has four requests for these dear believers and, my friend, we would do well to pray these for those we know who are caught up in false teaching.

> that their hearts may be encouraged, being knit together in love, and attaining to all riches of the full assurance of understanding, to the knowledge of the mystery of God, both of the Father and of Christ, (Colossians 2:2)

1. *The first prayer request from Paul is that their hearts might be encouraged.* Your translation might say comforted. *Hearts* would indicate one's thoughts or feelings, and to *be encouraged* means to be comforted or to draw near. Perhaps, you think this is a strange request from Paul, that their hearts would be encouraged. But think of this: those who are caught up in false teaching or who are being led astray by false teachers are discouraged because they are like children tossed to and fro, not knowing what to believe any more. Paul warns about this very thing in his letter to the Ephesians. Ephesians 4:14 says, "that we should no longer be children, tossed to and fro and carried about with every wind of doctrine, by the trickery of men, in the cunning craftiness of deceitful plotting." It's possible that the saints in Colossae were toiling in their minds too, thinking, "You know this Gnostic stuff sure sounds good, but in Christ I have everything I need … I think."

2. *Second, Paul prays that they would be knit together in love. Knit together* means to drive something or weld something together. This would unite them in association or affection, which is love. Paul is requesting that they would come together or be united with agape love. He's already told them in Colossians 1:4 that he and Timothy had heard of the love which they had for all the saints; that they were known for their love. So, Paul desires that they be knit together with that love! Now, why would they need to be knit together in love? When you consider that the false teachers were intending to deceive them with enticing words, you see how that deception could potentially cause division among them, and so they would need to be reminded to stick together in love. It's like James says in James 3:16, "For where envy and self-seeking exist, confusion and every evil thing are there." Where there is error or self-seeking, there is also confusion. When error tries to creep into a local church, you can almost count on a church split. You will have some who accept the error and others who will stand for the truth. We attended a certain church years ago which was allowing things in the church that should not be. My husband lovingly warned one of the elders that the church would split right down the middle if they did not put a stop to the nonsense going on, and sadly it did.

Paul was not only concerned for the Colossians' hearts, but for their minds as well. His third and fourth requests pertain to that.

3. *His third request is that they would attain to all riches of the full assurance of understanding. The full assurance of understanding* refers to entire confidence or conviction of something. *Understanding* is a mental putting together of something. Paul wants the Colossians to have confidence, or conviction, of the Christian doctrines. He wants them to be convinced of what Christ taught. Why? This is self-explanatory: they must have conviction of the truth so that they will know how to confront the dangerous error creeping into their church. In Titus, Paul speaks of this as an absolute necessity for a leader in the church. He writes in Titus 1:9, "holding fast the faithful word as he has been taught, that he may be able, by sound doctrine, both to exhort and convict those who contradict." My friend, this conviction concerning the truth isn't just for elders but for all of God's children. If you are not rooted and grounded in the Word yourself, you will not be able to discern false teachers or even confront them.

4. *Paul's fourth and last request for the Colossians is that they would know the mystery of God, both of the Father and Christ.* Paul wanted them to have a clear knowledge of the mystery of *God* and of *Christ*, His Son, who died for their sins. This would probably be the most important of Paul's requests, as the Gnostics taught that Christ was not enough. They, being "in the know," taught that one needed more and more knowledge. This "superior knowledge" the false teachers claimed to have, however, led them into all kinds of creepy error. The church at Colossae did not need more knowledge, as the Gnostics taught; they needed the knowledge of God, which was Christ. It was not Christ plus something else; it was—and is— the Master and Nothing Else! He is the mystery that Paul wrote of in 1:26-27, "the mystery which has been hidden from ages and from generations, but now has been revealed to His saints. To them God willed to make known what are the riches of the glory of this mystery among the Gentiles: which is Christ in you, the hope of glory." Paul goes on to remind them in verse three of just what they

have in Christ. I mean, why would you search for something else when you have what is described in verse 3?!

> in whom are hidden all the treasures of wisdom and knowledge. (Colossians 2:3)

Paul says in Him *are hidden all the treasures of wisdom and knowledge.* The word *hidden* means kept secret, and *treasures* refers to wealth that has been deposited. In Him is all the wealth we need, both of wisdom and of knowledge, not just a limited amount. *Knowledge* is the apprehending of truth, whereas *wisdom* is application of that truth to life. Wisdom is the ability to apply knowledge to the best advantage. The Gnostics taught that knowledge was an end in itself; they boasted of their secret hidden writings. But Paul contrasts their worthless secrets to the real hidden treasure, that being Christ alone. In Christ are hidden *all* the treasures of wisdom and knowledge, and yet, the Colossians must pursue that knowledge of Him, just as you and I must pursue it. It doesn't come by osmosis. This poses a question that each of us must consider, and that, is, "Are we growing in our knowledge of Christ?" We have so many means in our day of learning about so many different things, but are we learning and growing in our knowledge of the most important thing, to know God and to know His Son Jesus? This should be our greatest pursuit in life as Paul says in Philippians 3:10, "That I may know Him and the power of His resurrection, and the fellowship of His sufferings, being conformed to His death." The false teachers did not have all the wisdom and knowledge, even though they claimed they did, and Paul knew this. And so, he begins to warn in verse four, by saying:

> Now this I say lest anyone should deceive you with persuasive words. (Colossians 2:4)

Paul tells them he's writing this letter to them to prevent them from being *deceived* or led astray. The KJV uses the term beguile. Paul doesn't want the Colossians to be deluded into thinking something that isn't true. The Gnostics were deceiving these believers with enticing or *persuasive* words, a reference to fine-sounding arguments. They were being led astray by false reasoning. The apostle John, who also writes concerning this same false teaching, warns his readers in 1 John 2:26, "These things I have written to you concerning those who try to deceive you." Apparently, the Gnostics were good at enticing others with their persuasive speech. We, too, need to be on guard against those things that might sound really good, because, my friend, that is how Satan appears, as an angel of light. Jude warns of this very kind of speech among false teachers, in Jude 1:16, "These are grumblers, complainers, walking according to their own lusts; and they mouth great swelling words, flattering people to gain advantage." This certainly was not the speech of the apostle Paul. He writes 1 Corinthians 2:4, "And my speech and my preaching were not with persuasive words of human wisdom, but in demonstration of the Spirit and of power." My friend, we preach Christ and His Word, as Paul has already written, not our own mysterious and novel ideas. Beware! Just because someone can convince you by their smooth-sounding speech doesn't mean they're right. Even the adulterous woman of Proverbs 5:3-4 was persuasive with her speech, "For the lips of an immoral woman drip honey, and her mouth is smoother than oil; but in the end she is bitter as wormwood, sharp as a two-edged sword." David speaks of this very thing when talking about his so-called "trusted" friend, Ahithophel, who betrayed him. David writes of him in Psalm 55:21, "The words of his mouth were smoother than butter, but war was in his heart; his words were softer than oil, yet they were drawn swords." We would do well to listen to those who are empowered by the Spirit, and whose words line up with the Word of God and not with flowery, flattering, smooth speech.

In fact, let me give you four characteristics that are evident in those whose words are smooth but who have heresy in their heart. Maybe this will help you if you are caught up in any false teaching. It may also enable you to help those you love who are caught up in heresy. (These are not Paul's four recommendations, by the way, that is still yet to come!) Jesus gives us some helps in Matthew 23:1-7, where he confronts the false teachers of His day, the scribes and Pharisees.

> Then Jesus spoke to the multitudes and to His disciples, saying:
> "The scribes and the Pharisees sit in Moses' seat. Therefore
> whatever they tell you to observe, that observe and do, but do
> not do according to their works; for they say, and do not do. For
> they bind heavy burdens, hard to bear, and lay them on men's
> shoulders; but they themselves will not move them with one
> of their fingers. But all their works they do to be seen by men.
> They make their phylacteries broad and enlarge the borders
> of their garments. They love the best places at feasts, the best
> seats in the synagogues, greetings in the marketplaces, and to
> be called by men, Rabbi, Rabbi."

According to Jesus, we can spot a false teacher by four specific characteristics. He says they lack integrity (v 3), sympathy (v 4), spirituality (v 5), and humility (v 6).[14]

The news of the false teachers deceiving the saints at Colossae was weighing heavily on the apostle Paul and added to that burden was the fact that he could not be with them, as he mentioned in verse 5. I know when I have a burden for someone, the phone or email just doesn't suffice; I want to be face to face with that person to endeavor to help them. So, Paul writes in verse 5.

> For though I am absent in the flesh, yet I am with you in spirit,
> rejoicing to see your good order and the steadfastness of your
> faith in Christ. (Colossians 2:5)

Yet even though Paul is *absent* from them *in the flesh*, he is with them *in spirit*, which is a reference to his human spirit. We might phrase it this way: "My heart is with you." At the time I was writing this lesson, I had a dear friend in California who lost her mother. I wrote this very thing on her card: "For though I am absent in the flesh, yet am I with you in the spirit." Paul wanted to be with the Colossians but was providentially hindered from doing so. I, too, wanted to be with my friend but was unable to do so.

---

14 John MacArthur, "Exposing the Marks of Counterfeit Authority." Grace Community Church, Sun Valley, CA. *Grace to You. https://www.gty.org/library/sermons-library/90/353/Exposing-The-Marks-Of-Counterfeit-Authority.*

Even though Paul is absent, he is *rejoicing*. Why? He says it is *to see your good order and the steadfastness of your faith in Christ*. I find it interesting that Paul has just warned the Colossians and now he commends them. We saw the opposite of this in chapter one, where he first commended them and then warned them. The order is not essential, but the balance of warning and commending is. What is Paul saying here when he says he is rejoicing to see their good order and the steadfastness of their faith in Christ? He is *rejoicing*, which means to be calmly happy, and it is specifically related to two things: their *good order* and the *steadfastness of their faith*. *Order* is a military term which speaks of an orderly array of soldiers. *Steadfastness* is another military term which means to make solid. Keep in mind that Paul wrote this letter from prison where he had constant contact with soldiers, and so perhaps this is why he uses these military terms here. He is beholding with joy the Colossians' orderly array and the solid front of their faith in Christ. In 2 Timothy 2:3, Paul refers to saints as soldiers. He writes, "You therefore must endure hardship as a good soldier of Jesus Christ." Here in Colossians, he reminds them to continue the work of a good soldier, to be steadfast in an orderly array. He's saying, "Don't waver, don't doubt, and don't give in to the Gnostic teaching!"

Notice that the steadfastness of their faith was *in Christ*. Without Him, they would be wobbly, double-minded, and in disarray. That same steadfastness was also evidence that they had truly been reconciled to God, as Paul has already mentioned in Colossians 1:23, "If indeed you continue in the faith, grounded and steadfast, and are not moved away from the hope of the gospel which you heard, which was preached to every creature under heaven, of which I, Paul, became a minister." Paul wants them to remain steadfast, but how will they do that? And how will you and I remain steadfast in a world that is increasingly riddled with false teachers and false teaching? Paul answers that question by shifting from his requests for those caught up in heresy to his four recommendations to avoid being caught up in heresy. Let's look at verse 6.

Four Recommendations to Avoid Being Caught Up in Heresy

Colossians 2:6-7

As you therefore have received Christ Jesus the Lord, so walk
in Him, (Colossians 2:6)

1. *As you have received the Lord, now walk in Him; this is Paul's
first recommendation for avoiding heresy.* What does it mean that
they had *received Christ Jesus the Lord*? The word *receive* means
to associate oneself or to join oneself to another. They had received
Christ Jesus and notice that He is *Lord*! This is a tad bit different
than the typical gospel message we hear today which tells us to
receive Christ by asking Him into our heart (which, by the way,
is nowhere mentioned in the Bible). We who are God's children
have joined ourselves with One who is our Lord, who is our Master
and Owner, who is supreme in authority. Because the Colossians
had received Christ as the supreme authority in their life, Paul
says they are to *walk in Him*. Walking with God is the first step
to avoid heresy. The term *walk* is used as a metaphor in Scripture
to describe one's manner of life. It includes not only the activities
of an individual's life but also the progress that individual makes,
because when we think of walking, we think of progress. Paul was
reminding the Colossians that their walk must be in harmony with
the fact that they have embraced Christ as Lord. One cannot receive
Christ without walking with Him. If we are truly walking in the
Spirit and walking with the Lord, we will not allow ourselves to be
persuaded by false teachers. Unfortunately, many in our day are not
daily walking with the Lord. Many spend no time in the Word or
prayer and then they wonder why they are swept away by the novel
and new ideas that creep into the church. Walking with the Lord is
essential, and yet Paul goes on to give three more recommendations
for avoiding heresy, in verse 7.

rooted and built up in Him and established in the faith, as
you have been taught, abounding in it with thanksgiving.
(Colossians 2:7)

2. *The second recommendation we must heed if we are to avoid heresy is to be rooted and built up in Him.* The Greek reads, "Having been rooted." The Colossians believers had been firmly established, firmly rooted. One man has said, "strong roots stabilize growth."[15] We only need to be rooted once; it is an action that happens once and has continuing, ongoing results. Paul is reminding the Colossians that they have already been rooted in Christ. Being confident of this truth would be essential as they faced the Gnostic heresy.

The phrase *built up in Him* is a present participle, indicating continuous action. It reads, "Being constantly built up." And note that it's *in Him*, in Christ. Paul writes of this same idea in Ephesians 2:19-22, "Now, therefore, you are no longer strangers and foreigners, but fellow citizens with the saints and members of the household of God, having been built on the foundation of the apostles and prophets, Jesus Christ Himself being the chief cornerstone, in whom the whole building, being fitted together, grows into a holy temple in the Lord, in whom you also are being built together for a dwelling place of God in the Spirit." Paul's desire for the believers at Colossae is the same as his desire for the believers at Ephesus. We need to be built up in Him. Our foundation rests on Christ, who is the Chief Cornerstone.

You might be wondering how exactly we are built up in Christ. The answer: by the Word of God. Listen to what Paul says in Acts 20:32: "So now, brethren, I commend you to God and to the word of His grace, which is able to build you up and give you an inheritance among all those who are sanctified." But we also build ourselves up by something else. Consider what Jude says in Jude 1:20-21, "But you, beloved, building yourselves up on your most holy faith, praying in the Holy Spirit, keep yourselves in the love of God, looking for the mercy of our Lord Jesus Christ unto eternal life." When you marry these two passages together, the answer is simple. We build ourselves up by the Word, prayer, faith, and love.

---

15 Charles R Swindoll, *Growing Strong in the Seasons of Life (Portland: Multnomah Press, 1983), 116.*

3. Paul's third recommendation is the outcome of the first two. *As saints are rooted and built up, it is only natural that they will be established in the faith; this is the third recommendation to follow if one wants to be kept from error. Established* means to be strengthened, making firm or stable. It is also a present participle, which indicates a continuous action. The Colossians were not to be tossed to and fro by various false teachings; they were to be firm and stable in what they believed. Being established, being steadfast in the faith, would be a reminder to them that they were genuine in their faith.

4. *Paul gives one last recommendation to keep them from heresy: They are to abound in thanksgiving. Abounding* means to super-abound or to be in excess. Paul adds the word *with* before the word thanksgiving; it indicates a fixed position. *Thanksgiving* means to offer grateful language to God as an act of worship. You might wonder how abounding with thanksgiving can help one to avoid heresy. One who is thankful and content in their relationship with Christ is not on the lookout for the new and novel ideas that false teachers present. They have such a firmly grounded relationship with Christ that they are not on the lookout for anything enticing. They have their Master, and He is enough!

These four recommendations build upon each other. Being rooted leads to being built up, which leads to being established in the faith, which leads to abounding with thanksgiving. As believers are built up in Christ, they become more and more grateful, so that they are overflowing with thanksgiving. A thankful heart is a content heart. A thankful heart is not always on the lookout for something new and enticing. The thankful heart is satisfied with Christ, with Him alone and nothing else! This such a contrast from the false teachers who rarely are thankful to God but spend most of their time praising themselves! If we would cultivate a thankful spirit, we would not desire to look for fulfillment anywhere else or be led astray by false teachers. One man says,

People who received and were taught the correct faith by a true teacher from God, people who go walking on in it, are rooted more deeply and built up more fully in it, are constantly confirmed in regard to it by daily testing of it, are thankful for all of it, especially for the renewed confirmation. What will they do? Why, laugh at all false teachers who come along and try to alter any part of that faith and doctrine. This is a most excellent summary, and it is placed in the proper place.[16]

Summary

Paul's *Four Prayer Requests for Those Caught Up in Heresy* (vv 1-5) include:

1. That their hearts would be comforted
2. That they would be knit together in love
3. That they would attain to the full riches of a complete understanding
4. That they would know the mystery of God

My friend, if you are wavering in your faith today, I would encourage you to pray these four truths for yourself. If you know of someone who is caught up in error, pray these four truths for them. False teachers and their teaching are dangerous, so dangerous that they can lead someone eternally astray.

Paul's *Four Recommendations to Avoid Being Caught Up in Heresy* (vv 6-7) include:

1. Walk with God
2. Be rooted and built up in Him
3. Be established in the faith
4. Abound with thanksgiving

What are you doing to avoid being caught up in the false teachings of our day? Are you walking with God? How have you been walking with Him this week? Are you rooted and built up in Him by a life of

---

16 R.C.H. Lenski, *The Interpretation of St. Paul's Epistles to the Colossians and Thessalonians* (Minneapolis: Augsburg Fortress, 2008), 95.

dedicated prayer, reading the Word, faith, and love? How often do you participate in these spiritual disciplines? Is your time in the Word and prayer growing or diminishing? Are you firm in your faith? Do you know what you believe, why you believe it, and how to defend the faith you believe in? If not, why not? What about abounding in thanksgiving? Are you so content in your relationship with Christ that when those false ideas come your way, you think, "Who are they kidding?! I have my Lord and He is enough! Why should I taste of their erroneous ideas when I have tasted of the Lord and found that He is excellent?!"

Questions to Consider
Colossians 2:1-7
Requests and Recommendations for Those Caught up in Heresy

1. (a) Read Colossians chapter two. From your reading and without referring to other helps, jot down the heresies Paul mentions in this chapter, of which the Colossian believers were in danger? (b) What is Paul's attitude about this?

2. Memorize Colossians 2:6.

3. (a) Locate the city of Laodicea on a map (online, or in a bible atlas or study Bible). How far is Laodicea from Colossae? (b) Why do you think Paul is concerned for Laodicea? (See Colossians 4:13-16 for some hints.)

4. (a) In Colossians 2:4, how does Paul define the Gnostics' speech? (b) How does that compare to what Paul says about his own speech in 1 Corinthians 2:1-8? (c) What other warnings do you see, in 1 Corinthians 2, about man's wisdom? (d) What does this teach you about listening to the words of men?

5. (a) What do false teachers look like, according to 2 Corinthians 11:13-15? (b) What do they desire to do to the saints, according to Ephesians 4:14-15 and 5:6-7? (c) As believers, what should be our response to false teachers, according to these Scriptures, as well as Titus 3:9-11?

6. (a) According to Psalm 1:3; 92:12-13; Isaiah 61:3; and Jeremiah 17:8, why is it important that we as believers be firmly rooted and grounded in the faith? (b) According to Jude 1:8-13, what is going to happen to those who have not been rooted and grounded in the faith and have, instead, fallen into error?

7. (a) Have you grown in your knowledge of Christ? (b) What have you learned about Him specifically this past year?

8. (a) If a false teacher was trying to entice you, what would you do? (b) How can you train your children, grandchildren, or those you are mentoring to be on the alert for false teachers? (c) What advice would you give them?

9. Does your heart ache for someone you know who is caught up in erroneous teaching? Turn your pain for them into a prayer request for them. (Please be discreet in sharing.)

Chapter 9

Are We Complete in Christ Alone?

Colossians 2:8-15

The following is the true story of a pastor who was staying with some friends while conducting a series of church meetings: One evening, the pastor had a friend pick him up for the meetings, leaving his hosts at their home where he was staying. As he was leaving, he told them he'd be back around midnight. After the meetings were over, the pastor's friend dropped him off at the house and said, "Goodbye." The pastor went to the door and knocked, assuming that his hosts would be up waiting because the porch light was still on. But as he knocked on the door no one answered. Harder and harder he knocked, and still no one answered the door. It was rather cold, and so he went around to the kitchen door and pounded and still no one answered. So, he decided to walk to a neighbor's house, but realized that probably was not such a good idea that late, so he walked for several miles before reaching a motel. The manager was kind enough to let him use the phone. He called his friends and woke them up to let them know he could not get in the house and ask if they could come and get him. The host replied by saying, "Friend, you have a key in your coat pocket. Don't you remember? I gave it to you before you left." Sure enough, the key was right there in his pocket!

We all have probably had experiences like that—looking everywhere for some personal item, like our keys or phone, only to find that it is within our reach. Experiences like these are perfect illustrations of what Paul endeavors to convey to the Colossian believers in this lesson. They have everything they need in Christ in their spiritual pocket. Jesus is the key to every spiritual blessing we could ever desire. To seek something more is like frantically knocking on a door, seeking what is inside and not realizing you hold the key in your own pocket. We are complete in Christ. But maybe you're wondering, as some at Colossae may have been, "Are we really complete in Christ alone? How can this be? Why don't we need anything else?" Let's discover the answers to these questions together as we read verses 8-15 of Colossians 2.

Colossians 2:8-15

> Beware lest anyone cheat you through philosophy and empty deceit, according to the tradition of men, according to the basic principles of the world, and not according to Christ. [9]For in Him dwells all the fullness of the Godhead bodily; [10]and you are complete in Him, who is the head of all principality and power. [11]In Him you were also circumcised with the circumcision made without hands, by putting off the body of the sins of the flesh, by the circumcision of Christ, [12]buried with Him in baptism, in which you also were raised with Him through faith in the working of God, who raised Him from the dead. [13]And you, being dead in your trespasses and the uncircumcision of your flesh, He has made alive together with Him, having forgiven you all trespasses, [14]having wiped out the handwriting of requirements that was against us, which was contrary to us. And He has taken it out of the way, having nailed it to the cross. [15]Having disarmed principalities and powers, He made a public spectacle of them, triumphing over them in it.

As we consider the question, "Are we complete in Christ alone?" we will find the answer in the text we've just read, with the main points forming an acrostic spelling the word COMPLETE. (These are not in order, however.)

Paul is still warning the Colossians about the dangerous heresy being presented to them and he encourages them in these next few verses by reminding them they have everything they need in Christ alone. Why would anyone want to be caught up in heretical teaching when we having everything we need in Christ? Let's consider our first reason why we are complete in Christ alone from verse 8.

> Beware lest anyone cheat you through philosophy and empty deceit, according to the tradition of men, according to the basic principles of the world, and not according to Christ. (Colossians 2:8)

Paul begins by saying *beware*, which means take heed to this, be constantly looking out, keep a watchful eye ever open for this. What are they to beware of? That *anyone* might *cheat* them *through philosophy and empty deceit*. The Greek tense is future indicative, which means that this has not necessarily happened yet, but Paul fears it could happen and so he warns them of it. Notice also that Paul mentions the word *anyone*, which is a repeat from verse 4, where he writes about anyone deceiving them. This is a warning to each of us that Satan always is on the prowl and he uses people to attempt to deceive God's children.

Now what does Paul mean by the words *cheat you*? To *cheat* means to seduce or kidnap and it has the idea of carrying someone off as a captive and slave. In other words, Paul is saying don't let anyone lead you away as prey. Ladies, this is exactly what false teachers do! Peter is clear about this in 2 Peter 2:1-3, where he writes

> But there were also false prophets among the people, even as there will be false teachers among you, who will secretly bring in destructive heresies, even denying the Lord who bought them, and bring on themselves swift destruction. And many will follow their destructive ways, because of whom the way of truth will be blasphemed. By covetousness they will exploit you with deceptive words; for a long time their judgment has not been idle, and their destruction does not slumber

Jesus Himself said in Matthew 7:15, "Beware of false prophets, who come to you in sheep's clothing, but inwardly they are ravenous wolves." Paul, in Acts 20:29-31, warned the elders at Ephesus of the same thing: "For I know this, that after my departure savage wolves will come in among you, not sparing the flock. Also, from among yourselves men will rise up, speaking perverse things, to draw away the disciples after themselves. Therefore watch, and remember that for three years I did not cease to warn everyone night and day with tears."

So, how do false teachers deceive? Paul says they do so *through philosophy and empty deceit*. *Philosophy* means being fond of wise things or the love of wisdom, but Paul uses it to describe the sense of vain speculation. The Colossians were in danger of relying on reasoning and not on truth. Philosophy can sound so good, and yet it is deceptive. In fact, it amounts to *empty deceit*, Paul says. This means it is empty delusion; it is void of truth. It is deceptive because it cannot redeem its promises. Empty deceit tends to take men away from Christ and to weaken their trust in Him as the all-sufficient Savior. Now, I could spend a lot of time (and I won't) speaking to you about the dangers of Christian psychology and psychiatry. It is a dangerous trap that has captured many a believer, and I would encourage you to flee from it. Paul says in Romans 15:14 that those of us who are Christians are filled with knowledge and goodness, and because of that we are able or competent to counsel one another. We don't need a Christian psychologist, but we do need a Christian friend who will admonish us in love when it is needed. This is very, very important, because there are more than 250 types of counseling in America alone that offer absolutely no biblical help!

Paul says such nonsense is nothing but *the tradition of men*. This is a reference to the Jewish law which had been handed down from generation to generation. You will see in the Questions to Consider what Christ thought about keeping the traditions of men, especially when those traditions contradicted the commandments of God. He called those "keepers of traditions" hypocrites. Just because something is a tradition does not make it biblical. Paul says these things are not only the traditions of men, but they are *according to the basic principles of the world*. The word *principles* is translated in the KJV as rudiments, which refers to elementary principles. This is a reference to something simple and rudimentary, like the alphabet … a, b, c, d … or numbers … 1, 2, 3, 4. These things are childish, elementary things. One man puts it well: "To abandon biblical truth for empty philosophy is like returning to kindergarten after earning a doctorate."17 Paul warns of this very thing when

---

17 John MacArthur, *The MacArthur New Testament Commentary: Colossians and Phile-mon (Chicago: Moody Press, 1992), 102.*

he writes to the church at Galatia; he says in Galatians 4:3 and 9, "Even so we, when we were children, were in bondage under the elements of the world. … But now after you have known God, or rather are known by God, how is it that you turn again to the weak and beggarly elements, to which you desire again to be in bondage?" Hebrews 5:12 also speaks of those who should be teachers and yet they have returned to the milk of the Word rather than the meat of the Word! To remain under such legalistic bondage is not a sign of spiritual maturity, though some will try and convince you that it is. On the contrary, it is actually a sign of spiritual immaturity. Paul says this is not according to Christ—this is not Christianity! *We are complete in Christ alone. Why? According to this verse, it is because man's ideas are foolish. This is the **M** on your acrostic.* My friend, man's ideas are foolish and will keep you from being complete in Christ. In verse 9, Paul gives yet another reason we are complete in Christ.

> For in Him dwells all the fullness of the Godhead bodily; (Colossians 2:9)

Paul says of Christ that *in Him dwells all the fullness of the Godhead. Dwell* means to house permanently. The divine nature dwells fully in Christ, in His human body, and it is there permanently. John 1:14a says, "the Word became flesh and dwelt among us." In John 14:9, Jesus told Philip that to see Him was to see the Father. The Gnostics, however, taught that all matter was evil and therefore Jesus' body was evil. They diminished Christ to a mere angel and nothing more. But Paul confronts this error by writing that in Christ dwells all the fullness of the Godhead *bodily*, that is, in His physical body. *This is yet another reason why we are complete in Christ, and this is the first **E** on your acrostic: Entirety is in Christ.* Everything that God is, Christ is! He is entirely all we need. Why would we seek anything apart from Him? Paul moves on to yet another reason we are complete in Christ in verse 10.

> and you are complete in Him, who is the head of all principality and power. (Colossians 2:10)

Paul reminds the Colossians that they are *complete in Him*, that is, in Christ, which means that they are full in Him alone or satisfied in Him alone. The meaning is that they have been filled already and the present result is that they are in a state of always being filled with Him. It is like being so full of food that you can't eat another bite. You have no more room for anything else in your stomach. It should concern us when we look for our satisfaction in people or things when we already have everything we need in Christ. There is no lasting pleasure except in Christ. *This is the **P** on your acrostic in considering why we are complete in him: Pleasure is found in Him alone!*

Paul goes on to remind us of what he's already referred to in Colossians 1:16, when he wrote that Christ created all principalities and power. He created all principalities and powers, so doesn't it also make sense that He would be *head* over what He created? Why should one put trust in principalities and powers, when one can put trust in the One who is *head over all principality and power*? Paul goes on in verse 11 to remind them of yet another reason why they are complete in Christ alone.

> In Him you were also circumcised with the circumcision made without hands, by putting off the body of the sins of the flesh, by the circumcision of Christ, (Colossians 2:11)

Now, what is Paul talking about when he says we *were also circumcised with the circumcision made without hands*? The word *circumcised* means to cut around and for those of us who have birthed baby boys we know exactly what this is. In the biblical world, all Jewish boys were to be circumcised on the eighth day because circumcision was a sign that they were now under the covenant. Some Jews took that so far as to say that if one was not circumcised, then they could not be saved. Paul refuted that notion in Romans and states very plainly in Romans 2:28-29, "For he is not a Jew who is one outwardly, nor is circumcision that which is outward in the flesh; but he is a Jew who is one inwardly; and circumcision is that of the heart, in the Spirit, not in the letter; whose praise is not from men but from God."

Paul reminds us here in Colossians that we are circumcised but not with human circumcision. We, as Christians, have a different kind of circumcision; it is not physical, but spiritual. We have a circumcision of the heart, a *putting off the body of the sins of the flesh. Putting off* means to strip off from oneself, as with clothes or armor. It is like throwing off dirty clothes. Yes, there is a cutting away and throwing off, but it is not of skin but of sin. *The circumcision of Christ* is a circumcision of the heart, and it cannot come without putting off the body of the sins of the flesh. It means a total break from them. In fact, when we get into chapter three of Colossians, we'll see a list of things we are to put off and a list of what we are to put on. Do we want a work from the human surgeon or a work from the divine Spirit? Do we want an inward change or an outward change? Do we want removal of excess skin or removal of excess sin? My friend, Christ is always interested in your heart and not in the outward manifestations of religion. The heresy that was creeping into the church in Colossae, as well as many other New Testament churches, was that circumcision was necessary for salvation. Peter argued with the Jews in Acts 15:10 because the Jews were trying to put this yoke on the neck of the disciples. We are not saved by the yoke of circumcision but by being yoked to our Lord. He tells us in Matthew 11:30 that His yoke is easy and His burden is light; it is not like the yoke of circumcision. *So, why are we complete in Christ? Because of the C on your acrostic: our Circumcision is in Christ.* We have been circumcised once in our heart and that's all we need. Paul goes on with yet another reason we are complete in Christ in verse 12.

> buried with Him in baptism, in which you also were raised with Him through faith in the working of God, who raised Him from the dead. (Colossians 2:12)

To help us better understand what Paul is saying here in verse 12, let's consider what he writes in Romans 6:1-7:

> What shall we say then? Shall we continue in sin that grace may abound? Certainly not! How shall we who died to sin live any longer in it? Or do you not know that as many of us as were baptized into Christ Jesus were baptized into His death?

> Therefore we were buried with Him through baptism into death, that just as Christ was raised from the dead by the glory of the Father, even so we also should walk in newness of life. For if we have been united together in the likeness of His death, certainly we also shall be in the likeness of His resurrection, knowing this, that our old man was crucified with Him, that the body of sin might be done away with, that we should no longer be slaves of sin. For he who has died has been freed from sin.

In water baptism, immersion portrays being *buried* with Christ, which means that we have entered into company with Him in His death. Coming out of the water depicts the resurrection by the power of God to live a new life. Water baptism is an outward sign of an inward work. We are *raised with Him* by the working of God, which is His resurrection power that raised Jesus from the dead. Ladies, this same energizing power that raised Jesus has raised us to newness in life! *So, why do we not think we are complete in Christ? We are! Because of the E on your acrostic: the Energizing power of God raised Christ and raised us!* The false teachers and their teaching offer nothing of that value; they cannot energize you with anything other than the doctrines of demons. Paul continues to write in verse 13 and says,

> And you, being dead in your trespasses and the uncircumcision of your flesh, He has made alive together with Him, having forgiven you all trespasses, (Colossians 2:13)

The uncircumcision of your flesh pictures our moral and spiritual condition before we knew Christ. We were guilty, sinful, and hopeless. Before we knew Christ, we were spiritually *dead*, unresponsive to any spiritual understanding, just like a physically dead person cannot respond to any physical touch or reason. That was what we were before we knew Christ. But praise God, He has made us alive together with Him and forgiven all our sins! *Forgiven* means having been pardoned or rescued. You and I were dead in our sins, but Christ *has made us alive together with Him.* Can the false teachers do that? Can they make you alive? Can they forgive your sins and trespasses? No! *So, another reason we are complete in Christ is the T on your acrostic: our Trespasses have been forgiven!*

Paul continues to write in verse 14 that Christ is complete, and he demonstrates that in a very real way.

> having wiped out the handwriting of requirements that was against us, which was contrary to us. And He has taken it out of the way, having nailed it to the cross. (Colossians 2:14)

How did Christ demonstrate that He is enough, that in Him we are complete? By *having wiped out the handwriting of requirements that was against us* and *was contrary to us. The handwriting of requirements* is a reference to the Mosaic Law; it was against us. And *wiping away* means blotting out the handwriting of ordinances that was opposed to us, that was a hindrance to us. Paul writes in 2 Corinthians 3:3-6,

> clearly you are an epistle of Christ, ministered by us, written not with ink but by the Spirit of the living God, not on tablets of stone but on tablets of flesh, that is, of the heart. And we have such trust through Christ toward God. Not that we are sufficient of ourselves to think of anything as being from ourselves, but our sufficiency is from God, who also made us sufficient as ministers of the new covenant, not of the letter but of the Spirit; for the letter kills, but the Spirit gives life.

And again, in Galatians 3:13, he writes, "Christ has redeemed us from the curse of the law, having become a curse for us (for it is written, 'Cursed is everyone who hangs on a tree')." And what did Christ do with the handwriting of requirements that was against us? *He has taken it out the way, having nailed it to the cross*! To have *taken it out the way* means that he wholly removed it. Paul is telling the Colossian believers that those ordinances were done away with when Christ died. They tried to keep the moral law, as they understood it, but the burden of trying to keep it was difficult, and the more they tried, the more it became against them and contrary to them. Christ took those IOUs against the written law and nailed them to the cross. Christ wiped out the debt we owed and totally erased it by nailing it to the cross.

It's an interesting picture that Paul has painted for us here, because it was customary under Roman law to write out a copy of the law that a criminal had broken and nail the inscription above the person's head on the cross on which he was hanging. Just as Christ's accusation was nailed to the cross, so Christ nails our accusations to His cross. Matthew records for us in Matthew 27:37, "And they put up over His head the accusation written against Him: THIS IS JESUS THE KING OF THE JEWS." It was also customary during this time to thrust a nail through papers, declaring them old and obsolete. That's what Christ did with our sins. He declared them old and obsolete; He wiped them away when he nailed them to the cross. One translation says, "Christ has utterly wiped out the damning evidence of broken laws and commandments which always hung over our heads and has completely annulled it by nailing it over His own head on the cross."18 *Here we have the L on our acrostic, in answer to why we are complete in Christ alone: the Law was nailed to the cross.* Because of this, we don't need a psychologist to help us get in touch with our feelings and tell us what to do with those bad behaviors we all have or to help us drudge up all our sinful past so that we can blame it on others or on our circumstances. Christ nailed all of them to His cross and forgave us all of our sins. Praise God, we are complete in Him! We come to the final reason we are complete in Him, and it is the **O** in your acrostic.

> Having disarmed principalities and powers, He made a public spectacle of them, triumphing over them in it. (Colossians 2:15)

Oh, my friend, Christ *disarmed principalities and powers*, those fallen spirits! This is Paul's third reference to principalities and powers in this letter. We see in 1:16 that Christ created them; in 2:10 that He is the head of them; and here in 2:15 that He has disarmed them. Now, what did He do after He disarmed those principalities and powers? *He made a public spectacle of them, triumphing over them*! Christ made a *public* exhibit of them, *triumphing over them in it*, which means to lead them in a triumphal procession. Disarming the principalities and powers is the picture of conquered soldiers

---

18 J.B. Phillips, *The New Testament in Modern English.*

having stripped off their clothes and their weapons to symbolize total defeat! This *public spectacle* and *triumphing over them* resembles a Roman general leading his captives through the streets of his city for all the citizens to see as evidence of his complete and total victory. This was an open, public triumph! Paul says Christ had the final victory over all principalities and powers and he made an open public triumph over them! Since God created all principalities and powers, and since He is head of all principalities and powers, it only makes sense that He can also disarm them. Christ disarmed these demonic powers and triumphed over them. *So, the final reason that Christ is enough and we are complete in Him, and the O in our acrostic, is this: He Overcame all principalities and powers.*

Summary

Dear one, why do we want anything else besides Christ when we are complete in Him? We need nothing else. Let's look at our acrostic for COMPLETE.

Circumcision in Christ. Has your heart been circumcised? Has there been a cutting away of your old life? Are you counting on any outward works of righteousness to get you into heaven?

Christ *Overcame all principalities and powers.* He has disarmed all evil powers. Is that disarmament evident in your life? Do Satan and any of his cohorts have any hold on you? What spiritual battles have you been victorious over this week?

Man's ideas are foolish! My dear sister, are you being deceived today by the ideas of man? Have you fallen prey to the Christian psychology of our day? Please remember, you have everything you need for life and godliness in Christ.

Our *Pleasure is in Him.* Are you so full of Christ that you need nothing else? Do you have the Lord and is He enough for you? If not, in what or in whom are you seeking to find pleasure?

The *Law was nailed to the cross*. Have you been freed from the curse of the law? Are you making spiritual check-lists for yourself and others? Have you been saved by grace and grace alone?

Entirety is in Christ. Christ is God in the flesh. Do you believe that? If so, does it flesh out in how you conduct your life? Do you think you need Christ plus something else, or is He truly enough?

Our *Trespasses have been forgiven*. Have your sins been forgiven? Have you been freed from the bondage of guilt? Have you thanked God for His sacrificial gift of His Son on the cross?

We are complete in Christ because His *Energizing power raised Him and raised us*. Has your old life been buried with Him and has His energizing power raised you to newness of life? How does it show itself in your life? In what ways have you seen that power this week?

Are you complete in Christ? Does your life demonstrate that you are complete in Him? Or are you caught up in the trends of our day? The problem with philosophy, legalism, mysticism, and all the other -isms is that they cloud our perception of what Christ has done for us. Our salvation and our sanctification are complete in Him. We do not need Christ plus something. Peter is clear in 2 Peter 1:3, "His divine power has given to us all things that pertain to life and godliness, through the knowledge of Him who called us by glory and virtue."

Perhaps this lesson is nothing new to you. If that is the case, allow me, by way of closing, to say a word of caution to you. It is possible for healthy believers to be led astray; it happens every day, and more and more as we approach the day of our Lord's return. My prayer for each of us is that we won't go after all the new and novel ideas that are out there but that we will cling to the truth that we have what we need in Christ alone. How I pray that neither you, nor I, will be a casualty of the -isms of our day. The ideas of man are dangerous to the soul, but the law of the Lord is perfect, reviving the soul.

Questions to Consider

Colossians 2:8-15

Are We Complete in Christ Alone?

1. (a) Read Colossians 2:1-15. According to these verses, why is Christ sufficient? (b) What other verses come to your mind when you think of our sufficiency in Christ alone?

2. Memorize Colossians 2:10.

3. (a) What did Jesus say was the danger of keeping traditions, according to Matthew 15:1-9 and Mark 7:1-13? (b) What did Christ desire instead of their traditions? (c) In Matthew 23, what else did Jesus say about those who are more interested in the outward show of tradition than the inward purification of the heart?

4. (a) According to the following Scriptures, what are the differences between outward circumcision and inward circumcision? Genesis 17:11; Deuteronomy 30:6; Jeremiah 9:25-26; Romans 2:25-29; 1 Corinthians 7:17-19; Galatians 5:1-12; 6:11-15; and Philippians 3:3? (b) Why is outward circumcision unnecessary for salvation? See Acts 15. (c) How could you use what you have just learned to teach someone who thinks outward circumcision, or any other work, is necessary for salvation?

5. In Colossians 2:8 (KJV), Paul warns of the dangers of the "rudiments" of the world (NKJV, "basic principles; NASB, "elementary principles"). In Galatians 4:3, he calls this the "elements of the world." From Galatians 4, answer the following questions: (a) Why was Paul so concerned about this? (b) What is the danger of putting oneself under bondage? (c) What does Paul say is true freedom or liberty?

6. Why is Christ sufficient for the believer, according to Psalm 84:11; Romans 8:32; 1 Corinthians 1:30; 3:21-23; Colossians 2:3, 10; and 2 Peter 1:3?

7. (a) Using discretion, recall a time when you or someone else you know got caught up in philosophy, legalism, traditions of men, or the like. What was the result? (b) What did you or they learn? (Please avoid using names here unless you're sharing about yourself.)

8. What are some modern-day forms of philosophy, vain deceit, traditions of men, and rudiments of the world?

9. (a) What does it mean to you personally that "you are complete in Him"? (b) Is that truth evident in your life, or would others say, "She needs Christ plus something else"?

10. Please examine yourself before the Lord, asking Him if your life is demonstrating that He alone is sufficient. After thorough examination, please write a prayer request based on what God has revealed to you.

Chapter 10

Two Isms to Avoid!

Colossians 2:16-19

By way of introduction to this lesson, I would like to pose two statements, and I would like you to answer whether they are true or false.

1. God placed Adam and Eve in a garden immediately after creation and told them in Genesis 1:29 that their source of nourishment was to be raw fruits and vegetables; Christians who eat anything else have turned their back on God's diet and adopted the world's diet. True or False?

2. Christians should not celebrate Christmas, Easter, or any other such holidays. True or False?

You'd probably like to know if you've passed the test or not. Well, you'll have to be patient and wait until the end of the lesson to see.

We have been on a journey through Colossians chapter two. In our last lesson, we discovered how Paul had warned the Colossians of the danger of philosophy and vain deceit, which followed the traditions of men and not after Christ. In this lesson, Paul continues to warn us of the danger we are in if we deny the fact that we are indeed complete in Christ. He writes in Colossians 2:16-19,

Colossians 2:16-19

let no one judge you in food or in drink, or regarding a festival or a new moon or sabbaths, [17]which are a shadow of things to come, but the substance is of Christ. [18]Let no one cheat you of your reward, taking delight in false humility and worship of angels, intruding into those things which he has not seen, vainly puffed up by his fleshly mind, [19]and not holding fast to the Head, from whom all the body, nourished and knit together by joints and ligaments, grows with the increase that is from God.

As Paul nears the end of chapter two of his letter, he begins a three-fold warning for the Colossian believers. In this lesson, the warning will be against legalism and mysticism. And as we finish chapter two in our next lesson, we will see the warning against asceticism. The outline for this lesson is this:

The Warning Against Legalism (vv 16-17)
The Warning Against Mysticism (vv 18-19)

The Warning Against Legalism

Colossians 2:16-17

So let no one judge you in food or in drink, or regarding a festival or a new moon or sabbaths, (Colossians 2:16)

Because you have been made complete in Christ, and because you have been delivered from the observances of the law, *let no one judge you*, Paul says. In the Greek, Paul is literally saying here, "God forbid, never no, that any man should ever sit in judgment of you or try to condemn or damn you." Stop letting those Gnostics, those false teachers, sit in judgment of you. Why would the false teachers *judge* them? Because of their diet, which Paul describes as *in food and in drink*, and because of their days, which Paul describes as *a festival or a new moon or sabbaths*. The Colossians were enjoying their new freedom in Christ alone, but the false teachers were coming along and endeavoring to entice them to follow the restrictions of legalism, mysticism, and asceticism.

The first area in which the false teachers were judging the Colossians was their diet. They were instructing them to return to the observance of Old Testament dietary laws, claiming that doing so would lead them to God and to spiritual fulfillment. The word *food* simply refers to the act of eating and the word *drink* refers to the act of drinking. The Levitical law was given for physical reasons as well as spiritual reasons. It was given to mark Israel as God's distinct people and to discourage them from intermingling with the surrounding nations. God gave them those laws so that they would be able to distinguish between purity and impurity. But when Jesus came, those Old Testament dietary laws were abolished. (Hopefully, you saw that as you looked at Mark 7 and then at Luke's words regarding Peter in Acts 10.) Another important passage to consider in this regard is what Paul writes to the church at Ephesus in 1 Timothy 4:1-5:

> Now the Spirit expressly says that in latter times some will depart from the faith, giving heed to deceiving spirits and doctrines of demons, speaking lies in hypocrisy, having their own conscience seared with a hot iron, forbidding to marry, and commanding to abstain from foods which God created to be received with thanksgiving by those who believe and know the truth. For every creature of God is good, and nothing is to be refused if it is received with thanksgiving; for it is sanctified by the word of God and prayer.

Did you catch the seriousness of what Paul is saying? Those who command others to abstain from certain foods Paul calls apostates, saying they have departed from the faith! This is a very serious issue! Paul calls this type of teaching demonic, referring to it as the doctrine of demons. He is unmistakably clear that "*every* creature of God is good, and *nothing* is to be refused if it is received with thanksgiving" (emphasis mine). Also, in 1 Corinthians 8:8, Paul writes, "But food does not commend us to God; for neither if we eat are we the better, nor if we do not eat are we the worse." We can see clearly from the New Testament that all food and drink is lawful. Now, this doesn't mean that you should be a glutton and gorge yourself because we know Scripture does speak to that issue. We also know that our body is God's temple, and we should do things in moderation, endeavoring to keep our bodies fit for the service of the Lord. But, as one writer put it well, "Eat too may Twinkies and you will no longer be twinkle toes. Too many Snickers are no laughing matter. But dietary discipline is not a sign of spirituality."[19]

Not only were the Colossians not to let the false teachers judge them concerning their diet, but they were also not to let others judge them concerning their observance of days. Paul refers to these as *a festival or a new moon or sabbaths*. *A festival* would refer to observances like Passover, Pentecost, and The Feast of Tabernacles. *A new moon* would refer to the monthly new moon festival. Messengers would be placed at high places to watch the sky, and as soon as it was clear that the new moon had arrived, they would rush to let everyone know, even if they had to travel on the Sabbath to do so. The new moons indicated the beginning of a new month, and the Israelites would celebrate by blowing trumpets, offering special sacrifices, and feasting. This would also be a time of religious instruction and all labor would be suspended.

Paul also mentions the observance of *sabbaths*, a word that means cessation from exertion. The sabbath was established when God created the heavens and the earth, as He Himself rested on the seventh day. The Sabbath was given for man to rest and as a symbol for Israel of the Old Covenant. We, however, are no longer commanded to keep the Sabbath because we are under the New Covenant. Paul wrote of this when he was concerned about the Galatians wanting to be under bondage again. In Galatians 4:10-11, he says, "You observe days and months and seasons and years. I am afraid for you, lest I have labored for you in vain." Nowhere in the New Testament are we commanded to keep the Sabbath and yet all the other commandments are repeated. Now, if you want to keep the Sabbath day, that is up to you. I personally think a day to rest your body and mind is a great idea. But again, keep in mind that Christians are free from the law's legalistic requirements. We have liberty as Christians regarding what we can do in terms of diet and days. We can keep days and diets, or we can forget them altogether. But we cannot judge others for what they do! Legalism breeds judgmentalism. Legalism focuses on the outward as a means

19 R. Kent Hughes, *Colossians and Philemon: The Supremacy of Christ (Westchester: Crossway Books, 1989)*, 82.

of producing spirituality and doesn't deal with the inward sins, like justice, mercy, and faith.

I remember hearing a sermon as a young teen during which the speaker actually handed out a list of things you should and should not do in order to be spiritual—things like the kinds of clothes one should and shouldn't wear; certain places one should or should not go; the length of one's hair; and on and on. There was no mention of the undeniable realities that Christians shouldn't kill, shouldn't commit adultery, shouldn't steal, shouldn't lie, etc. Isn't it interesting that James says in James 1:27 that true religion is a tad bit different than legalism? He writes, "Pure and undefiled religion before God and the Father is this: to visit orphans and widows in their trouble, and to keep oneself unspotted from the world." True religion is not found in the clothes we wear, the food we eat, or the days we celebrate. Legalism has the potential to be so dangerous and so misleading, especially to those who are new Christians, who easily can be led astray into thinking that Christianity is a list of dos and don'ts. I know by experience the danger of such thinking because for years I thought I was on my way to heaven because I was an outwardly righteous person. I followed the lists of dos and don'ts, but inwardly my heart was impure and wicked. How I praise God that He delivered my soul from hell and from the deadly trap of legalism! In verse 17, Paul explains for us why such rules about diets and days are dangerous. He says of them,

> which are a shadow of things to come, but the substance is of Christ. (Colossians 1:17)

These things, Paul says, are just *a shadow* of things to come; they were meant only to be a dim outline of reality. The writer to the Hebrews speaks of this in Hebrews 10:1: "For the law, having a shadow of the good things to come, and not the very image of the things, can never with these same sacrifices, which they offer continually year by year, make those who approach perfect." The law was only a shadow of what was *to come*, that being Christ. When you see a shadow, that's all it is. It's not the real image, but it is shadowing the real image.

You can step outside and make a shadow if it's a sunny day, but that shadow is not you. A shadow has no real substance, right? The reality, your body, is what makes the shadow. These regulations, the law, were just shadows; the reality was Christ. Paul puts it like this: *but the substance is of Christ.* In contrast to these shadows, the reality is Christ. One commentator said, "Once one finds Christ, he no longer needs to follow the old shadow."[20] Christ is sufficient, complete; there is no need to go back to the dietary laws and the honoring of days and feasts. Paul is saying: don't settle for a shadow when you can have the real thing, when you can have Christ. We are complete in Him; it is Christ plus nothing else! However, the Colossians were not only being led astray into legalism. There was another -ism with which the Gnostics were enticing the Colossians: mysticism. Paul writes of this in verses 18 and 19.

The Warning Against Mysticism

Colossians 2:18-19

> Let no one cheat you of your reward, taking delight in false humility and worship of angels, intruding into those things which he has not seen, vainly puffed up by his fleshly mind, (Colossians 1:18)

Paul says *let no one cheat you of your reward.* This is a repeat of what he said in verse 16, *let no one.* To *cheat* one out of their reward is to act as a judge or an umpire, to be the one who disqualifies anyone not following the rules. This judge or umpire had the ability to decide against a competitor, or to declare them unworthy of the prize. Essentially, a judge could deprive someone of their *reward.* What is Paul saying here? He's saying that the Colossians were running the race—just like many of us—but the false teachers were trying to trip them up in the race, by acting as judges over the Colossians and thus robbing them of their just reward. The Gnostics were doing this, Paul says, by *taking delight in false humility and worship of angels, intruding into things which he has not seen.*

---

20 Norman L. Geisler, *Bible Knowledge Commentary (Wheaton: Victor Books, 1983), 678.*

They devoted themselves to false humility. Now, ladies, that is sick. Humility is a wonderful virtue, but false humility, when it is self-conscious, ceases to have any value. These false teachers were putting on the appearance of modesty. And not only that, but they were practicing *worship of angels*, and judging those who were not following suit. The attitude of the false teachers was that of sitting in judgment as to the future reward of those who refused their doctrine of angel worship. Paul has already told the Colossians that Christ is above all the angelic beings. In fact, He created them, as we saw in Colossians 1:16, and He did not create them to be worshiped. The angels worship God, but they are not to be worshiped—just like we should worship God, but we are never to be worshiped. In Revelation, we read of the apostle John and the vision he received while he was exiled on the isle of Patmos. As he relates his vision, he explains in Revelation 19:9-10 how he fell down to worship an angel and was rebuked for it. He writes,

> Then he said to me, "Write: 'Blessed are those who are called to the marriage supper of the Lamb!'" And he said to me, "These are the true sayings of God." And I fell at his feet to worship him. But he said to me, "See that you do not do that! I am your fellow servant, and of your brethren who have the testimony of Jesus. Worship God! For the testimony of Jesus is the spirit of prophecy."

Church history records for us how Colossae was for quite some time involved in the worship of angels. The archangel Michael was worshiped in Asia Minor as late as AD 739 and was given credit for miraculous cures. At that time, angels were seen as God's powerful agents to protect people from evil powers. Worshippers called on angels to make their lives successful or to bring vengeance on their enemies. But this is just as much a trend in our day, and we would do well to be cautious. Angel worship is very much alive today, all you need to do is go in to any gift shop and you will find angels to be one of the primary categories of gifts you can purchase. That's not to say that buying angel decor is bad in and of itself but simply to point out that there seems to almost be an obsession with them. There are even some interesting books on the subject, like *The ABC's of*

Angels. This book will help you, in case you're in any trouble, to know how to ask an angel to guide the way. Then there's *100 Ways to Attract Angels.* You might also pick up *Angelic Healing,* which explains how angels can inspire humans to mend and heal. Last, but certainly not least, there's *What You Should Know About Angels,* a book which tells you how angels make their presence known to us and how to include them in our daily worship. I hope you know I'm being cynical and sarcastic with these examples—but, seriously, we need to be aware and to take heed, lest we get caught up in such nonsense! Believe me, even in our day there are people who would love to trip you up.

Not only did the Gnostics practice angel worship, but they also claimed to have special visions and even went into great detail about what they claimed they had seen. But Paul says that the one who does this is actually *intruding into those things which he has not seen, vainly puffed up by his fleshly mind.* These false teachers prided themselves in the supposed visions they'd seen. But Paul addresses this very thing in 1 Timothy 1:6-7, where he writes, "from which some, having strayed, have turned aside to idle talk, desiring to be teachers of the law, understanding neither what they say nor the things which they affirm." Paul had a vision himself, according to 2 Corinthians 12, but he says that he would not glory about such a vision, because it would be foolish to do so. In fact, just to make sure he would not glory in that heavenly vision, the Lord gave Paul a thorn in the flesh to keep him humble. Not so with the false teachers; they weren't even humble about the things they hadn't really seen. They were involved in mysticism, which is the belief that spiritual reality can be perceived apart from the human mind and natural senses. Mysticism weighs heavily on feelings or intuition and not on fact. (That is why it is wise to avoid questions like, "How do you feel?" when dealing with biblical truth! Feelings cannot always be trusted, but the truth of God's Word can always be trusted.) Extreme forms of mysticism are found today in Hinduism and New Age philosophy. These false teachers—both in Paul's day and in ours—claim to have some superior knowledge, but in reality, they have nothing more than an exalted opinion of themselves. Their humility is self-imposed and far from genuine.

The word *intruding* means to scrutinize minutely. These false teachers scrutinized minutely the things which they imagined or professed to have seen in a vision. Paul says they have *not seen* these things but rather are *vainly puffed up by their fleshly mind*. *Vainly* means without a cause, without reason, without success or effort. To be *puffed up* is to be inflated or proud. And a *fleshly mind* is a carnal mind. This is a person whose mind is puffed with pride because of his visions that he claims to have seen. But, do not be deceived by what they are saying, Paul says; the result might just be that you would be disqualified from the reward, which is the prize. For a believer to allow anyone to lead him away from his or her completeness in Christ could result in being robbed of their reward. My friend, this is serious. In our day, we have many who follow and listen to speakers and authors who are claiming to have had all kinds of supposed visions about things that do not measure up to God's Word! Why do we give them a voice?! Many are following after them, and I fear they are losing their reward, becoming disqualified! This is serious stuff!

The problem with those who worship angels and those who follow dietary laws and observe holy days, is that they have lost their connection with the head. And it's not their physical head (though sometimes I wonder!); it's their spiritual head. Look at how Paul puts it in verse 19.

> and not holding fast to the Head, from whom all the body, nourished and knit together by joints and ligaments, grows with the increase that is from God. (Colossians 1:19)

These people are *not holding fast to the Head. The Head* here is Christ. Consider Ephesians 1:22-23, "And He put all things under His feet, and gave Him to be head over all things to the church, which is His body, the fullness of Him who fills all in all." Also consider Ephesians 4:15-16, "but, speaking the truth in love, may grow up in all things into Him who is the head—Christ—from whom the whole body, joined and knit together by what every joint supplies, according to the effective working by which every part does its share, causes growth of the body for the edifying of itself in love." My friend, Christ is the head that holds all aspects of the body together. Paul says the problem with these guys is that they are not holding on to the Head. The word for *holding* means to seize or retain and has the idea of a firm grasp and a tenacious hold. These false teachers are not keeping a firm hold on the Head; they are not clinging to Christ. They have forsaken Him to follow ridiculous shadows!

Christ our Head is enough; in Him we are complete. Why? Paul says that from the head *all the body* is *nourished and knit together by joints and ligaments*, which means we are fully supported and united together by the Head. We can't be nourished or supported or anything without Him. The words *knit together* and *nourished* picture well the wonderful unity in the body that is achieved as the various cells, muscles, arteries, veins, nerves, skin, organs, and glands work together. It is a marvelous machine working together under the direction of the head. Just as the human head controls the human body, our head, Christ, controls His body, the church. If our physical head isn't working, neither is our body. It simply won't function properly. I have a great nephew who has cerebral palsy, a disease that affects the brain. Because of it, his body doesn't work as it ought to; he isn't able to sit up on his own, and yet he's an adult. In the same way, Christ is the spiritual head, and He controls the spiritual body, the church. Without Christ our Head, we can do nothing.

Paul ends by saying that the body, connected to the Head and nourished and knit together by the joints and ligaments, *grows with the increase that is from God.* Ladies, the only way we *grow* is *from God.* Paul is not talking about the numerical growth of the church but individual spiritual growth. What Paul is saying here is that the new man is increasing, and it is growing not by legalism and mysticism but by the increase of God, by an increase of grace which is from God as its author. You will not grow by rules. You will not grow by visions. You will not grow by worshiping angels. But you will grow by knowledge of Christ. It only makes sense, doesn't it? You can follow diets or days, which are a mere shadow, or you can follow the reality, which is Christ. Worship angels or worship Christ.

Summary

Having now looked closely at these verses, how did you fare with the two true/false questions at the beginning of this lesson?

1. Do Christians need to get back to the garden? Should we be eating only fruits and veggies? Biblically, you'd have a hard time proving that. But, if that is what you desire for yourself, it is no more sinful than for those who choose to eat meat and chocolate and drink coffee. What you *are forbidden* to do is to judge others for what they eat or what they don't eat. (On the way to the airport recently, I noticed a bumper sticker that said, "Eat right. Exercise regularly. Die anyway—so enjoy!" I thought, "Oh, how true!")

2. Should Christians celebrate Easter and Christmas and other holidays? Again, if you are under the conviction that you and your family should not celebrate such holidays, then don't. And if you don't celebrate those days, don't try to use Jeremiah 10 to prove your case for not having a Christmas tree, unless you plan to fall down and worship it! If you celebrate Christmas and Easter, that is okay. Paul tells us in Romans 14 that each of us should be persuaded in our own mind in how we regard each day. But again, what we are forbidden to do is judge one another in the areas of food and drink and observance of days. These are not matters of spirituality. Judging others, however, is a matter of spirituality and shows that one is weak in the faith.

Are you in danger of being deprived of genuine Christianity because of legalism? Legalism, as one man has said, demands uniformity, produces a surface faith, spawns judgmentalism, and produces a joyless life.[21] Do you demand that others conform to the way you celebrate certain days of the year? Do you look down on others who don't follow the same dietary plan you follow? If so, my friend, you have bought into legalism. Is your faith superficial? Do you have a deep and meaningful relationship with Christ alone, or has your Christianity become hum-drum? Have you lost your joy? Examine yourself to see if you have bought into the legalism of our day.

Are you in danger of being deprived of genuine Christianity by mysticism? Do you value experience over truth, especially biblical truth? Do you value intuition over truth? Do you value your own inner power over the inner working power of God? If so, my friend, you are in danger, and you have bought into mysticism.

Both legalism and mysticism crept into the church at Colossae, but, my friend, they are prevalent in the 21st century church, too! I beg you to turn away from any iota of legalism and mysticism and to turn completely to Christ alone! Why settle for these things when you can have Him?

---

21 R. Kent Hughes, *Colossians and Philemon: The Supremacy of Christ* (Westchester: Crossway Books, 1989), 83.

Questions to Consider
Colossians 2:16-19
Two Isms to Avoid!

1. (a) Read Colossians 2 and list all the commands you see. (b) Why do you think Paul listed these commands for the Colossian believers?

2. Memorize Colossians 2:16.

3. (a) Write down at least five dietary laws mentioned in Leviticus 11. (b) What do Christ and Luke tell us about these dietary laws in Mark 7:14-20 and Acts 10:9-15?

4. (a) Why was the Sabbath given, according to Exodus 31:14-17; Leviticus 16:31; Leviticus 23:1-3; and Ezekiel 20:12? (b) What did Jesus say and illustrate in the New Testament about the Sabbath in the New Testament, specifically in Mark 2:23-3:5? (c) Are Christians required to keep the Sabbath? Prove your answer from the Word of God.

5. (a) Read Romans 14. What does Paul say here about judging others for what they eat, and for how they live? (b) What is Christ mainly interested in, according to verses 6, 8-9, 13, and 17?

6. (a) In the following verses, what are the angels described as doing? Luke 2:9-14; Hebrews 1:6-7, 14; Revelation 5:11-14. (b) What did John try to do to the angel in Revelation 22:6-9? (c) What was the angel's response? (d) Do you think we should worship angels? Why or why not?

7. (a) Do you look down on those who do not follow the same dietary laws as you do? (b) What about those who choose to celebrate or not to celebrate certain holidays? (c) What have you learned from this lesson about the danger of doing so?

8. How would you describe humility?

9. What has God shown you through this lesson? Write down any thoughts you might have in the form of a prayer request.

Chapter 11

Warning Against Asceticism!

Colossians 2:20-23

We have come to our final lesson in the second chapter of Colossians. In our last lesson, we saw the first two parts of Paul's three-fold warning to the church at Colossae, in which he specifically warned against legalism and mysticism. In those verses, Paul warned the Colossians   not to let anyone judge them regarding diets and days or to persuade them to involve themselves in angel worship. The danger in observing days and diets is that they are merely a shadow of what is real, of Christ Himself. In addition to this, both legalism and mysticism carry inherent within them the danger of causing us to lose sight of the Head, that is, Christ. He is the One who holds all things together. He is sufficient. There is no lasting joy or spiritual growth when one gets caught up in these heresies, these two -isms.

But we must also consider the third part of Paul's warning, the third -ism we must avoid, and that is asceticism. Perhaps you're reading that word and wondering just what asceticism is. By way of introduction, I'd like to share a personal experience which I think will help you to understand this third -ism.

Early in my so-called Christian life, I met a lady whom I deeply admired, who was extremely thin. When she found out I was a walker, she was overjoyed, and even introduced me as a "walker" to another Christian lady whom I also highly respected. Because of my respect for her, I wanted to be like her. She was very thin, and her diet was extremely important to her. So, I began my journey to lose some weight, thinking, "Ah! This is the key to my spiritual growth!" Now, keep in mind, I wasn't obese or anything like that at the time, but losing 5-10 pounds would not have hurt me either. The only problem with my new mission was that as I began to lose weight, I couldn't stop—or wouldn't stop, I would say. "Just five more pounds," I would say, except that "five more" was never enough. This went on for a good year, and I would go days without eating; other days I would only eat 200-300 calories a day. I became very, very thin, to the point that my husband was seriously concerned, warning me that I was doing irreversible damage to my body. My hair was falling out, I stopped menstruating, and my teeth were decaying. I was pinning my size 1 jeans to make them fit! My daughter, who was about 7 at the time, wanted to know what "those things" were sticking out of my back. I can remember, during this time, that just riding in a car would hurt my bones. I thank the Lord that he used my husband, my father, and a dear friend to awaken me to what I was doing. Without their confrontational concern and prayers, I probably wouldn't be here today.

This true illustration helps us in our definition of asceticism. An ascetic is someone who lives a life of rigorous self-denial as a means of earning forgiveness and favor with God. In fact, I really thought this was my key to spiritually growth; I had adopted the false idea that rigid asceticism would be a key to my spiritual growth. The reason I referred to this time in my life as my "so-called Christian life" is that, even though I thought I was a believer at that time, the truth is that God did not save me until about a year after this experience. Asceticism. What is it? The encyclopedia describes it this way:

> Asceticism (Greek askesis, "exercise"), practice of self-denial and renunciation of worldly pleasure in order to attain a higher degree of spirituality, intellectuality, or self-awareness. Among the ancient Greeks, the term originally denoted the training practiced by athletes and soldiers. Asceticism is practiced to some extent by the adherents of every religion. It often requires abstinence from food, drink, or sexual activity, as in fasting or celibacy. It may also require physical pain or discomfort, such as endurance of extreme heat or cold or self-punishment. It may require withdrawal from the material world to a life of meditation, as in the practice of Yoga.[22]

---

22 "Asceticism." *Resources for Life. http://www.resourcesforlife.com/groups/ simpleliving/glossary.*

Legalism, mysticism, and now, asceticism. These were all forms of heresy that were invading the church in Colossae. And there's nothing new under the sun—they have invaded the church today, as well. Now, before you think that this lesson has nothing to do with you, I would ask you to consider that everyone at one time or another practices denial of something, thinking that it will earn them favor with God. Let's read Colossians 2:20-23 and see what the Holy Spirit has to say about asceticism through the apostle Paul.

Colossians 2:20-23

> Therefore, if you died with Christ from the basic principles of the world, why, as though living in the world, do you subject yourselves to regulations—²¹"Do not touch, do not taste, do not handle," ²²which all concern things which perish with the using—according to the commandments and doctrines of men? ²³These things indeed have an appearance of wisdom in self-imposed religion, false humility, and neglect of the body, but are of no value against the indulgence of the flesh.

In this lesson, we'll ask and answer the following questions:

What is Asceticism? (vv 20-21)
Why is Asceticism Dangerous? (vv 22-23)

What is Asceticism?

Colossians 2:20-21

> Therefore, if you died with Christ from the basic principles of the world, why, as though living in the world, do you subject yourselves to regulations (Colossians 2:20)

Paul begins with the word *therefore*, which begs us to ask why it's there. Paul is essentially saying, in view of everything I've written thus far, and because Christ is sufficient, then remember that you have *died with Christ from the basic principles of the world*. The word *if* is actually more accurately translated as *since*. In other words, since you *died with Christ,* why *do you subject yourself to regulations?* The Greek word *died* speaks of a past action that has already taken place. The Colossian believers had died with Christ, which meant that their old way of life was gone. Paul already reminded them of this in verse 14. There he mentioned that Christ had blotted out those ordinances which were against us and nailed them to the cross. Why would we want to take them up again? Paul also puts it well in Galatians 2:20, when he clearly states, "I have been crucified with Christ." The death of a believer with Christ is a death to sin, to the law, to guilt, and to the world. Paul says, you have died to legalism, to mysticism, and to asceticism, so why do you want to revive it? Why do you want to put yourself under bondage again? In Galatians 2:20, Paul goes on to say, "I have been crucified with Christ; it is no longer I who live, but Christ lives in me; and the life which I now live in the flesh I live by faith in the Son of God, who loved me and gave Himself for me."

Paul is very clear that children of God do not live by rules or self-denial, but we live by faith. The just shall live by faith! We do not live by a list of dos and don'ts; we do not live by worshiping angels; and we do not live by rigid asceticism, by self-denial of our bodies. We live by faith in Christ and Christ alone. Paul already explained in verses 12 and 13 that the Colossians had died to all those -isms when he wrote that they had been buried with Christ in baptism and had been raised with Him to newness of life. The picture is one of coming out of the grave! They had died to those rudiments of the world. We learned that the rudiments of the world referred to the elementary teachings and practices of the world; the word itself means anything in a row, like the letters of the alphabet. These are the basic principles of the world, which man practices in the vain hope of achieving salvation. And yet, as Paul said in verse 8, these things are not after Christ.

Now, he says, since you are dead to these things, then *why, as though living in the world, do you subject yourself to regulations?* Why are you following the world's ways? Why are you subjecting yourself to man's rules? Why are you listening to the false teachers? Now, it's possible that you are wondering what regulations Paul is speaking of here. The answer is found in verse 21.

"Do not touch, do not taste, do not handle," (Colossians 2:21)

Don't touch this; don't taste that; and, by all means, don't handle! Paul is describing, with these three *do not do* commands, the third -ism we must avoid—asceticism. Asceticism is a man-made system of rules based on human commands and teachings; it is the attempt to achieve holiness through rigorous self-neglect, self-denial, and even self-infliction. History records that those who practiced asceticism rejected good things that God created, like marriage, sex, parenthood, and even their own selves. Ancient Jewish writings give us a sense of what this would have looked like: "They allowed themselves no food that was pleasant to the taste, but ate dry, coarse bread, and drank only water. Many of them ate nothing until sunset, and if anyone touched them who did not belong to their sect, they washed themselves as if they had been most deeply defiled."[23] Many ascetics abstained from sexual relations with their mate, and that is perhaps why Paul includes the reference to "touch not" and "handle not." Some ascetics abstained from marriage altogether, which is interesting in light of Paul's warning in 1 Timothy 4:1-3: "Now the Spirit expressly says that in latter times some will depart from the faith, giving heed to deceiving spirits and doctrines of demons, speaking lies in hypocrisy, having their own conscience seared with a hot iron, *forbidding to marry,* and *commanding to abstain from foods* which God created to be received with thanksgiving by those who believe and know the truth" (emphases mine). These man-made ordinances and doctrines were not only worthless but actually harmful. And they had crept into the church at Colossae, threatening to steal them away from Christ.

Ladies, we can punish our body in such ridiculous ways, but it does not take care of the real problem, which is in the heart and the mind. God is interested in a transformed mind, not a buff body. God is interested in a regenerated heart, not rigorous affliction of one's

23 Albert Barnes, *Barnes' Notes: Ephesians to Philemon (Grand Rapids: Baker Book House, 1983), 270.*

body. Paul states in 1 Timothy 4:8 that exercise just profits a little, but godliness is profitable not only in this life but in the life to come. Also keep in mind Romans 14:17, "For the kingdom of God is not eating and drinking, but righteousness and peace and joy in the Holy Spirit." These latter things—righteousness, peace, and joy—are the things we should be pursuing, not legalism, mysticism and asceticism. Growing in Christlikeness will come through the things of the Holy Spirit, not some mystical spirit. So, what is asceticism, according to the Bible? It is a system of regulations that require one to not touch, not taste, and not handle. And Paul helps us to understand why asceticism is so dangerous, in verses 22 and 23. Do you want to understand what's going to happen to all those man-made rules? Paul says they are all going to perish.

Why is Asceticism Dangerous?

Colossians 2:22-23

> which all concern things which perish with the using—according to the commandments and doctrines of men? (Colossians 2:22)

These things are all going to *perish*; they are all going to corrupt and decay. And notice that Paul says they are *all* going to perish, not just some of them. We know from 2 Peter that everything is going to perish. Listen to what Peter writes in 2 Peter 3:10-13:

> But the day of the Lord will come as a thief in the night, in which the heavens will pass away with a great noise, and the elements will melt with fervent heat; both the earth and the works that are in it will be burned up. Therefore, since all these things will be dissolved, what manner of persons ought you to be in holy conduct and godliness, looking for and hastening the coming of the day of God, because of which the heavens will be dissolved, being on fire, and the elements will melt with fervent heat? Nevertheless we, according to His promise, look for new heavens and a new earth in which righteousness dwells.

All this stuff is going to burn up. So why we are so insistent on being involved with such nonsense—touch not, taste not, handle not? Peter even says the same thing Paul says, that the new earth will be where righteousness dwells. Paul says the kingdom of God is not food and drink but righteousness and peace and joy in the Holy Spirit (Romans 14:17). We should be focusing on things that will last, like the Word of God and the souls of men. Our focus should be on the eternal, not the temporal. As Paul states in 2 Corinthians 4:18, "we do not look at the things which are seen, but at the things which are not seen. For the things which are seen are temporary, but the things which are not seen are eternal."

Paul goes on to say that these things will perish *with the using*. The idea is that all these -isms are all going to be used up, or burned up, as Peter would say. And Paul says that these things are *after the commandments and doctrines of men*. *Commandments* are precepts and *doctrines* are instructions. Paul says these are after *men*, not after God. These are man-made rules, not God-made rules. Again, ladies, God is not interested in rules, but He is interested in the heart! Isaiah mentions this same problem in Isaiah 29:13; he says, "these people draw near with their mouths and honor Me with their lips, but have removed their hearts far from Me, and their fear toward Me is taught by the commandment of men." As you can see, it was going on in Isaiah's day, it was going on in Paul's day, and it's still going on in our day. Isaiah says that they who are following the commandments of men, have hearts are far from God. My friend, this is why it is so important for us to spend the bulk of our time and energies on the inward woman, not the outward woman. But why are these things of no use? Why shouldn't I practice self-denial by not touching, not tasting, and not handling? Paul tells us why in verse 23.

> These things indeed have an appearance of wisdom in self-imposed religion, false humility, and neglect of the body, but are of no value against the indulgence of the flesh. (Colossians 2:23)

These things, these regulations, *have an appearance of wisdom* in self-imposed religion, false humility, and neglect of the body. They have the appearance of holiness. They make us appear to be religious, when in fact we are not. They make us appear humble, but they only inflate our pride. In fact, I know people who measure the spiritual value of other Christians by what they weigh on a bathroom scale. One woman told me that while she was trying to find a new church, she pulled into the parking lot of a church she intended to visit and noticed that some of the people going into the church building were overweight by her standard, so she drove away. She told me that she could never go to a church where people were overweight. My friend, that is not wisdom; that is judgmentalism.

These things have the appearance of wisdom but, Paul says, are self-imposed *religion*. This is a religion someone devises and prescribes for himself; it is self-imposed ritual and nothing more! These things appear to be wise and a means of worship, but truly they are not—just as I thought I would be more spiritual by achieving thinness. Where did I get that idea? From man. Certainly not from God! And yet, some Christians give us the idea that these things are worship.

Not only are these things self-imposed religion, but Paul says they're also *false humility*, mock humility. It is like the so-called humility mentioned in verse 18 that the false teachers possess. This kind of humility had them talking about things they had never seen, vainly puffed up by their fleshly mind. They substituted a self-manufactured humility that glorified self, not God. When humility becomes self-conscious, it ceases to be humility. True humility is found not in drawing attention to yourself but in death to self. It is the humility that Paul writes about in Philippians 2:7-8 when he speaks of our Lord, "but made Himself of no reputation, taking the form of a bondservant, and coming in the likeness of men. And being found in appearance as a man, He humbled Himself and became obedient to the point of death, even the death of the cross." Genuine humility dies to self and lives for others. That's quite a contrast to the false teachers, isn't it? They pamper themselves and want to take others down the heretical path with them. This was the issue that Jesus addressed in the Sermon on the Mount, in Matthew 6:1-18, when He rebuked the religious of the day who did their acts of righteousness, like fasting, giving, and praying, only to be seen by others. They had a false humility. They were puffed up.

Paul says these things have the appearance of piety, but you know what they really are? They are *neglect of the body, but are of no value against the indulgence of the flesh.* These things *neglect* the body. They do cruelty to the body. They are hard on the body. God made the body and practicing asceticism treats the body harshly. When we practice asceticism, we do not consider that we are fearfully and wonderfully made and that our bodies are the temple of the Holy Spirit. Paul writes in 1 Corinthians 6:19-20, "Or do you not know that your body is the temple of the Holy Spirit who is in you, whom you have from God, and you are not your own? For you were bought at a price; therefore glorify God in your body and in your spirit, which are God's." We have been bought with a price, the precious blood of Jesus, and therefore we are to glorify God with our bodies, but glorifying Him with our bodies does not mean abusing them or neglecting them. One man writes,

> Commenting on the futility of asceticism, the great nineteenth-century Scottish preacher Alexander McClaren wrote, "Any asceticism is a great deal more to men's taste than abandoning self. They will rather stick hooks in their backs and do the 'swinging poojah' than give up their sins and yield up their wills. There is only one thing that will put the collar on the neck of the animal within us and that is the power of the indwelling Christ. Ascetic religion is godless, for its practitioners essentially worship themselves."[24]

Some, both in the past and even in the present, have taken this to the ridiculous. History records for us that the founder of Christian monasticism (monks) never changed his vest or washed his feet. Another monk outdid him, however, spending the last 30 years of his life on top of a 60 foot pillar; he thought the path to spirituality lay in exposing his body to the elements and withdrawing from the world. Even Martin Luther, prior to his salvation, almost wrecked his health through asceticism. What I was doing by starving my body could have eventually led to my death. Who knows what damage was done in that one year? My teeth had started decaying, my hair

---

24 John MacArthur, *The MacArthur New Testament Commentary: Colossians and Philemon* (Chicago: Moody Press, 1992), 123-124.

was falling out, and I didn't menstruate for a year. My husband was doing some study at the time on eating disorders, and he explained to me that my heart and lungs probably suffered damage as well. Was that glorifying God with the body He gave me? No. Was that the means to my spiritual growth? No.

Please understand that I am not saying there aren't times when we must deny ourselves physically. Often, missionaries, for example, must go without food for various reasons. Or you might choose to fast for physical or spiritual reasons. These are good and godly things. But we should not do these things if we think that the end will bring us favor with God, or if we think it will be the means to our spiritual growth. Even Paul himself said in 2 Corinthians 11 that he went hungry and thirsty, and that he was cold and naked and weary. Why did he do such things? To gain favor with God? No. Those were the circumstances God divinely allowed for him at that time in which he was serving God. They were not self-inflicted, like these false teachers who choose to do such things to their bodies. Paul even says that he glories in these sufferings so that the power of Christ would rest on him; he wasn't seeking self-glorification. We have a responsibility to take care of our bodies, not to abuse them with neglect and harsh treatment.

In fact, Paul says these things *are of no value against the indulgence of the flesh*. These things do nothing in the battle against gratifying the flesh. When we endeavor to live by self-made rules and religion, we think we are being wise, but there is absolutely no value in them other than feeding our flesh. When you and I deny our body certain things, it only makes our flesh want those things more. These practices do not help our spiritual life, but rather, hinder it. One man put it this way, "A man might whip and fast himself into a walking skeleton, and yet the spirit within him might have all its lusts unconquered."[25] It is like trying to stick to a rigid diet only to find that it arouses the flesh's desire for food. You know exactly what I mean! It feeds the flesh by starving it. When I was anorexic, I

25 John Eadie, *Greek Text Commentaries: Colossians (Grand Rapids: Baker Book House, 1979), 200.*

was starved for days at a time, wishing desperately to be thin enough to eat, and yet I was very, very thin. I wasn't battling the insatiable desires of the flesh, by any means; I was lusting for food all day long. I was sinning. I remember having a conversation with my husband one time regarding weight, and he said, "Susan, when we get to heaven, God may get on to me about my weight, but He is going to get on you for your obsession with being thin." Paul says that such obsession only serves to puff you up!

Summary

Asceticism is dangerous. Why? Because it will perish; because it is after the commandments of men, not God; because it feeds man's pride; because it promotes the harsh treatment of the body; and because it does not aid in the fight against gratifying the flesh.

Do you have any forms of asceticism in your life? Do you think that by denying yourself certain things you will be more spiritual? Do you treat your body in harsh ways, thinking that it will earn you favor with God? My friend, asceticism promotes pride, not humility. It also is a substitute for a meaningful personal relationship with Christ; it leads you away from Christ and the fullness of salvation that we have in Him. You see, if I can soothe my conscience with a list of dos and don'ts, then I do not have to be forced to face the living God and have my sin exposed. Usually, those who practice any of these -isms do so out of a guilty conscience, but Christ died for our guilty conscience. He came to take away the sins of the world. In addition to these things, we also need to remember that when we practice mysticism, legalism, or asceticism, we send a confusing message to new Christians, tempting them to think that these things are the answer to a fulfilled Christian life. What happens is that we end up worshiping self, not God.

The biggest reason, however, why all these -isms are dangerous is the heart. They reveal where the heart truly is. The writer to the Hebrews says it well in Hebrews 13:8-9: "Jesus Christ is the same yesterday, today, and forever. Do not be carried about with various and strange doctrines. For it is good that the heart be established by grace, not with foods which have not profited those who have been occupied with them." Our hearts should be established by grace, nourished with the good-producing works of Christ, not with the guilt-producing works of men. One man has put it better far than me:

> The answer to legalism is the continual realization of the grace of Christ. The answer to mystics is an understanding of how profoundly we are related to Christ. The answer to asceticism is the reckoning that we have died, been buried, and are resurrected with Christ. The answer is where it all began, at the foot of the Cross.

> I have seen in my own life and the lives of those I have counseled that there is a tendency to move away from where we had our beginning: the Cross. All our theology, all our preaching, all of our singing hymns together, the disciplines of the life experienced in family and relationships are meant to keep us right at the foot of the Cross—simply drinking long and deep from the Fountainhead, Jesus Christ.[26]

---

26 R. Kent Hughes, *Colossians and Philemon: The Supremacy of Christ (Westchester: Crossway Books, 1989), 87.*

Questions to Consider

Colossians 2:20-23
Warning Against Asceticism

1. Read Colossians 1 and 2, and list all the new truths you have learned.

2. Memorize Colossians 2:20-21.

3. (a) Read Galatians 3. According to verse 24, what was the purpose of the law? (b) According to this passage, what is the danger of putting oneself back under the law? (c) What does Paul exhort his readers to do instead, according to Galatians 5:1?

4. (a) In Romans 7:1-6, what analogy does Paul use to explain our death to the law? (b) What happened when we died to the law?

5. (a) In 1 Corinthians 6:13, what does Paul say is going to happen to food? (b) In John 6:27, who else says the same thing? (c) What did Jesus say would last forever? (d) What was He talking about? (e) What did Jesus say was His food, in John 4:34-38? (f) What do these verses teach you about where our time should be invested?

6. (a) In 1 Timothy 4:1-10, what does Paul warn about? (b) What does he say should be our attitude toward exercise? (c) What is more important? (d) According to Romans 12:1-2, how should we treat our bodies? (e) What else does Paul emphasize in these verses? (f) With all that in mind, what do you think is the biblical mandate regarding our bodies? (g) What dangers do you see in our culture in regard to the body?

7. Are there any man-made rules or traditions that you are following in the hope of aiding your spiritual growth?

8. What are some of the dangers in following a list of dos and don'ts?

9. What changes have you made thus far as a result of our study? Please write them down in the form of praises to God.

10. What changes would you still like to see? Please write one or two down in the form of a prayer request.

Chapter 12

Where is Your Affection?

Colossians 3:1-4

It has been my joy over the years to disciple and counsel women. It is a blessing to encourage them to follow the Lord in all things and just downright fun to watch them grow to be more like Christ. One of the most common issues I deal with when trying to help women is to be more disciplined in the management of their time. An exercise I've found helpful is to assign women the task of journaling everything they do for a week. I have them jot down how much time they spend on shopping, cleaning, doing laundry, cooking, surfing the internet, social networking, entertainment, etc. compared to how much time they spend in the Word, with God's people, in ministry, and in other spiritual disciplines. It is helpful in aiding them to see the things that rob their time and how they can better manage their days. And sometimes it reveals a much bigger issue: their hearts and where their affections lie. Do they have an affinity for spiritual things or are their affections for worldly things? As daughters of the King, our lives should be different than the daughters of the world because we have been called out to glorify God!

As we begin chapter three of Colossians, the apostle Paul writes to us regarding this important but forgotten truth! Paul has ended the doctrinal portion of Colossians and he now begins the duty portion. Most of the Pauline epistles are written in this fashion: first doctrine, then duty. Now that we have been instructed regarding proper doctrine, we need to understand how to live out what we believe. Since we have been convinced that Gnosticism is dangerous, and we reject all aspects of it, how should we live? Now that we have learned to put off legalism, mysticism, and asceticism, what should we put on instead? Let's listen in as Paul answers these questions from Colossians 3:1-4.

Colossians 3:1-4

If then you were raised with Christ, seek those things which are above, where Christ is, sitting at the right hand of God. ²Set your mind on things above, not on things on the earth. ³For you died, and your life is hidden with Christ in God. ⁴When Christ who is our life appears, then you also will appear with Him in glory.

As we consider the question, "Where is *your* affection?" we will discover in these verses

> *Where Our Affections Lie* (vv 1-2)
> *Why Our Affections Lie There* (vv 3-4)

Where Our Affections Lie

Colossians 3:1-2

If then you were raised with Christ, seek those things which are above, where Christ is, sitting at the right hand of God. (Colossians 3:1)

Paul begins verse one with the word *if*. Paul does not doubt these Colossian believers, but he is speaking in a way that is similar to what we saw in 2:20. The word is not accurately translated as *if* but *since*. Since you were raised, or since you were raised with Christ, seek the things that are above. Notice that it here reads *if* you were raised, and yet in 2:20 it reads if you died. You might think that this is odd, but it is not. Why not? Because I am dead to sin and self but have been raised to new life in Christ. So, Paul says since *you were raised with Christ, seek those things which are above*. The phrase *raised* (or risen) *with Christ* means to arouse from death to be in company with. Paul writes of this truth in Romans 6:5, "For if we have been united together in the likeness of His death, certainly we also shall be in the likeness of His resurrection." We have died with Christ, and we have risen with Him to new life.

Because of this fact, Paul says we should *seek those things which are above*. This is a command that Paul is giving, not an option. The verb *seek* implies a persevering effort; it means to seek or strive for earnestly, and to be constantly seeking. We are to be constantly seeking the things that are above. It is not just a seeking to discover but a seeking to obtain. It is very similar to what Jesus says in Matthew 6:33, "But seek first the kingdom of God and His righteousness, and all these things shall be added to you."

What are these *things which are above* that Paul is writing about? *Above* is a word that means upward or on the top. This would be in direct contrast to what the Gnostics were seeking. They were seeking earthly things: traditions, asceticism, legalism, mysticism, angel worship, philosophy, and other such earthly things. They were in pursuit of the things of man, not the things of Christ. But Paul says no, you have died to those things and have been raised with Christ. Seek His character, His presence, and His heavenly joys. You are no longer under the rule of earthly things, like angel worship, philosophy, traditions, and the things that produce false humility. You are under the rule of heavenly things, the things of Christ, which produce genuine humility.

It's possible that some of the Colossian believers might have been wondering if Paul was referring to things like astrology, angel worship, and the like. Paul is most certainly not talking about seeking those kinds of "heavenly" things. Instead, he defines heavenly things a little differently, by saying *where Christ is, sitting at the right hand of God*. We know that God is in heaven and so Paul is saying seek those things that are truly heavenly, the things that pertain to *God* and *Christ*. The *right hand* indicates a position of authority. We are to be seeking the person of Christ who sits at God's right hand. He is equal with God! In Ephesians 1:20, the sister epistle to Colossians, Paul writes, "which He worked in Christ when He raised Him from the dead and seated Him at His right hand in the heavenly places." A person of high rank who puts anyone on his right hand gives that person equal honor with himself and recognizes him as having equal dignity. Paul has already told us in Colossians 2:9 that in

Christ dwells the fullness of the Godhead. He has already told us in Colossians 1:15 that Christ is the image of the invisible God. Paul is making it clear here, once again, that Christ must be supreme above anything else. It is *With the Master and Nothing Else*! So, how can we know where our affection lies? By what we seek! Do we seek eternal things or earthly things? There's a second way, though, in which we can know where our affection lies. It's not only in what we seek but also in what we think. Let's read verse 2.

> Set your mind on things above, not on things on the earth. (Colossians 3:2)

Paul gives a second command for those who have died with Christ and are risen with Him, and that is *set your mind on things above*. Some translations translate *mind* as affections, referring to the will or moral consideration. Paul is basically saying exercise your mind. We are not to simply seek heaven but to think heaven. This command is in the present imperative, which means this is to be a continuous, ongoing effort. It doesn't mean that I only think about things above occasionally or when I read about Heaven or hear a sermon about heaven, but I am to keep on thinking about the things above; we are to seek Christ because He is the highest. At first glance, it might seem to you that seeking things above and setting your affections on things above are one and the same, but they're not. The first suggests striving, while the second suggests concentrating.

After Paul states the positive, that is, where we are to be placing our affections, our minds, he then states the negative, where we are not to be setting our affections, our minds. We are *not* to set our minds *on things on the earth*. My friend, heaven and earth are complete opposites. This is a definite contradiction to all that the Gnostics taught and practiced. Their whole lives were consumed in earthly stuff, the traditions of men, legalism, asceticism, mysticism. All these regulations to touch not, taste not, handle not, took their attention off Christ and the world to come. Can you imagine how much time the Gnostics wasted on thinking, "Now, should I touch this or not? Hmm, should I taste that or not?" Legalism requires a lot of wasted time and thinking, and it takes one's thought off Christ and on to self and things.

Now, lest you think, "Susan has lost it! She's proposing that we be so heavenly minded that we are of no earthly good!" I beg you to hear me out! Paul does not mean that we should never think about the things upon the earth, but rather that these should not be our aim, our goal, or our master; we should not be engrossed in these things. Consider this example: Most of us have had the experience of moving. I think I've moved at least 12 times in my 40+ years of marriage. I remember moving once and during that move asking myself, "How are you going to keep your mind fixed on things above during this move? There is so much to do—the packing, the unpacking, turning off utilities, turning on utilities, buying a house, selling a house, purchasing things for the new house, and giving things away from the old house." The Lord, in His kindness, helped me to see how even in a move on this earth my mind could be fixed on the heavenlies. I began to view the move in light of eternity. I began to ask, "How can this new house be best used for the kingdom?" I began to pray about who would occupy the old house, asking God that it would go on being used for His glory. I asked myself, "How can I be a blessing to others during the packing process? Who could use some of these things that we no longer need? How can I represent Christ during every minute detail?" I also thought about the blessing it will be on that final move, my move to glory, when I will not have to take with me any of the stuff I've accumulated on earth. Praise God! I really believe that no matter what earthly things we must be involved in while we are passing through, it is possible to remain heavenly minded in them. One man puts it well: "The Christian has to keep his feet upon the earth, but his head in the heavens. He must be heavenly-minded here on earth and so help to make earth like heaven."[27]

Our mindset is a deliberate act of our will. Paul helps us to understand how we do this, in 2 Corinthians 4:18, when he says, "we do not look at the things which are seen, but at the things which

---

27 A.T. Robertson. *Robertson's Word Pictures: http://www.bibletools.org/index.*

are not seen. For the things which are seen are temporary, but the things which are not seen are eternal." We should keep in mind that we are strangers and pilgrims on earth, as Peter explains in 1 Peter 2:11. We should also consider studying Hebrews 11, so that we can observe how those who've gone before us lived. How did they set their affections upward? They certainly remembered that they were strangers and pilgrims here on this earth, as Peter said. They also desired a better country, a heavenly country, as Hebrews reminds us. Perhaps if we were being faced with the possibility of being sawn in half, as they were, we would be more heavenly-minded. We are an indulgent and pampered people and know little about suffering or the threat of persecution. But this does not mean that all things will continue as they have been. Wise women will prepare themselves now for the day of adversity by being women who are committed to seeking heaven and thinking heaven. We need to keep in mind that this world is not our home, that we are simply passing through. Heaven is where you and I will be forever, so why not seek it and think of it?

We have two answers to the question of where our affections lie. First, the answer lies in what we seek, eternal things or heavenly things. Second, the answer lies in what we think. Do we think of heaven, or do we think of earth? But why does the redeemed woman seek and think heavenly things? The answer is also two-fold and is found in verses 3 and 4.

Why Our Affections Lie There

Colossians 3:3-4

> For you died, and your life is hidden with Christ in God.
> (Colossians 3:3)

Paul says *you died.* The word *died* comes from the Greek word apethanete, which refers to a definite act. *You* died! Your former life died, and all the evils of that life died, when you came to Christ. You are dead to yourself, and you are dead to sin! You also died to the elementary things of the world; you are dead to the traditions of men, Judaism, rules, legalism, and the like. It is just like someone who is dead physically; they don't care what you do with their earthly possessions because they are dead! I remember when my mom passed away suddenly 10 years ago in Irkutsk, Russia. She had been on a tour heading to Mongolia when she suffered two heart attacks in Russia. We had to wait weeks to have her body prepared and shipped back to the states for the funeral. It was a confusing time for our family and so we did our best to make the memorial and burial what we thought our mother would like. A few months afterward, one of my sisters called to tell me that she had been going through my mom's things and discovered that mom had wanted to be buried in a yellow dress that she had knitted. I told my sister that mom was gone and that she did not care about that now. I told her that I thought it would not be wise or financially prudent to exhume mom's body and take off her purple dress to put on the yellow dress. Mom was dead, and she did not care about the dress her body was wearing. That's what Paul is saying regarding the spiritual realm. We have died spiritually, and our life is hidden with Christ; we have died to all those earthly trappings, and they should not matter to us. (Paul has already alluded to this in 2:12 and 2:20.) We must consider ourselves dead to the things of this world.

Not only does Paul add that you died but also that *your life is hidden with Christ in God.* Your life has been hidden with Christ in God, and it should remain that way. *Hidden* is a wonderful word that implies concealment and safety, as well as security. It refers to a treasure which is hidden or concealed in a secure place. The idea is that your eternal life is a treasure which has been laid up with Christ in a secure place, which is heaven. And, ladies, that is the best safe there is! Your eternal life has been safely deposited; nothing can reach it, and no one can take it away. Your life is preserved intact, and no harm can come to it. What a wonderful truth! When we consider this precious fact, it should cause us as believers to live with heaven in mind because that's where our treasure is; that's where it has been safely deposited.

Jesus mentions this concept in the Sermon on the Mount. Consider His words in Matthew 6:19-21: "Do not lay up for yourselves treasures on earth, where moth and rust destroy and where thieves break in and steal; but lay up for yourselves treasures in heaven, where neither moth nor rust destroys and where thieves do not break in and steal. For where your treasure is, there your heart will be also." If your treasure is here on earth, then your heart is here on earth, as well. If your treasure is in heaven, then your heart will be there also. This reality begs us to consider what occupies our hearts, our minds, our time, and our energies. Is your mind occupied with clothes, food, the internet (and all that it includes)? Is your mind occupied with your body, your marriage, your children, or your job? What occupies your mind? My friend, this is the first reason why you think and seek heaven: You are dead to self and alive with Christ. There is a second reason, though, that we should be heavenly minded, and it is found in verse 4.

> When Christ who is our life appears, then you also will appear
> with Him in glory. (Colossians 3:4)

Paul goes on to say *when Christ who is our life appears*. Now what does that mean? Paul is saying that all these things that you hold so dear here on earth, these rules and regulations which have become your life, they're not your life. Christ is your life. Your life has been hidden with Christ in God. And we need to remember that this One, this Jesus, who is our life, will *appear*. That life that has been hidden with Christ in God will then be made visible, as we appear with Him in glory. It is not going to matter how many times you have denied your body, or whether you have circumcised your sons, or how many visions you claim to have seen, or if you have followed all those ABC rules. But it will matter whether Christ is your life, and it will matter if your life is hidden with Him.

Paul is reminding the Colossians of the hope they have in heaven. Hope was one of the four characteristics the Colossians believers were known for, as we saw in Colossians 1:4-5. That same hope is reserved for them in heaven. And Paul states that when Christ comes *you also will appear with Him in glory*! Perhaps we need to remind ourselves of this blessed truth, this blessed hope. Consider what Paul writes in 1 Thessalonians 4:13-18:

> But I do not want you to be ignorant, brethren, concerning those who have fallen asleep, lest you sorrow as others who have no hope. For if we believe that Jesus died and rose again, even so God will bring with Him those who sleep in Jesus. For this we say to you by the word of the Lord, that we who are alive and remain until the coming of the Lord will by no means precede those who are asleep. For the Lord Himself will descend from heaven with a shout, with the voice of an archangel, and with the trumpet of God. And the dead in Christ will rise first. Then we who are alive and remain shall be caught up together with them in the clouds to meet the Lord in the air. And thus we shall always be with the Lord. Therefore comfort one another with these words.

The apostle John writes of this same truth in 1 John 3:2-3: "Beloved, now we are children of God; and it has not yet been revealed what we shall be, but we know that when He is revealed, we shall be like Him, for we shall see Him as He is. And everyone who has this hope in Him purifies himself, just as He is pure." (Other passages we would do well to consider include: 1 Corinthians 13:12; Philippians 3:20-21; Colossians 1:27; and 2 Thessalonians 1:10-12.) C.S. Lewis described this glory as "a longing all human beings have for something that can hardly be expressed." He called it "a desire which no natural happiness will satisfy."[28] We should look not only upward to Christ in heaven where He reigns over us but also look forward to His return for us in glory. Unfortunately, too many believers are so caught up in the here and now that they simply do not long for heaven. When I was growing up, bible prophecy was taught and talked about often. But nowadays, people really aren't all that interested in sermons about heaven or prophecy. They're not popular because our minds are set on the here and now, not on heaven and the future. We want sermons that appeal to our felt

---

28 As quoted in: Andrew Spencer. "C.S. Lewis and the Surprising Reason We Desire Fulfillment at Work." *Institute for Faith, Work & Economics. https://tifwe.org/c-s-lewis-surprising-reason-fulfillment-at-work/*

needs, rather than those that press us to think about eternity. No wonder our churches are weak and our parishioners spiritually sick. Oh, my friend, why do we seek to find contentment and joy in this life, which passes so quickly, when our eternal life is forever? Why are we laying up stuff here when this is a merely a shadow of what is to come: our Lord and His glory?

Summary

Where Our Affections Lie (vv 1-2): When we answer the question, "Where do my affection lie?" we must consider two things. First, the answer lies in what we seek, eternal things or heavenly things. Which do you seek after? If you were to keep a time journal this week of all your activities, what would it reveal about your pursuits? Would they be heavenly or worldly? Second, the answer lies in what we think. Do you think heaven, or do you think earth? As you go through your day, where does your mind wander? Are you thinking of heaven or thinking of earth? Or are your days so crowded with noise and activity that you can't think? My friend, I pray heaven is truly what you seek and think.

Why Our Affections Lie There (vv 3-4): Why do we seek and think heaven? First, because we are dead to self and alive with Christ. In what ways has your life manifested that you are dead to your sin and yourself? In what ways does your life exhibit that you are alive to Christ? Second, we should think and seek heaven because we are going to appear with Christ in glory. Does the fact that Christ will appear one day motivate you to pursue heavenly things? If not, why not?

Perhaps you are wondering how one goes about practically setting their mind on things above? How can I practically do this as a woman when my life is so busy that all I can think about is raising my children, cooking meals, doing laundry, meeting my family's needs, paying the bills, cleaning the house, and a myriad of other responsibilities? Let me give you four practical suggestions as we close. First, a heavenly mind-set must begin with prayer. Have you asked the Lord to make you more heavenly minded? You might pray something very simple like, "Lord, help me set my mind on things above."

Second, a heavenly mind-set is a deliberate act of our will. We can set our minds on a lot of things, like a vacation, or having lunch with a good friend, or on what we're going to fix for dinner. These things occupy our thoughts, no doubt, but why not discipline yourself to think of these things from a heavenly perspective? For example, when you plan a trip, set your mind on your final trip, the one which will take you home to heaven. When you're having lunch with a friend, think about the fact that one day you will be able to have perfect fellowship with this friend forever (if she's a believer)! When you're cooking a meal for your family, set your mind on the Marriage Supper of the Lamb and on the Lamb Himself.

Third, a heavenly mind-set must hold loosely to the things on earth. Remember the rich young ruler in Luke 18, who went away very sad when Jesus told him to go and sell all that he had and give it to the poor? His mind and heart were set on earth. He would not give up earthly things for the Kingdom. Are there any earthly possessions that you're holding on to tightly? I remember one time asking myself this very question and the only thing I could think of was my house—not the one we are in now, but the one we were in for 10 years—and guess what? We are there no more! A good exercise you might try, in an effort to discipline yourself to hold the things of earth loosely, is to regularly give away something that you value very much.

Fourth, a heavenly mindset wisely commits to memory Scriptures that pertain to the things of heaven. Passages like Matthew 6:19-21; Philippians 2:9-11; Colossians 3:1-4; 1 Thessalonians 4:16-5:11; 1 John 3:1-3; and Revelation 21:1-7 would be beneficial. These are but a few of them, and perhaps you would want to look up some of your own by searching in a concordance for the word "heaven." Commit the Scriptures to memory and meditate on them throughout your day.

Fixing my attention on things above involves centering my life on the ascended, glorified Christ, who is seated at the right hand of God. When we think about it, what is there here on earth that makes us so fond of it? Heaven is so much better, and it is where our hearts should be drawn. Why? Because our Head is there, our home is there, our treasure is there, and we who have committed our lives to His Lordship will be there forever! One of my husband's favorite quotes is framed and hanging in our living room; it says, "If we insist on keeping hell or even earth, we shall not see heaven. If we accept heaven, we shall not be able to retain even the smallest and most intimate souvenirs of hell."[29]

29 Ibid.

Questions to Consider

Colossians 3:1-4
Where is Your Affection?

1. (a) Read Colossians chapter three and list all the commands you find. (b) Are you obeying these commands?

2. Memorize Colossians 3:2.

3. (a) What things does Paul mention about Christ in Colossians 3:1-4? (b) What do you think each one of these means? (c) Why does Paul emphasize the person of Christ so much here in chapter three? (Hint: look back at chapter two.)

4. (a) In Colossians 3:1, Paul mentions that Christ is sitting at the right hand of the Father. What insights do the following verses give you as to why Jesus is at the right hand of the Father? Acts 2:33; Romans 8:34; Hebrews 1:3; 1 Peter 3:22. (b) Why do you think Christ is described as standing at the right hand of God, rather than sitting, in Acts 7:54-60? (c) What hope does this give you as you think of the day that you too will "appear with Him in glory"?

5. (a) The men and women listed in Hebrews 11 had some challenges in keeping their thoughts heavenward. Write down at least three people mentioned in Hebrews 11, as well as the challenges they were facing as they lived here on earth. (b) How did they keep their mind set on things above, according to verses 13-16? (c) How does this encourage you to keep your focus heavenward and not earthward?

6. (a) Make two columns on the back of your paper, one with the heading of "Heaven" and the other with the heading of "Earth." (b) Read the following passages and list under the proper heading what Heaven and Earth each have to offer. Psalm 73:25; Hebrews 10:34; 1 Peter 1:4; 1 John 2:15-17; 5:19; Revelation 21:9-27. (c) Looking back over these lists, which place do you prefer? (d) How do you think these passages could help you to stay focused on the kingdom to come?

7. (a) Think back over this past week and ask yourself if you have set your affection on things above or on things on the earth. (b) What changes do you need to make in order to be more eternally minded?

8. (a) If the Lord came back today, would you be ready? (b) Why or why not?

9. (a) What do you think is keeping you from being more heavenly-minded? (b) Write your thoughts in the form of a prayer request.

Chapter 13

Putting Sin to Death! (Part 1)

Colossians 3:5-7

It goes without saying, but I'll say it anyway: The Unites States is in serious trouble. The moral decline of our nation is staggering! It seems like a day doesn't go by in which I don't hear of someone who has fallen morally. Sexual sin runs rampant in the workplace, in the government, in the home, and yes, sad as it is, in the church! Accurate statistics on extra-marital affairs (adultery, as the Bible calls it) are nearly impossible to establish because so many people are unwilling to admit to it. Of those who will admit to it, statistics show that approximately two out of every three married men commit adultery and one out of every two married women. Other studies propose even higher numbers. Whatever the actual numbers are, the point to be made is this: adultery is much more common than we would like to admit. One man has stated: "There may be as many acts of infidelity in our society as there are traffic accidents."[30] He argues that the reality of adultery becoming so commonplace has actually altered society's perception of it. He says, "We won't go back to the times when adulterers were put in the stocks and publicly humiliated, or become one of those societies in which adultery is punishable by death. Society in any case is unable to enforce a rule that the majority of people break, and infidelity is so common it is no longer wrong."[31]

Perhaps you're thinking, "This is just a problem with non-believers, right? It can't be a problem in the church. Certainly, the moral standards of Christians are higher than this!" I wish that were true. But an article published in Newsweek magazine more than 20 years ago (1997) noted that various surveys suggest that as many as 30 percent of male Protestant ministers have had sexual relationships

---

30 "Adultery." *Probe Ministries. https://probe.org/adultery/?print=print*
31 Ibid.

with women other than their wives. One survey of Southern Baptist pastors reported that 14 percent acknowledged they had engaged in "sexual behavior inappropriate to a minister." It also reported that 70 percent had counseled at least one woman who had had intercourse with another minister. In a recent Leadership magazine poll of pastors, 18 percent of pastors completing the survey admitted to sexual immorality or immoral acts. Of these pastors, 12 percent admitted to adultery (and only 4 percent were discovered by their congregation). Six percent more had engaged in other forms of immorality. This means that possibly one pastor in every five has a major moral problem! But the researchers also interviewed nearly 1000 subscribers to Christianity Today who were not pastors. The numbers found in this group were nearly double those found among the pastors: 45 percent indicated having done something sexually inappropriate, and 23 percent acknowledged having had extramarital intercourse. Adultery is in society, and it is in the church, as well.[32]

Twenty years later we're not any better off. A recent poll revealed that 95 percent of born-again Christians say that they've looked at pornography, with 54 percent indicating that they view it at least on a monthly basis, and 44 percent admitting that they'd seen it at work within the last three months. Twenty-five percent of these believers confirmed that they hide their internet browsing history by erasing porn URLs from their computers and electronic devices. Furthermore, this born-again group proved that, when it comes to infidelity, they're not much better than the general consensus of professing Christians that included nominal believers; nearly a third of the self-proclaimed born-again Christians admitted to having had an extramarital sexual affair while they were married. "The rate of extramarital affairs appears to have a correlation to frequency of viewing pornography. A married person who views porn several times a month is ripe to have an affair."[33]

My friend, have we forgotten the seriousness of sexual sin?! When

---

32 Ibid.
33 *One News Now.* https://www.onenewsnow.com/culture/2014/10/09/survey-alarming-rate-of-christian-men-look-at-porn-commit-adultery

did we forget that God said no adulterer will enter the kingdom of God?! Perhaps we would do well to remind ourselves of what God says about these things by studying Colossians 3:5-7. Let's read these verses together.

Colossians 3:5-7

> Therefore put to death your members which are on the earth: fornication, uncleanness, passion, evil desire, and covetousness, which is idolatry. ⁶Because of these things the wrath of God is coming upon the sons of disobedience, ⁷in which you yourselves once walked when you lived in them.

When we began the third chapter of Colossians in our last lesson, we answered the question, "Where are my affections?" We saw, first, that the answer lies in what we seek: eternal things or heavenly things. We saw, second, that the answer lies in what we think: do we think of heaven or do we think of earth? We also considered a second question: "Why do we seek and think heaven?" First, we seek and think heaven because we are dead to self and alive with Christ. Second, we seek and think heaven because we are going to appear with Christ in glory.

These first four verses of chapter three are imperative to our understanding of the verses we'll study in this lesson. In them Paul sets forth where our minds and our affections should be. If we are indeed setting our minds and our affections heavenward, as Paul explains in verses 1-4, then it follows that we will not be pursuing the sexual sins Paul lists in verses 5-7. Paul isn't going to mince words with the church at Colossae or with us, regarding the sins we are to put off. The sins we will deal with in this lesson are mainly sexual sins; in our next lesson, we'll deal with social sins. In this lesson, we will consider

> *The Murder of Five Deadly Sins* (v 5)
> *The Motivations for Murdering These Sins* (vv 6-7)

The Murder of Five Deadly Sins

Colossians 3:5

> Therefore put to death your members which are on the earth: fornication, uncleanness, passion, evil desire, and covetousness, which is idolatry. (Colossians 3:5)

Paul begins by saying *therefore put to death your members which are on the earth*. The *therefore* is there because of what he has already written in verses 1-4. Because you are dead and your life is hidden with Christ in God, because Christ is your life and you will appear with Him in glory, then put to death your flesh! Now, you may be wondering if there is perhaps a contradiction in what Paul has just said; first, he said we died and our life is hidden with Christ in God, and now he says we need to put to death our sins! Well, we have died to sin and risen to new life, but we also still live on in the flesh until we reach glory, and while the spirit is willing the flesh is often weak. So, we must regularly put to death those earthly desires.

The words *put to death* mean to subdue, to kill or put to death; one translation (KJV) uses the term mortify. My friend, we are to reckon our flesh as dead; we are to consider it a corpse. This means that we deprive our flesh of its power, and we destroy it. And the Greek indicates that we are to do it now—this is not something we put off until a later time! As Christians, we do not have the luxury of being apathetic about the sin in our lives. Some people claim that they are gradually weaning themselves from a certain sin. That is not only unbiblical; it is also foolish. Paul is clear in Romans 6:1-16 as to what our attitude should be concerning these sins. He says,

> What shall we say then? Shall we continue in sin that grace may abound? Certainly not! How shall we who died to sin live any longer in it? Or do you not know that as many of us as were baptized into Christ Jesus were baptized into His death? Therefore we were buried with Him through baptism into death, that just as Christ was raised from the dead by the glory of the Father, even so we also should walk in newness of life. For if we have been united together in the likeness of His death,

certainly we also shall be in the likeness of His resurrection, knowing this, that our old man was crucified with Him, that the body of sin might be done away with, that we should no longer be slaves of sin. For he who has died has been freed from sin. Now if we died with Christ, we believe that we shall also live with Him, knowing that Christ, having been raised from the dead, dies no more. Death no longer has dominion over Him. For the death that He died, He died to sin once for all; but the life that He lives, He lives to God. Likewise you also, reckon yourselves to be dead indeed to sin, but alive to God in Christ Jesus our Lord. Therefore do not let sin reign in your mortal body, that you should obey it in its lusts. And do not present your members as instruments of unrighteousness to sin, but present yourselves to God as being alive from the dead, and your members as instruments of righteousness to God. For sin shall not have dominion over you, for you are not under law but under grace. What then? Shall we sin because we are not under law but under grace? Certainly not! Do you not know that to whom you present yourselves slaves to obey, you are that one's slaves whom you obey, whether of sin leading to death, or of obedience leading to righteousness?

Paul says that we must put to death our *members which are on the earth.* The *members* here refers not to church members but to a limb or part of a body; it refers to that which belongs to your earthly nature. One translation, The Twentieth-Century New Testament, puts it this way: "kill all your animal appetites." Some have taken the term members to not mean literal parts of the body that we are to put to death but instead see it as a reference to the sins mentioned in the next part of this verse. Indeed, we do need to be putting our sins to death, as well as the sinful appetites of our physical members. We use parts of our body as instruments of sin: hands to do things that are ungodly; feet to go places we should not go; eyes to look on things that are unrighteous; mouths to speak words that are not godly; ears to hear things that are inappropriate; and minds to think on unwholesome thoughts.

This concept would be very important to Paul's readers because the Gnostics were teaching that it did not matter what your earthly members did. The body, in their view, was evil and therefore was not responsible for its actions. Therefore, they taught that you could do anything you wanted with your members, your physical body. You could fornicate; you could covet; you could lie; you could murder; you could be involved in any kind of evil and not be responsible for it. It's this ridiculous idea that Paul confronts here in Colossians.

Now, some will try to kill their members in an ungodly way, as we studied in chapter two when we considered rigid asceticism, which is extreme self-denial of the body. Some have gone to the ridiculous extreme of scourging themselves in penance for their sins. In fact, I read of a man who wore a belt studded with nails that constantly tore his flesh; he felt that by doing so he was both killing the flesh and suffering to atone for his sins. Is that what Paul means here by put to death your members which are on the earth? Are we to be mutilating the members of our body so that we don't sin? Is that what Jesus means in Matthew 5:27-30 when He states that we are to cut off those members that are sinning because it is better to go into heaven without an eye or a hand than to have our whole body cast into hell? No. Jesus was not speaking literally, though some teach that and practice that. One famous theologian named Origen had himself castrated in order to fulfill what he believed Jesus was saying here. But if that is what Jesus meant, then all of us would limb-less! We would also be brain-less since all sin begins in the mind! Neither Jesus nor Paul are calling for self-mutilation, but for self-mortification, a death to self and to the desires of the flesh. Mutilation is the easy way to deal with sin; mortification is wrestling and struggling with our sin. Sin cannot be dealt with by legalism, pharisaism, celibacy, rosary beads, or any other external means. A blind man can still lust; an angry woman can still murder in her heart. Sin is an internal issue, an issue of the heart and mind, not an external issue. If you and I cannot control our thought lives, we cannot control what we do with the members of our bodies. We must learn to wrestle, as Paul writes in Romans 7, because, my friends, we are at war with our members, and we must kill them!

With this in mind, let's look more closely at the five sins we are to murder. The first sin we are to murder is *fornication*. The Greek word is <u>porneia</u>, from which we get our English word pornography. In the New Testament, however, the word has a broader meaning, including any kind of illicit sexual activity. This would include every kind of immoral sexual act there is: fornication; adultery, homosexuality, incest, bestiality, and the like. As we think about sexual sins, ladies, we must admit that we are faced with this temptation in a way like no other generation has been faced with due to the availability of porn on the internet, television, books, magazines, billboards, and even store front windows. Countless marriages and families have been ruined by pornography. With the tap of a finger, we can have access to it. Internet Porn is a 57-billion-dollar industry worldwide. Twelve billion of that is US revenue—more than the combined revenues of all professional football, baseball, and basketball franchises, and of the combined revenues of ABC, CBS, and NBC. Forty million people in the US are involved in something sexual on the internet. Sex is the number one topic searched on the internet, and twenty-five percent of all search engine requests are porn-related. Ladies, these statistics should motivate you to guard yourself and your family!

What does the Bible say about this awful sin? In Matthew 15:19, Jesus tells us where this terrible sin comes from. He says, "For out of the heart proceed evil thoughts, murders, adulteries, fornications, thefts, false witness, blasphemies." Paul writes in 1 Corinthians 5:1, "It is actually reported that there is sexual immorality among you, and such sexual immorality as is not even named among the Gentiles—that a man has his father's wife!" Paul says this kind of fornication isn't even practiced among the pagans and certainly shouldn't be practiced among Christians. He even tells us later in verse 11 that we ought not even hang out with fornicators: "But now I have written to you not to keep company with anyone named a brother, who is sexually immoral, or covetous, or an idolater, or a reviler, or a drunkard, or an extortioner—not even to eat with such a person." In Ephesians 5:3, Paul says, "But fornication and all uncleanness or covetousness, let it not even be named among you, as is fitting for saints." In 1 Corinthians 6:9-11, Paul writes about what will happen to those who practice sexual sins.

> Do you not know that the unrighteous will not inherit the kingdom of God? Do not be deceived. Neither fornicators, nor idolaters, nor adulterers, nor homosexuals, nor sodomites, nor thieves, nor covetous, nor drunkards, nor revilers, nor extortioners will inherit the kingdom of God. And such were some of you. But you were washed, but you were sanctified, but you were justified in the name of the Lord Jesus and by the Spirit of our God.

When my husband and I were living in California, he shared this verse with a homosexual who was cutting his hair; needless to say, he came home with a very interesting haircut. Paul goes on to tell us in 1 Corinthians 6:13b, "Now the body is not for sexual immorality but for the Lord, and the Lord for the body." He goes on to write in verses 18-20 of the same chapter, "Flee sexual immorality. Every sin that a man does is outside the body, but he who commits sexual immorality sins against his own body. Or do you not know that your body is the temple of the Holy Spirit who is in you, whom you have from God, and you are not your own? For you were bought at a price; therefore glorify God in your body and in your spirit, which are God's." In 1 Thessalonians 4:3-4, Paul writes, "For this is the will of God, your sanctification: that you should abstain from sexual immorality; that each of you should know how to possess his own vessel in sanctification and honor." My friend, if we refuse to heed these admonitions, we will have an even worse thing happen; consider the warning of Revelation 21:8: "But the cowardly, unbelieving, abominable, murderers, sexually immoral, sorcerers, idolaters, and all liars shall have their part in the lake which burns with fire and brimstone, which is the second death."

The second sin we are to put to death is *uncleanness*. This word means to have a lucid imagination or speech that comes from a sensual heart or a filthy mind. These are evil thoughts and intentions of the mind. It's the idea expressed in what Jesus said in Matthew 5:27-28: "You have heard that it was said to those of old, 'You shall not commit adultery.' But I say to you that whoever looks at a woman to lust for her has already committed adultery with her in his heart." It may not be outwardly committing a sexual act, but it is certainly thinking or talking about it.

The third sin we are to murder is *passion*, or as the KJV says, inordinate affection. This is a longing for what is forbidden. These are lusts that dishonor those that are involved in them. It is what Paul speaks of in 1 Thessalonians 4:3-5, where he calls it the passion of lust. Paul refers to it as vile affections in Romans 1:26-27: "For this reason God gave them up to vile passions. For even their women exchanged the natural use for what is against nature. Likewise, also the men, leaving the natural use of the woman, burned in their lust for one another, men with men committing what is shameful, and receiving in themselves the penalty of their error which was due." These are unnatural desires; even bestiality falls under this category.

The fourth sin that should die is *evil desire*. Evil desire is a wicked, self-serving, greedy kind of lust. This person is only out for their own sexual interests. Peter writes in 1 Peter 2:11, "Beloved, I beg you as sojourners and pilgrims, abstain from fleshly lusts which war against the soul." We all should echo what Job said in Job 31:1. "I have made a covenant with my eyes; why then should I look upon a young woman?" It may mean turning your head at the checkout stand to avoid filthy magazines; it may mean not gazing at billboards and store front windows. Maybe you need to get rid of your television. Perhaps you need to get some new friends. I am grieved when I see what I think are devoted Christian women talking in sexual overtones or joking of such things. Just the other day, I heard a group of people laughing about porn. My friend, porn is not a laughing matter! The sexually immoral are certainly not laughing in hell right now. Paul tells us in Ephesians 5:12 that "it is shameful even to speak of those things which are done by them in secret."

The fifth sin we need to murder is *covetousness, which*, Paul says, *is idolatry*. Covetousness is the desire to possess more than one has, particularly that which belongs to someone else. Exodus 20:17 mentions this in one of the 10 commandments that God gave Moses: "You shall not covet your neighbor's house; you shall not covet your neighbor's wife, nor his male servant, nor his female servant, nor his ox, nor his donkey, nor anything that is your neighbor's." A man may desire to have sexual relations with a girl to whom he is not married. In doing so, he is coveting by wanting something that is not his to have. In the biblical world, some tried to fight this sin in the most ridiculous ways. Rabbis taught that if a man wanted to keep his mind on the Law, he should not walk on a road behind a woman, even if that woman were his own wife. Such advice is ridiculous, because it fails to solve the problem of lust, which begins in the mind and the heart. The solution for lust is not to cover up women in gunnysacks, but to transform the way a man looks at a woman—to transform his mind. Those who lust after another—who covet another—must come to see others as persons for whom Christ died, not as objects for physical gratification. (This applies as much to women as it does to men.) Why then does Paul say that covetousness *is idolatry*? Coveting is wanting something that is not yours. Any longing for something that is not ours turns our hearts away from God and toward the object we covet. That is idolatry. What we crave we worship, and God says He will have no other gods—no other objects of our desire, no other idols—before Him.

Dear one, we are to murder these sins. As one man has said, "Carry out this principle of death, and kill everything that is mundane and carnal in your being."[34] And, as another man has said, "Use sin as it will use you; spare it not, for it will not spare you; it is your murderer, and the murderer of the world, use it, therefore as a murderer should be used. Kill it before it kills you and though it bring you to the grave as it did your Head, it shall not be able to keep you there."[35] Now, it's possible that you don't really want to kill these particular sins—or any other sins you're holding on to—because sin does have its pleasure for a season. Well, in verses 6 and 7, Paul gives us two motivations for murdering these five deadly sins. Notice what he writes in verse 6.

---

34 J.B. Lightfoot, *Paul's Epistles to the Colossians and Philemon (Peabody: Hendrickson, 1993), 211.*

35 Richard Baxter, *www.bartleby.com. http://www.bartleby.com/349/authors/13.html*

The Motivations for Murdering These Sins

Colossians 3:6-7

> Because of these things the wrath of God is coming upon the
> sons of disobedience, (Colossians 3:6)

The first motivation for murdering these terrible sins is that the
wrath of God is coming on those who disobey! Paul says *because
of these things*, because of the sins he's just mentioned, *the wrath of
God is coming. Wrath* is a word for violent, passionate punishment.
The words *is coming* are in the present tense and suggest that God's
wrath has already begun and will culminate in the future. Paul
speaks of God's wrath in Romans 1:18: "For the wrath of God is
revealed from heaven against all ungodliness and unrighteousness
of men, who suppress the truth in unrighteousness." In Ephesians,
Paul writes about the wrath of God falling on those who practice
sexual sins. Ephesians 5:3-7 states,

> But fornication and all uncleanness or covetousness, let it
> not even be named among you, as is fitting for saints; neither
> filthiness, nor foolish talking, nor coarse jesting, which are
> not fitting, but rather giving of thanks. For this you know, that
> no fornicator, unclean person, nor covetous man, who is an
> idolater, has any inheritance in the kingdom of Christ and God.
> Let no one deceive you with empty words, for because of these
> things the wrath of God comes upon the sons of disobedience.
> Therefore do not be partakers with them.

In Hebrews 13:4, the writer to the Hebrews is clear regarding sexual
sin when he writes, "Marriage is honorable among all, and the bed
undefiled; but fornicators and adulterers God will judge."

Paul says this wrath, this anger of God, has come and will come *on
the sons of disobedience. Disobedience* is a word that describes the
obstinate and rebellious. This would indicate that when believers
are involved in these kinds of sins they are behaving as sons of
disobedience. God is holy, and He cannot allow sin; His wrath comes
because of sin. I think we can see even today some manifestation of

the wrath of God that has come on us as a nation, and it's no wonder when you consider what the average Christian believes. A recent survey among professing Christians revealed that most believe God is forgiving (97%) and loving (96%), but far fewer believe that God is judging (37%) or punishes those who do wrong (19%). I'm always amazed at people who tell me that have no fear of disobeying God. I have to assume that they do not take God seriously and they have no fear of His judgment. If we say we don't take God seriously, then we can safely say that we do not take our marriages seriously, the raising of our children seriously, or even faithfulness, sexual purity, humility, repentance, honesty, faithfulness, lying, cheating, or stealing. Why should we?! If we don't believe that God is serious about what He says He will do, then we won't take Him seriously. Dear ladies, we need to teach our children and our grandchildren to fear God and have them memorize Scripture that deals with this very topic. Hebrews 10:31 would be a good place to start: "It is a fearful thing to fall into the hands of the living God." Jonathan Edward's sermon, *Sinners in the Hands of an Angry God*, would fall on skeptical ears today.

> The Christian cannot move in and out of Christ's Lordship whenever it becomes convenient or inconvenient. Holy living is rarely convenient and we should never forget the looming wrath of God, which brings certain punishment. Even when it seems that we have gotten away with our sin, it gestates within us. Consequently, Paul insists, our unethical behavior, which belongs to our old life, must be discarded like old rags or cut out like a cancerous tumor before it destroys us.[36]

But the wrath of God isn't our only motivation for putting off these sins. Paul gives us another motivation in verse 7.

> in which you yourselves once walked when you lived in them. (Colossians 3:7)

Motivation number two for murdering these sins is that these sins are an indication of our old life, not our new life! The words *once walked*

---

36 David Garland, *NIV Life Application Commentary: Colossians and Philemon. Zondervan Academic, 2009. Google Books, https://books.google.com/books*

are an indication that Paul is writing to believers, some of whom are behaving like unbelievers! They *once* did these things, they once were occupied with these sins, but this is not how a genuine believer lives after salvation. Why? Because our life is hidden with Christ in God. Paul sheds light on this when he writes in Ephesians 2:1-6,

> And you He made alive, who were dead in trespasses and sins, in which you once walked according to the course of this world, according to the prince of the power of the air, the spirit who now works in the sons of disobedience, among whom also we all once conducted ourselves in the lusts of our flesh, fulfilling the desires of the flesh and of the mind, and were by nature children of wrath, just as the others. But God, who is rich in mercy, because of His great love with which He loved us, even when we were dead in trespasses, made us alive together with Christ (by grace you have been saved), and raised us up together, and made us sit together in the heavenly places in Christ Jesus.

Even though the Gnostics were telling them they were not responsible for the deeds done in the body, Paul makes it clear that they are responsible!

Summary

What are the five sins we must murder? Fornication, uncleanness, passion, evil desire, and covetousness. Are you murdering these five deadly sins? If not, why not? If your affection is set here on earthly things, then your earthly members, more than likely, have not been put to death.

Perhaps you need some motivation for killing these sins. Paul gives us two motivations. First, the wrath of God is coming on the sons of disobedience, on those who disobey. Second, these sins are an indication of the old life, not the new life. Do you believe that God's wrath will come on you if you choose to live as a son of disobedience, if you choose to live in ongoing disobedience to Him? Does your walk look more like the new woman or the old woman?

If you are struggling with these sins or any others, I want to encourage you as we close out this lesson by giving you 8 helps for putting off these sins.

1. *Make no provision for the flesh.* Romans 13:14 speaks to this very issue. Simply refuse to accommodate your fleshly lusts. If you struggle with lust, then determine where your temptation comes from and flee from it. You might have to throw away all your devices or your television, but wouldn't you rather lose the world than lose your soul?

2. *Fix your heart on Christ.* Jesus says that where our treasure is our heart will be also. You will become like the object you worship.

3. *Memorize God's Word.* Psalm 119:11 says, "Your word I have hidden in my heart, That I might not sin against You." Think about God's Word throughout the day. Adjust your schedule to have to have ample thinking time.

4. *Pray without ceasing.* When you are tempted in any area of sin, pray about it, plead for God's mercy and help, and fast if necessary.

5. *Exercise self-control.* Self-control is one of the fruits of the spirit, according to Galatians 5:23. Just say no!

6. *Be filled with the Holy Spirit.* Yield to His promptings, and don't grieve or quench Him, or you will become insensitive to your sin— you will sear your conscience and it will grow desensitized to sin. You cannot have victory over sin without the Holy Spirit's enabling.

7. *Find someone to hold you accountable and pray for you.* I cannot emphasize enough the importance of accountability in the area of sin. I have seen its benefits repeatedly in my own life. The Christian life is not meant to be tackled alone.

8. *Keep an attitude of humility.* Don't ever think these sexual sins will never tempt you. First Corinthians 10:12 says, "Therefore let

him who thinks he stands take heed lest he fall." Many a man and woman has fallen prey to sexual sin because of pride. Pride is at the root of all sin.

I close with the words of John Owen, "Are you putting to death your sin? Do you make it your daily work? Be always putting it to death while you live, cease not a day from this work. Be killing sin or it will be killing you."[37]

---

37 John Owen. "John Owen Quotes." *Crossroad. http://www.crossroad.to/Quotes/faith/ owen.htm*

Questions to Consider

Colossians 3:5-7
Putting Sin to Death! (Part 1)

1. (a) Read Colossians 3:1-9. Compare this list of evil deeds with Romans 1:29-31; 1 Corinthians 5:11; 6:9-10; Galatians 5:19-21; and Ephesians 5:3-5. (b) Which of the evil deeds listed in these other passages are similar to those listed in Colossians? (c) Which of them are different?

2. Memorize Colossians 3:5.

3. (a) Why is it necessary that we "put to death" our sin, according to Romans 6:6; 8:13; Galatians 5:24; and Ephesians 5:3-6? (b) What are we to be doing with our "members" instead? See Romans 6:13.

4. (a) Paul says we are to put to death our sins. How does Jesus communicate the same idea in Matthew 5:27-30? (b) Do you think Jesus intends for us to take His words literally? (c) Why or why not?

5. (a) Name the sinner and the sin in the following passages. Also, describe the manner in which God's wrath was shown on each sinner mentioned? (Note: These should fall under one of the sins listed in Colossians 3:5.) Genesis 19:15-29; 2 Samuel 11:1-17 *with* 12:13-14; Acts 5:1-11; 1 Corinthians 5:1-8. (b) What does this teach you about sin and its consequences?

6. (a) According to Ephesians 6:11-18, how are we as believers to fight against sin? (You should find several ways listed here.) (b) How could you use Ephesians 6:11-18 to help yourself or someone else in waging war against one of the sins mentioned in Colossians 3:5? List some practical things you could do.

7. (a) Have you put to death the 5 sins Paul mentions in Colossians 3:5? (b) If not, why not? (c) What will you do about it? (I would encourage you to confess your sin before God and anyone you have sinned against. Then determine to repent. Also, you might consider asking someone to hold you accountable.)

8. (a) Based on what you have learned in this lesson, how would you counsel a professing Christian who is engaged in one of the sins listed in Colossians 3:5? (b) If they refused to repent, what would you do?

9. (a) Is there an area of sin (not necessarily one Paul mentions in Colossians 3:5-7) which the Spirit of God is challenging you to "put to death"? Perhaps it is spiritual pride, selfishness, lack of submission to husband, anger, or something else. (b) How may we pray for you about it? Please write it down to share with your group.

**Recommended Reading: *The Vanishing Conscience*, by John MacArthur

Chapter 14

Putting Sin to Death! (Part 2)
Colossians 3:8-11

Most of us have heard of Jonathan Edwards, one of the greatest preachers of the 18th century. He is widely known for his profound and fruit-bearing sermon, *Sinners in the Hands of an Angry God!* But most of us probably do not know the following story about his daughter.

Jonathan Edwards had a daughter with an uncontrollable temper. It is said that when a certain young man came to ask Mr. Edwards for this daughter's hand in marriage, Mr. Edwards responded with a frank "No." Quite upset, the young man replied, "But I love her, and she loves me!" pleading with Mr. Edwards to let him marry her. Mr. Edwards simply responded, "That makes no difference. She is not worthy of you." "She is a Christian, isn't she?" the young man inquired. Mr. Edwards responded that yes, she was, but then added, "The grace of God can live with some people with whom no one else could ever live." Apparently, his daughter had quite a problem with her temper.

Jonathan Edwards's response to this young man indicated that he knew that the presence of selfish anger indicates the absence of genuine love. I'm not so sure, however, that the apostle Paul would agree with Mr. Edwards' evaluation of his daughter's eternal destiny; Paul says in 1 Corinthians 13 that love does not get angry, nor is it easily provoked. We also know from 1 Corinthians 6:9-10 and Galatians 5:19-21 that the sin of ongoing anger can be an indication of an unregenerate heart. Even in the verses we will cover in this lesson, we will discover that Paul says anger should no longer be a part of the new man. Habitual anger is a part of the old man, not the new man. Consider carefully what Paul writes in Colossians 3:8-11.

Colossians 3:8-11

> But now you yourselves are to put off all these: anger, wrath, malice, blasphemy, filthy language out of your mouth. 9Do not lie to one another, since you have put off the old man with his deeds, 10and have put on the new man who is renewed in knowledge according to the image of Him who created him, 11where there is neither Greek nor Jew, circumcised nor uncircumcised, barbarian, Scythian, slave nor free, but Christ is all and in all.

In our last lesson, the sins we looked at were sexual sins; in this lesson, we will deal with social sins. By way of an outline, we will consider

> *The Murder of Six More Deadly Sins* (vv 8-9a)
> *Three Motivations for Murdering these Sins* (vv 9b-11)

The Murder of Six More Deadly Sins

Colossians 3:8-9a

> But now you yourselves are to put off all these: anger, wrath, malice, blasphemy, filthy language out of your mouth. (Colossians 3:8)

Paul writes *but now*, which indicates a contrast from the previous verse. In contrast to what you used to be, to how you used to walk, which was in sin, you are now to walk differently, you are to put off these sins. The words *put off* mean to rid yourself of something. Paul says throw off *all these* sins just like you would throw off a dirty shirt or a worn-out garment. And notice that he says *all* of these, which means every single one of them. The writer to the Hebrews says the very same thing in Hebrews 12:1: "Therefore we also, since we are surrounded by so great a cloud of witnesses, let us lay aside *every* weight, and the sin which so easily ensnares us, and let us run with endurance the race that is set before us." James states in James 1:21, "Therefore lay aside *all* filthiness and overflow of wickedness, and receive with meekness the implanted word, which is able to save your souls." Peter also reiterates the same truth in 1 Peter 2:1: "Therefore, laying aside *all* malice, all deceit, hypocrisy, envy, and all evil speaking." (All emphases mine.) We are never told in Scripture to treat sin lightly or to hold on to any sin that we deem small or insignificant. All sins are to be put to death!

The command in this verse is in the aorist tense, which means it's conveying the idea that we should do this once for all. In other words, do not pick up these sinful habits again! In saying this, Paul may have had in mind a practice that would occur in the New Testament times. When a believer was baptized, they would lay aside their old clothes before their baptism and were given a new white robe for their baptism. This would symbolize that the old is gone and the new is come. When I was growing up, in my father's church we had white robes that individuals would wear when they were baptized. Like this change in garments, we must lay aside all sin and, instead, put on all Christ-like virtues.

I think this list of sins may come as a surprise to some, because these sins have become respectable sins among many believers—but they are not respectable to God!

1. The first sin on Paul's death list is *anger*. This means to be quick tempered. This is one who has a violent passion or a deep smoldering bitterness. One man describes anger like this: "growing, inner anger, like sap in a tree on a hot day which swells the trunk and branches until they are in danger of bursting."[38] We would all have to admit that we have experienced that inner feeling of anger. I had a real problem with this before my new life in Christ. If you don't believe me, just ask my husband. He used to tell me he was going to put on my tombstone, "She did it her way!" That tells you a bit about my life before salvation! In fact, my husband almost called off the wedding the night before we got married due to my anger. Jesus is clear in Matthew 5:22, "But I say to you that whoever is angry with his brother without a cause shall be in danger of the judgment.

---

38 "The Seeking of Things Above." *Word Search Bible. https://www.wordsearchbible.com/products/15294/sample_text.*

And whoever says to his brother, 'Raca!' shall be in danger of the council. But whoever says, 'You fool!' shall be in danger of hell fire." Anger is a sin that can send someone to hell. Anger is a serious sin! Now, allow me to clarify that there is such a thing as righteous anger, which is anger against sin in your own life or in the lives of others. But there should be no unrighteous anger in the life of the believer. We must not feed it; we must flee it! If we don't, it will have ramifications not only for our own souls, but also for those who are the recipients of our anger. We can do physical damage not only to ourselves, as it wreaks havoc on our health, but we can also do damage to the relationships we have with others. I read once that a fit of anger exerts the same amount of energy as half a day of housework! Wise Solomon wrote in Ecclesiastes 7:9, "Do not hasten in your spirit to be angry, for anger rests in the bosom of fools."

2. The second sin we are to murder is *wrath*. Wrath is indignation. Like a roaring furnace, it has the idea of a fierce passion, as when one breathes hard. The Greeks would liken wrath to straw that had been set to fire; it would flare up briefly and then be gone. Perhaps this has you wondering what the difference is between wrath and anger. Anger often lies smoldering below the surface, giving rise to periodic eruptions of wrath. Wrath, then, is anger which has boiled over. Not only are these two sins dangerous, but they also have to the potential to be extremely hurtful. I have counseled many women who deeply regret things they've said in a moment of rage. I have also counseled women who can't shake words that a spouse or someone else has spoken to them in a fit of rage. These words can never be taken back and often are hard to forget. Whoever said "Sticks and stones may break my bones, but words can never hurt me" must never have been the recipient of another person's anger and wrath. My daughter-in-law once told me that murder is the number one cause of death among pregnant women, and it is usually the result of a husband or boyfriend's fit of rage.

3. The third sin Paul mentions that we are to put off is *malice*. Malice is badness or moral evil, and it begins with an evil habit of the mind. A malicious person has a vicious nature bent on doing

harm to others. It's like the man mentioned in Micah 2:1, who plots evil on his bed at night and carries it out the next day. A malicious person also rejoices when misery falls on the one who is the object of their hatred. Haman is an excellent example of this in the story of Esther; he plotted against the Jews and diligently tried to carry it out. King Saul was malicious toward David, attempting many times to kill him. As a young bride of 19 years of age, I worked with a woman who was bent on doing evil to me; I'd come home in tears and complain to my husband about her.

4. The fourth sin Paul says we are to murder is *blasphemy*. This word means to wound another's reputation by evil speaking; it is like slander. James tells us in the third chapter of his epistle that a tongue bent on slander is from the pit of hell. This type of speech spreads like a fire out of control and before you know it, life has become unbearable for its victim. In fact, even as I was writing this lesson, I was personally reminded again of the deep hurt of slander by someone. What we too often don't realize is that slander has a way of getting to the one who's being slandered, even though we don't think that it will. In 1 Timothy 1:13, Paul says that before his conversion he was a blasphemer, but after his salvation that was no longer a part of his life, because he had obtained mercy. We, as women, have the greater challenge in this. It was Calvin who said that "talkativeness is a disease of women, and it gets worse with age."

5. The fifth sin Paul tells us to put to death also pertains to our speech: *filthy language out of your mouth. Filthy language* would be speech that is foul, obscene, vile, or abusive. The words *out of your mouth* mean to hurl out of one's mouth. In Ephesians, the sister epistle of Colossians, Paul writes of this very thing: "But fornication and all uncleanness or covetousness, let it not even be named among you, as is fitting for saints; neither filthiness, nor foolish talking, nor coarse jesting, which are not fitting, but rather giving of thanks" (Ephesians 5:3-4). It is very grieving to hear believers use foul language and tell dirty jokes, and I've been shocked at the number of believers who do and think nothing of it—or even think it funny!

I cannot see my Lord doing that. Can you? Perhaps a good reminder for us would be what Jesus said in Matthew 12:36-37: "But I say to you that for every idle word men may speak, they will give account of it in the day of judgment. For by your words you will be justified, and by your words you will be condemned." But Paul has one more on his list of social sins to put off; it's number six on the list and it is found in verse 9.

> Do not lie to one another, (Colossians 3:9a)

6. *Do not lie to one another*, Paul writes. *Do not lie*, stop lying, he says. It's an imperative in the Greek, so that it means God forbid. To *lie* is to utter an untruth or attempt to deceive by falsehood. In John 8:44, we're told that lying is from the devil. And because Titus 1:2 clearly tells us that God is a God who cannot lie, lying should have no part in the lives of those who follow Him. Psalm 58:3 says that we come out of the womb speaking lies, and, my friend, it is our responsibility to train our children not to lie and to discipline them when they do. I will never forget one spanking my father gave me for lying. He asked me one morning at breakfast why I had a Band-Aid on my face, and I told him that my brother had sliced my face with a knife. Of course, it was a lie, and I remember that spanking very well! I do believe it cured me from lying to my dad again because it is the last spanking I remember receiving as a child. As we age, however, we become more sophisticated in our lying, don't we? We pretend to be spiritual in church when we aren't so spiritual at home. My friend, that is a lie, and your kids and your husband will see right through it. Some of us have sold a house or a car or some other personal item and lied about its value. I've been in homes where mothers have encouraged their children to lie for them. I remember, years ago, waiting in a lobby while my car was being washed. The woman sitting next to me was also waiting for her car, talking on her phone to someone, and I overheard her say, "I'm on my way as we speak." She was not on her way at all, and I was dumbfounded at how blatantly she would lie! Some of us might not be as blatant as that woman was, but we'll easily color a story to make us look good. That is exaggeration, which is a lie. Some of us

tell others we'll do something for them or be there at a certain time and yet we fail to do so. That is not keeping one's word, which is a lie; that falls right into the category of lying. In Ephesians 4:25, Paul says, "Therefore, putting away lying, 'Let each one of you speak truth with his neighbor,' for we are members of one another." We speak truth to each other because we belong to each other; we are members of the same body whose head is Christ.

Three Motivations for Murdering These Sins

Colossians 3:9b-11

> … since you have put off the old man with his deeds, (Colossians 3:9)

1. *Paul now shifts to the first motivation for putting these sins to death. The first reason is that we have put off the old man with his deeds.* This is very similar to one of the motivations for putting off sexual sin that we saw in verse 7. *The old man with his deeds* is how we used to walk or live. This is the old woman; it is not who we are now. These are interesting words Paul uses here in verse 9. *Old* means antique, recent, worn out. The *old man* is not who we are now. We've been redeemed and have been set free from sin. *Deeds* here refers to practices, specifically the sinful habits we practice. Paul writes of this, too, in Ephesians 4:22: "that you put off, concerning your former conduct, the old man which grows corrupt according to the deceitful lusts." We already put off that old, worn-out man, so why do we want to put it back on? You took that dirty filthy garment off; now, don't put it back on! It simply doesn't make sense to put it back on, does it? Paul continues by giving us a second motivation for murdering these ugly sins:

> and have put on the new man who is renewed in knowledge according to the image of Him who created him, (Colossians 3:10)

Paul says we *have put on the new man*; we are now new creatures.

Paul reminds the church at Corinth of this truth in 2 Corinthians 5:17; he says, "Therefore, if anyone is in Christ, he is a new creation; old things have passed away; behold, all things have become new." The words *put on* have the sense of sinking into a garment. We're not wearing that filthy garment any longer but, rather, a new garment, a robe of righteousness.

2. Paul then us gives a second reason why we should put off these sins: our new man is renewed in knowledge after the One who saved us! The *new man* is the regenerate man. You have put on the new man *who is renewed in knowledge according to the image of Him who created him.* The word *renewed* means to be renovated; it is in the present tense, a past action with present results. We are not there yet but are constantly, presently, being renewed. This renewal is *in knowledge*, which is <u>epignosis</u>, a full knowledge, not gnosis, which is what the Gnostics taught. We are being renovated with a knowledge that comes from God. This is a true knowledge which is in Christ, as opposed to the knowledge of the false teachers. How are we renewed in knowledge? Paul says we are renewed *according to the image of Him who created him. The image* means likeness or resemblance. The words *who created him* have caused some debate. Some think this is referring to the creation that took place in Genesis when it states that man was created in the image of God. I don't think that's what Paul is saying here because the context is talking about the new man, the new creation that took place when we bowed the knee to Christ's Lordship. We are new creations, as Paul wrote in 2 Corinthians 5:17. We are constantly being renewed in the knowledge of God and changing to be more and more conformed to His image. Second Corinthians 4:16 puts it well, "Therefore we do not lose heart. Even though our outward man is perishing, yet the inward man is being renewed day by day." Also, 2 Corinthians 3:18 states how that renewing process happens: "But we all, with unveiled face, beholding as in a mirror the glory of the Lord, are being transformed into the same image from glory to glory, just as by the Spirit of the Lord." We are renewed in knowledge and changed to His image by His Spirit. The best way to be renewed is by the Word and the application of it! What a blessed hope and an encouragement it is as

I walk through this life that those sins of anger, wrath, lying, malice, filthy communication and the like will be changed, they will be put off, as I walk in obedience to the Spirit's promptings. Well, there is one more motivation for putting off these sins, in verse 11.

> where there is neither Greek nor Jew, circumcised nor uncircumcised, barbarian, Scythian, slave nor free, but Christ is all and in all. (Colossians 3:11)

3. *The third motivation for murdering these sins is that there is no distinction with God,* and there should be none with us. We are not given liberty to speak evil, to lie, or to be angry at others just because they are of a different race or social status then we are.

This verse was blasphemed not long ago by a lesbian Unitarian "pastor" at my brother's funeral by being ripped out of its context; I quote, "For him (my brother) there was no distinction of Jew or Gentile, male and female, gay and straight, Unitarians and Trinitarians, barbarian or Scythian, Levite or Samaritan, formerly incarcerated or free." Interestingly, Christ was left out of her misquotation of this verse. Now, you might be wondering, like I did when I first studied this verse, what this verse has to do with sin. The first thing we should consider is that all of God's children are to put off these things because God is no respecter of persons. This is a true statement, but I do not believe that it is the meaning of this verse. As we consider the contrasts in these classes of people, it becomes clear what Paul is meaning to convey. Sins of anger, wrath, malice, filthy communication, and lying are often directed at people who are not like us. Often, we are more likely to be angry, hateful, to use evil speech, and even lie to those whom we deem to be different than ourselves—of a different race, religion, culture, social status, or political persuasion than we are. I am amazed at the prejudices of some so-called Christians. We teach our children to sing, "Jesus loves the little children, all the children of the world; red and yellow, black and white, they are precious in his sight; Jesus loves the little children of the world." We teach that to our children, but do we live it? Paul's statement here would have been startling to the church at Colossae, because there were a great many barriers in the early church between people who were different racially, religiously, culturally, and socially. But Paul reminds them that there are no distinctions with God; He is not partial in His love nor in His gift of salvation. Galatians 3:28 states, "There is neither Jew nor Greek, there is neither slave nor free, there is neither male nor female; for you are all one in Christ Jesus."

The groups Paul lists are complete opposites. Because with God there are no ethnic distinctions, there ought to be no ethnic distinctions between God's people either. *Greeks* and *Jews* were opposed to each other. Jewish people refused to enter Gentile (Greek) homes; they wouldn't even eat a meal cooked by Gentiles or buy meat prepared by Gentile butchers.

There also should be no religious distinctions between the *circumcised* and *uncircumcised*. These two groups were also commonly opposed to each other. In the second chapter of Colossians, we learned in our study that this barrier was so big between the circumcised and the uncircumcised that the leaders of the church had to call a Council meeting in Acts 15; the dissension was so great that it created sharp dispute and debate. Of course, we know the outcome was that circumcision was deemed to be not necessary for salvation.

Paul is also clear that there are no cultural distinctions between *barbarian* and *Scythian*. A barbarian was someone who did not speak Greek and were thought by the Greeks to be uncivilized. Their speech was stammering, sounding to the Greeks like "bar-bar-bar." Scythians were known especially for their brutality and were considered by many to be little better than wild beasts. It was the Jewish historian Josephus who said of them, "The Scythians delight in murdering people and are little better than wild beasts."[39] Herodotus described them as living in wagons, offering human sacrifices, scalping and sometimes flaying slain enemies, drinking

---

39 John MacArthur, The MacArthur New Testament Commentary: Colossians and Philemon (Chicago: Moody Press, 1992), 152.

their blood, and using their skulls for drinking cups.[40] But Paul reminds the church that there is no distinction, and we are not to judge someone based on their past life.

There are also no economic or social distinctions to be made between *slave* and *free*. A slave would be someone in a permanent relation of servitude to another. Someone who was free was independent of others, at liberty. Male Jews would bless the Lord each morning because God did not make him a Gentile, a slave, or a woman. Such distinctions are certainly nothing to be praising God for. Paul writes clearly in 1 Corinthians 12:13, "For by one Spirit we were all baptized into one body—whether Jews or Greeks, whether slaves or free—and have all been made to drink into one Spirit."

The idea of doing away with these barriers would be ludicrous to the Gnostics. Their so-called enlightened teaching was only for a select few—never for a Barbarian or the like. Yet, there is no place for such barriers in the church because Paul says *Christ is all and in all*. He breaks down barriers and with Him there are no distinctions. What ought to characterize the church of Jesus Christ is that there are no distinctions. We are all one in Christ, and Christ is all and in all of us. To show partiality or prejudice against those who are of different race, social status, or any other difference, is not demonstrating that we have been renewed in the image of God. Rather, it says loudly that I am still holding on to the old man.

Summary

What five sins are we to put to death? Anger, wrath, malice, blasphemy, and filthy communication. Are any of these sins a part of your life? May I lovingly remind you of the danger you are in if they are a part of your life? Paul is clear in Galatians 5:19-21, "Now the works of the flesh are evident, which are: adultery, fornication, uncleanness, lewdness, idolatry, sorcery, hatred, contentions, jealousies, outbursts of wrath, selfish ambitions, dissensions, heresies, envy, murders, drunkenness, revelries, and the like; of which I tell you beforehand,

---

40 Ibid, 152.

just as I also told you in time past, that those who practice such things will not inherit the kingdom of God."

What are the three motivations for murdering these sins? First, the old man is gone. Second, we are being renewed in the knowledge of Christ. Third, there are no distinctions with God and there should be none with us. Can you honestly say that you do not look down on those who are different from you; that you do not use your mouth to speak evil of them; that you are not as prone to lie to them or be angry with them? Has your knowledge of God grown so deeply that all sin of partiality has been eradicated? Is the old woman really gone?

For a moment, take yourself back in time a little (for some of us, we have to go way back) and imagine that your fiancée is asking your father for your hand in marriage. Would your father's response be similar to Jonathan Edwards', "No, you cannot have her. You see, she has a temper, and worse than that, she is given over to outbursts of anger! No, you cannot have her. She is bent on evil and engrossed in gossip and blasphemy, and every once in a while she comes up with the dirtiest jokes that aren't even fit for a sailor to tell. No, you cannot have her. She has a terrible prejudice and can't get along with anyone who isn't exactly like her in race, social status, or background. No, you cannot have her. She cannot be trusted to tell the truth."

I trust that this is not what would transpire. I trust that each of us would hear from the lips not only of our earthly father but from our Heavenly Father, "Yes, you can have her. She will do you good and not evil all the days of her life. She is full of compassion and kindness, and there is not a mean or prejudiced bone in that woman's body. She can be fully trusted; she is an honest woman. She is a virtuous woman, and her worth is far above rubies. She will make you a good bride, because her actions show her to be a part of the Bride of Christ."

Questions to Consider

Colossians 3:8-11
Putting Sin to Death! (Part 2)

1. (a) Read Colossians 3:8-11 and Ephesians 4:20-32. From these two passages, which of the sins listed are similar and which are different? (b) According to what Paul says in the Ephesians passage, how does one rid themselves of these sins?

2. Memorize 3:8-9.

3. Look up the following passages and note the sinner, the sin that is committed, and the result of the sin, if it is mentioned. These should fall under one of the sins Paul mentions in Colossians 3:8-11 (you may need to read further on in the passage for the answer): Genesis 4:1-15 (two sins here); Genesis 12:10-20; Leviticus 24:10-16; Numbers 20:1-13; Judges 16 (at least two here); 2 Samuel 16:5-14; Esther 3 (at least two sins here).

4. (a) Where does lying come from? See John 8:44. (b) What are we to do instead of lying? See Ephesians 4:25. (c) What will happen to all liars? See Revelation 21:8, 27; 22:15.

5. (a) According to Matthew 15:19, where does ungodly speech come from? (b) What does James say about our tongue in James 3:1-10? (c) What should we be doing with our speech instead? See Ephesians 4:29. (d) What have you done in the past and in the present to tame your tongue?

6. (a) What do the following passages have to say about God being a respecter of persons (or being partial)? Proverbs 22:2; Mark 7:24-30; Acts 10:34-35, 43; Romans 2:5-11; 3:28-30; 10:12-13; 1 Corinthians 12:13; Galatians 5:6; 6:15; Ephesians 6:8. (b) How does this help you to understand what Paul says in Colossians 3:11?

7. (a) How can we practically put to death the sins of anger, wrath, malice, blasphemy, filthy communication, and lying? (b) How are you training (or could you train) your children, grandchildren, or those you disciple in putting these off? (c) How can we as women set a good example in these areas for our children, grandchildren, or those we disciple?

8. (a) Do you have prejudices against those (even fellow believers) who are different in race, religion, social status, culture, or any other area? (b) What does Paul say about that in Colossians 3:11? (c) Why should there be no distinctions?

9. (a) How has God spoken to you through this lesson? (b) Please write down a prayer request based on what He has shown you.

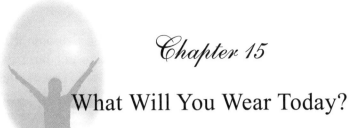

Chapter 15

What Will You Wear Today?

Colossians 3:12-14

Clothing is certainly an interesting phenomenon in our day, isn't it? There is so much emphasis on the style, color, and even the material of garments. I don't know about you, but I personally get overwhelmed by clothes shopping. One morning, I was walking at the mall with a friend, and I decided I should probably invest in a few tops. I quickly browsed at what was available and was unimpressed. Upon returning home, I went to my closet and thought, "I don't need any clothes! I think I'll be just fine!" As a child, I was happy to have one new clothing item each year. As one of seven children living in a pastor's home, we lived very frugally, and I shared a little, itty-bitty closet with three other sisters, so there wasn't a lot of decision about what I was going to wear.

Things have changed for most of us. We have so many clothes that at times it's hard to decide what to wear. We probably spend at least some time each day (hopefully not too much time) thinking about what we will wear. Should I wear that yellow dress or that old pair of jeans?? Usually, we decide what we will wear based on what we are doing or who we are seeing that day. For example, on Tuesdays and Sundays, you can almost be sure I will be in a dress, as Sunday is the Lord's Day and Tuesday night is ladies' Bible study. But, if you were to come over to my house on any other day, you would probably find me in casual clothes.

We put thought into what we will wear on the outer woman, but how many of us went to bed last night or woke up this morning thinking, "Hmmm … what should I put on in the inner woman tomorrow? How can I love my family more? How can I be kind to that neighbor who has treated me unjustly? How can I manifest a spirit of forgiveness toward that lady at church for that unkind thing she said about me?" How much time and energy do we spend on getting our physical body dressed and ready to go in comparison to the time and mental energy we spend on getting our spiritual man ready to go? And just what are we to put on the inner man? In Colossians 3:12-14, Paul gives us *Eight Virtues that We Should be Putting On*. Let's read from these verses what we should be wearing.

Colossians 3:12-14

> Therefore, as the elect of God, holy and beloved, put on tender mercies, kindness, humility, meekness, longsuffering; [13]bearing with one another, and forgiving one another, if anyone has a complaint against another; even as Christ forgave you, so you also must do. [14]But above all these things put on love, which is the bond of perfection.

There is a reason Paul mentions in the last chapter the sins we are to put off before he mentions the virtues we are to put on. Now that we have rid ourselves of certain things, we are to clothe ourselves with other certain things. Think of it this way: You would not want to put on a fresh garment over a soiled garment, would you? You would not put a beautiful wedding dress over some soiled, sweaty, workout clothes, would you? What would be the point? In the same way, now that we have put to death these ugly sins, what should we put on? Paul begins to tell us in verse 12 and writes,

> Therefore, as the elect of God, holy and beloved, put on tender mercies, kindness, humility, meekness, longsuffering (Colossians 3:12)

Paul begins by saying *therefore, as the elect of God, holy and beloved, put on certain virtues. Therefore*, because God has chosen you and you are elected to be holy and loved by Him, then resemble Him! Paul calls the church at Colossae *the elect of God*. The word *elect* means to select from a number. Paul writes in Colossians' sister epistle, Ephesians, something similar. In Ephesians 1:4, he says, "Just as He chose us in Him before the foundation of the world, that we should be holy and without blame before Him in love." This is in direct contrast to what the false teachers were teaching. To the Gnostics, the Colossians would not deserve such titles as "elect" because, in their thinking, only the enlightened ones were chosen and certainly not those who did not follow their rules and regulations. But Paul says yes, indeed, you are elect, and that election is from God, not the false teachers.

Paul not only refers to them as elect but also as *holy and beloved.* *Holy* means to be set apart for God. And *beloved* is the word <u>agapao,</u> which speaks of God's love that was shown at Calvary, a love that denies oneself for the one it loves. We who are called of God are loved by God in that we are the objects of His love. It is the idea spoken of in Deuteronomy 7:7-8, where it says, "The Lord did not set His love on you nor choose you because you were more in number than any other people, for you were the least of all peoples; but because the Lord loves you, and because He would keep the oath which He swore to your fathers, the Lord has brought you out with a mighty hand, and redeemed you from the house of bondage, from the hand of Pharaoh king of Egypt." The word beloved is also in the perfect tense, which gives the sense that the objects of this love—the Colossians, and by extension, every believer—will continue to be beloved now and forever. But we who are elect, we who are beloved of God, have a responsibility to also be holy; as 1 Peter 1:15-16 says, "but as He who called you is holy, you also be holy in all your conduct, because it is written, 'Be holy, for I am holy.'" Jesus Himself said in John 15:16, "You did not choose Me, but I chose you and appointed you that you should go and bear fruit, and that your fruit should remain, that whatever you ask the Father in My name He may give you." Part of the fruit we are to be bearing are the virtues that Paul mentions here in Colossians. Our manner of life should be in harmony with the kind of life that God's elect should live. He chose us and therefore we owe Him a life that is set apart unto Him. Even though it was Divine Sovereignty that chose us, that does not lessen our human responsibility to obey.

Because we are His daughters and we represent Him, we must dress our inner woman in a manner that pleases Him. (We should dress our outer woman in a manner that pleases Him, too!) Paul describes the way God's elect should dress by using the words *put on*. To put on means to envelop in, to clothe with. It has the sense of sinking into a garment. Thayer says it is "To become so possessed of the mind of Christ as in thought, feeling, and action to resemble Him, and as it were, reproduce the life He lived."[41] This word in the Greek, which is translated as put on, is in the aorist tense, which gives this command the meaning that it must be obeyed at once. There should be no dallying around when it comes to putting on these virtues. When you tell your children to go to bed or to brush their teeth or to get dressed, you do not mean for them to do it tomorrow, but right now, right? That's what Paul is saying. Do it now. Some people are under the delusion that after salvation they can be apathetic about their sin. They can't fathom that they must stop yelling at their wife, or stop sinning sexually, or stop cheating on their taxes, or stop lying to their employer. We must remind ourselves of what Paul says in Romans 6:1-2: "What shall we say then? Shall we continue in sin that grace may abound? Certainly not! How shall we who died to sin live any longer in it?" And Paul has just written something similar in Colossians 3:3. Let's look at the eight virtues we should be putting on:

1. *The first virtue we are to put on is tender mercies*, or as some translations say, bowels of mercies. In the Greek language, the bowels included the intestines, the spleen, and other internal organs, and were representative of deep passions, like anger and love. *Mercy* is compassion or kindness. We are to put on a heart of compassion, or heartfelt compassion. We should exemplify our Father who is full of compassion and tender mercies. When we see the hurts of others, it should cause us to act and do something about it.

2. *Paul says we are to put on kindness*. The word *kindness* means gentle, a gracious disposition. It was used to describe wine which

---

41 Kenneth Wuest, *Wuest's Word Studies from the Greek New Testament for the English Reader* (Grand Rapids: Eerdman Publishing, 1973), 223.

had grown mellow with age and had lost its harshness. This kindness is not to only to be shown toward our best friends but to all of God's creation. We are reminded in Luke 6:35, "But love your enemies, do good, and lend, hoping for nothing in return; and your reward will be great, and you will be sons of the Most High. For He is kind to the unthankful and evil." It's easy to be kind to those we love, but what about the unthankful and evil? Without the enabling grace of God, this would be impossible! Before my salvation, my husband would have to remind me that the meaning of my name, Susan, is "tender lily." He would gently say, "Tender lily," in a gracious way to convey to me that I was not living up to the meaning of my name. Thankfully, the Lord has helped me to grow up in the virtue of kindness. Proverbs 31:26 says of the virtuous woman, "She opens her mouth with wisdom, and on her tongue is the law of kindness."

3. *We are to clothe ourselves with humility. Humility* is having a humble opinion of oneself, a deep sense of one's littleness; it is modesty, or lowliness of mind. It is exemplified in a person who does not think highly of herself or, better yet, does not think of herself at all. It is interesting to note that the Greeks never applied this word to themselves. They had no symbol in their language to describe humility, though it is a virtue that should be characteristic of all Christians. But the Greeks aren't the only culture known for not prizing humility as a virtue; I think most Americans don't see it as a virtue either. Our country is filled with people who are engrossed in their own world, ignoring the concerns of others. "It's all about me" is the mantra of our day! But humility is the attitude Paul speaks of in Philippians 2:5-8 when he describes our Lord; he says, "Let this mind be in you which was also in Christ Jesus, who, being in the form of God, did not consider it robbery to be equal with God, but made Himself of no reputation, taking the form of a bondservant, and coming in the likeness of men. And being found in appearance as a man, He humbled Himself and became obedient to the point of death, even the death of the cross." Humility isn't only seen in the example of our Lord, though; it is also exemplified in a parable He spoke in Luke 18:9-14:

Also He spoke this parable to some who trusted in themselves that they were righteous, and despised others: "Two men went up to the temple to pray, one a Pharisee and the other a tax collector. The Pharisee stood and prayed thus with himself, 'God, I thank You that I am not like other men—extortioners, unjust, adulterers, or even as this tax collector. I fast twice a week; I give tithes of all that I possess.' And the tax collector, standing afar off, would not so much as raise his eyes to heaven, but beat his breast, saying, 'God, be merciful to me a sinner!' I tell you, this man went down to his house justified rather than the other; for everyone who exalts himself will be humbled, and he who humbles himself will be exalted."

Most of us can mask our pride and pretend to be humble, but Paul is calling here for a humility that no one sees but the Lord, a humility that takes place in our mind.

4. *The next virtue on our what-to-wear list is meekness. Meekness* is inward grace of the soul, a spirit in which we accept God's dealings with us as good, without disputing or resisting. It not only deals with our attitude toward God, but toward others as well, even when we are not treated like we would like to be treated. Someone who is meek is willing to suffer injury rather than to inflict it. Now, meekness is not weakness; rather, it is strength under control. We should strive to be like Moses who, according to Numbers 12:3, was meeker than any who were upon the face of the earth. And how did Moses exemplify meekness? Did he go around like a wimpy mouse? No, he showed strength under control—many, many times—in front of Pharaoh and in the presence of the murmuring Israelites. That's probably why he was chosen for such a difficult task. I look at Moses and wonder how he did it! Meekness is a virtue that is much needed for spiritual leaders; Paul tells Timothy in 1 Timothy 6:11 to pursue meekness: "But thou, O man of God, flee these things, and follow after righteousness, godliness, faith, love, patience, meekness" (KJV). But meekness is a needed virtue for us all, as well. In Titus 3:2, Paul says that we are to "speak evil of no man, to be no brawlers, but gentle, showing all meekness unto all men" (KJV). Also, when we exhort a sinning brother, this virtue must be present, as Paul writes in Galatians 6:1, "Brethren, if a man

be overtaken in a fault, ye who are spiritual restore such a one in the spirit of meekness, considering thyself, lest thou also be tempted" (KJV). Also, as a woman writing to women, let me give you a little tip: this virtue is a must in your marriage. Your husband doesn't want a nag for a wife, and he doesn't want a wimp for a wife either; he wants a meek woman, one who is strong and who has that strength under control. Consider 1 Peter 3:3-4, where Peter writes to wives: "Whose adorning let it not be that outward adorning of plaiting the hair, and of wearing of gold, or of putting on of apparel; but let it be the hidden man of the heart, in that which is not corruptible, even the ornament of a meek and quiet spirit, which is in the sight of God of great price" (KJV).

5. *We must put on the quality of longsuffering.* This word describes a person who is not easily provoked by others and does not get angry. Many times, it is expressed by patience under the abusive treatment of others. When we studied Colossians 1, we saw that this was part of Paul's prayer for the Colossians in Colossians 1:11, where he prayed that they would be "strengthened with all might, according to His glorious power, for all patience and longsuffering with joy." We learned then that longsuffering characterizes the person who, in relation to those who oppose or hurt him, exercises patience, refusing to yield to passion or to outbursts of anger. This would be one who does not allow himself to be provoked by people or to become angry. It is, as one would say, a long holding out of the mind before it gives room to action or passions. Hosea is a good example in Scripture of someone who was longsuffering toward his adulterous wife and even took her back after her unfaithfulness.

As we move on to number six, we observe what Paul writes in Colossians 3:13:

> bearing with one another, and forgiving one another, if anyone has a complaint against another; even as Christ forgave you, so you also must do (Colossians 3:13)

6. *Paul writes that we are to bear with one another.* Bearing with one another has the idea of enduring or holding out when burdens are heaped up. We should be willing to put up with one another. And, quite frankly, at times that can be difficult, because we often don't see eye to eye with one another. Even as I was writing this lesson, my forbearance was being tested toward a certain individual and I was reminded that I must be forbearing. As the poem goes, "To live above with the saints we love, oh that will be glory; but to live below with the saints we know, well, that's another story."

7. *The seventh and probably one of the more difficult things for us to wear and that is forgiveness.* Paul says we are to be *forgiving one another*, and then he tells us why we might need to forgive each other. *If anyone has a complaint against another*, he says, *even as Christ forgave you, so you also must do.* Obviously, this is not the only reason we might need to forgive someone, but it is the reason Paul lists here. *Forgiving* is the act of excusing or pardoning another despite his or her shortcomings or errors. It is to be shown with a gracious and kind spirit—not murmuring, "I forgive you," with a scowl firmly planted on our faces, but with sincerity. In the context here, forgiveness is to be extended to someone with whom we have a complaint or quarrel. This could be your son or daughter, your husband, your mother or father, your best friend, a church acquaintance, or even an enemy. In Galatians 2:11-21, Paul says that he and Peter had a pretty good quarrel over the issue of circumcision. He puts it this way in verse 11: "Now when Peter had come to Antioch, I withstood him to his face, because he was to be blamed." In Acts 15, Paul had another quarrel, with Barnabas, over whether John Mark should be taken along with them on their mission journey. Acts 15:39 tells us, "Then the contention became so sharp that they parted from one another." There must have been a change of heart somewhere, either with Paul or with John Mark, because at the end of Paul's life he says to Timothy in 2 Timothy 4:11, "Only Luke is with me. Get Mark and bring him with you, for he is useful to me for ministry." And then there are those two ladies mentioned in Philippians 4:2, Euodia and Syntyche, who could not get along, and Paul asks someone to help those women.

Christians are not exempt from having quarrels, but we are not permitted to allow resentment to fester. We must forgive. And how are we to forgive? Just as Christ has forgiven us. This means we forgive in the same degree, in the same proportion, as He did. And how did Christ forgive us? Was it a partial forgiveness? Did He say, "I will forgive you for that sin, but I can never forgive you for that one; that one is unforgivable"? No, He forgave us fully and completely. As the Lord's Prayer states, in Matthew 6:12, "forgive us our debts, as we forgive our debtors." Look at Matthew 18:21-22: "Then Peter came to Him and said, 'Lord, how often shall my brother sin against me, and I forgive him? Up to seven times?' Jesus said to him, 'I do not say to you, up to seven times, but up to seventy times seven.'" That's 490 times! Have you ever forgiven someone that many times for the same offense? It's doubtful! Has the Lord forgiven you and me 490 times for an offense that we repeat over and over again? Probably more than we would like to admit! And so should we. Jesus, from the cross, uttered, "Father, forgive them, for they do not know what they do" (Luke 23:34).

You might be thinking to yourself, "But that was Jesus. He was God in the flesh." Yes, but He was also human and had all the feelings and temptations that we have. Hebrews 4:15 tells us, "We do not have a High Priest who cannot sympathize with our weaknesses, but was in all points tempted as we are, yet without sin." We also have the many biblical examples to follow. Joseph is a good example; in Genesis 50:19-20, when his brothers sought his forgiveness for selling him into slavery, he said, "Do not be afraid, for am I in the place of God? But as for you, you meant evil against me; but God meant it for good, to bring it about as it is this day, to save many people alive." And Stephen, in Acts 7:59-60, while he was being stoned to death: "And they stoned Stephen as he was calling on God and saying, 'Lord Jesus, receive my spirit.' Then he knelt down and cried out with a loud voice, 'Lord, do not charge them with this sin.' And when he had said this, he fell asleep."

One man has said it well: "An unforgiving Christian is a contradiction of terms because we are the forgiven ones."[42] He then gives three practical steps for dealing with the sin of unforgiveness. If forgiveness is a problem for you, perhaps these will help you. He says,

1. First confess it to the Lord and ask him to help you mend the relationship.

2. Go to the person and ask forgiveness and seek reconciliation.

3. Give the person something you highly value. This is a practical approach as Jesus said where your treasure is, there will your heart be also (Matthew 6:21).[43]

Whatever you do, don't ignore the offense, because bitterness and resentment will set in, and it will rob you of your joy. And, in case you're tempted to think so, remember this: an attitude of avoidance is not forgiveness.

After having dressed ourselves with tender mercies, kindness, humility of mind, meekness, longsuffering, forbearance, and forgiveness, it would be natural to think, "That should do it. I'm dressed and ready to go." But not quite yet. There is one article that must go on above all those others. It would be like putting on your socks and shoes, your underwear, and your slip, but forgetting the most important garment to put on, that being the main garment, your dress or jeans or whatever you're going to wear. You would never think of going out in public without that final garment. And neither should we think of walking the Christian life without this most important piece of clothing. It is the one that is above the rest. *It is love. This is the eighth piece of clothing we must wear.* Paul writes,

> But above all these things put on love, which is the bond of perfection. (Colossians 3:14)

---

42 John MacArthur, *Drawing Near (Wheaton: Crossway Books, 1993), March 28.*
43 Ibid.

8. *Above all these things put on love.* What are the *all these things*? The things Paul has just mentioned: tender mercies, kindness, humility, meekness, longsuffering, forbearance, and forgiveness. Above all these, *put on love.* The Greek word for *love* is agape, which is the same kind of love that God has shown toward us, as we learned when we looked at verse 12. This love was shown by God toward all those who are holy and beloved by Him. And it is, Paul says, *the bond of perfection*; in other words, is it the uniting principle. It is the girdle that holds the other pieces of clothing together. It is the bond of perfectness, or what makes these virtues complete. Love is the binding factor here that holds all these other virtues together and makes them usable. One man says, "Love embraces and knits together all the virtues."[44] Another puts it this way, "Love is the outer garment which holds the others in their places."[45] When these other qualities are practiced without love, as Paul says in 1 Corinthians 13, it is like a sounding brass or a clanging symbol. It would be like making an empty, meaningless noise.

It is interesting to note that Paul doesn't say it is knowledge that binds all these virtues together, which is what the false teachers would've taught. Knowledge was the main piece of clothing the Gnostics were trying to put on. They were trying to steal the Colossians' reward (2:16-19), because they didn't think the Colossians measured up to the Gnostic rules about eating and drinking, festivals, angel worship, and the like. The Gnostics would never have thought of love as a virtue to be sought after at all—why, that would be ridiculous to them! But love is the harder attribute, and it is the attribute that focuses on the heart, the inner man. Legalism, what these false teachers were practicing, focuses only on the outer man.

Summary

When we consider the context of these eight Christ-like virtues, it's easy to understand why Paul presents them specifically to the

---

44 *Vincent's Word Studies in the New Testament. Biblesoft, 2006.*
45 J.B. Lightfoot, *St. Paul's Epistles to the Colossians and Philemon (Peabody: Hendrickson Publishers, 1993), 222.*

church at Colossae. If you've ever been exposed to false teaching or been a part of a church that allowed false teaching to creep in, you know how such teaching causes divisions and strife and arguments. In such a context, tender mercies, kindness, humility, meekness, longsuffering, forbearance, forgiveness, and love are sorely needed. I am often grieved at the strife caused among professing Christians by false teaching. We need to remember that these eight virtues must be practiced in our dealings with others; otherwise, we run the risk of becoming unnecessarily divisive.

Let me ask you: Do these eight characteristics describe you? When was the last time you extended tender mercy toward someone? Were your words kind today? In conversations, do you find yourself wanting to talk about you, or do you find yourself wanting to know about others? Are you a woman who exhibits meekness, that is, strength under control? Do you find yourself irritated most of the time, or do you bear long with others and with difficult situations? Do you endure under hard circumstances and difficult people? Is there anyone to whom you are not extending forgiveness? Is agape love your motive for showing tender mercy, kindness, humility, meekness, longsuffering, forbearance, and forgiveness?

Are you dressed for the day? Do you have tender mercies, kindness, humility, meekness, longsuffering, forbearance, forgiveness, and love clothing your inner man? I trust you will choose tender mercies over tongue lashings; kindness over knowledge; humility over hate; meekness over malice; longsuffering over lying; forbearance over filthy communication; forgiveness over fighting; and love over lust. What will you choose to wear today?

Questions to Consider

Colossians 3:12-14
What Will You Wear Today?

1. (a) Read Colossians 3:12-14. Who in Scripture, male or female (except our Lord), comes to mind when you read over these qualities? (b) What quality or qualities did they exemplify?

2. Memorize Colossians 3:12, 13, or 14.

3. (a) Compare and contrast Colossians 3:12-14 with Galatians 5:22-23. What virtues do you find in both passages? (b) What virtues are different? (c) How is it possible to put these virtues on, according to the Galatians passage? (d) What happens when you try to do these in your own strength? See John 15:5.

4. (a) Read the parable of the Good Samaritan, in Luke 10:30-37. Which one of these individuals demonstrated mercy, kindness, and humility? (b) Which individuals did not? (c) Put yourself in the parable for a moment. If you were the man who was stripped and beaten, how would you feel? (d) Being honest with yourself, if you came upon that half-dead man, would you respond like the priest, the Levite, or the Samaritan? (e) When looking at these three individuals, what makes this story so appalling?

5. (a) Read 1 Corinthians 13. What virtues are listed here that are also listed in Colossians 3:12-14? (b) What is similar about 1 Corinthians 13:13 and Colossians 3:14?

6. (a) Make 8 columns on a piece of paper. Write above each column the following: tender mercies, kindness, humility, meekness, longsuffering, forbearance, forgiveness, and love. (b) Read Matthew 27, Mark 15, Luke 23, and John 19, which all record the last hour of our Lord. Write in the appropriate column how Jesus Christ, our Supreme example, exemplified these eight qualities.

7. (a) Does your life manifest tender mercies, kindness, humility, meekness, longsuffering, forbearance, forgiveness, and love? (If you really want to know, ask your family members.) (b) How can we as God's daughters improve in these virtues?

8. (a) What has Christ forgiven you of? (b) Have you shown that same forgiveness toward others?

9. Write a prayer request based on your answers from question number 7. In other words, how can we pray for you regarding these qualities that should be evident in your life?

Chapter 16
Five Commands for the New Woman
Colossians 3:15-17

Billy Graham was once asked in an interview, "If you had to live your life over again, what would you do differently?" Mr. Graham replied with this sobering statement: "One of my great regrets is that I have not studied enough. I wish I had studied more and preached less. People have pressured me into speaking to groups when I should have been studying and preparing."[46] I don't know about you, but I found that to be an interesting and thought-provoking statement by a man whom most of us would assume had studied hours upon hours. And yet, he said he wasn't in God's Word enough, much to his own regret.

Would you and I say the same thing about ourselves? Do we come to the end of our day and wonder to ourselves what was so important that it kept us from the Word of God? Did we spend any time reading it? Studying it? Memorizing it? Meditating on it? Did we pass any of its truths on to our children, to our friends, our neighbors, and lost ones? How does our knowledge of God's Word compare to that of our brothers and sisters in Colossae? Does it dwell in us like it did in them? I think we'll be a little surprised when we consider what Paul is saying here in these few verses we'll cover in this lesson.

In our last lesson, we learned that we are to clothe ourselves with eight virtues: tender mercies, kindness, humility, meekness, longsuffering, forbearance, forgiveness, and love. Now that we have put off the ugly sins and have put on the beautiful virtues, we have work to do. As we have been clothed with the mind of Christ, we now have some things to do. Paul says we are just getting started:

---

46 Christianity Today, September 23, 1977.

Colossians 3:15-17

> And let the peace of God rule in your hearts, to which also you were called in one body; and be thankful. [16]Let the word of Christ dwell in you richly in all wisdom, teaching and admonishing one another in psalms and hymns and spiritual songs, singing with grace in your hearts to the Lord. [17]And whatever you do in word or deed, do all in the name of the Lord Jesus, giving thanks to God the Father through Him.

Now that we have put off those ugly-stained sins and have put on those beautiful Christ-like virtues, there are five commands for the newly dressed woman (or man) of God. In this lesson we'll consider *Five Commands for the New Woman*. Let's look at command number one.

> And let the peace of God rule in your hearts, to which also you were called in one body; and be thankful. (Colossians 3:15)

1. *The first command Paul gives for the newly dressed woman (or man) is to let the peace of God rule in their hearts.* The words *and let* mean in addition to. In other words, in addition to all the put-ons that Paul has just mentioned, we are to also let the peace of God rule in our hearts. We are to allow the peace of God to govern or rule our hearts. What is *the peace of God*? The word *peace* means quietness or rest. And it can only rule in the hearts of those who are redeemed. The world knows nothing of this type of contentment and rest. But as God's daughters, we can be at rest because we know that He is ever with us. It is said that when Bible translators were trying to find a word or phrase for peace in the language of the Chol Indians of South Mexico, they discovered the words "quiet heart" gave just the meaning they were looking for. My friend, a quiet heart can only come from God. It doesn't come from practicing Yoga or lighting a candle; it comes from God. It is one of the fruits of the Spirit that Paul mentions in Galatians 5:22-23: "But the fruit of the Spirit is love, joy, peace, longsuffering, kindness, goodness, faithfulness, gentleness, self-control. Against such there is no law."

Having the peace of God rule in our hearts is the same idea that Paul mentions in Philippians 4:6-7, where he writes, "Be anxious for nothing, but in everything by prayer and supplication, with thanksgiving, let your requests be made known to God; and the peace of God, which surpasses all understanding, will guard your hearts and minds through Christ Jesus." As we commit our anxious thoughts and circumstances to God, the peace He gives us keeps our hearts and minds. This idea of guarding our hearts and minds comes from a military term; it means that the mind will be guarded as a camp or castle is guarded. It will be preserved from the intrusion of anxious fears and alarms. What a wonderful mental picture Paul gives us! I am sure that we all can testify to times that this has been true in our own lives. There are times in our lives when you and I have experienced a peace that cannot be explained apart from God. The world would tell us to take anti-anxiety drugs to acquire peace, but the world doesn't understand that true peace is not found in a prescription we can buy; true peace is a gift that has been paid for by the blood of the Lamb (Colossians 1:20)!

The placing of this verse within the letter to the Colossians is important, because as we put on the virtues we saw in our last lesson—when we clothe ourselves with tender mercies, kindness, humility, meekness, longsuffering, forbearance, forgiveness, and love—then the peace of God follows. Peace is set in definite contrast to those who would practice fornication, uncleanness, inordinate affection, evil desire, covetousness, anger, wrath, malice, blasphemy, filthy communication, and lying. They certainly do not have peace! Isaiah puts it well in Isaiah 57:21, "'There is no peace,' says my God, 'for the wicked.'" Actor Harrison Ford was once asked in an interview if he had everything in this life he wanted, and he responded by saying he had everything he desired except for peace and that he hoped to find it when he died. What a sad reality, that one who doesn't have peace now thinks he will have it when he dies. This kind of peace is something the false teachers will never be able to deliver.

It is also interesting to note here that the word for *God* is <u>Christos,</u> or Christ. It is not Theos, which is the Greek word for God, but

Christos, the Greek word for Christ. Why? Because this peace is from Christ and was given by Him. In Christ's final hours with His disciples in the upper room, He stated in John 14:27, "Peace I leave with you, My peace I give to you; not as the world gives do I give to you. Let not your heart be troubled, neither let it be afraid." It was a gift from Jesus to His disciples as He left them to go back to the Father. And in Colossians 1:20, Paul tells us how Jesus made that peace possible: "and by Him to reconcile all things to Himself, by Him, whether things on earth or things in heaven, having made peace through the blood of His cross."

It's also interesting to note that the word *rule* can refer to an umpire. The peace of God is to umpire my heart amidst the conflicts of life. It should rule my heart, my thoughts, my feelings, my mind. Let peace decide what is right. Remember, it was the false teachers who were trying to sit as umpire to judge the Colossian believers regarding their reward, as we saw in 2:18. But Paul says, "Don't let them umpire you or rule you; let the peace of God rule you!" "The false teacher, as a self-constituted umpire, defrauds you of your prize; but if the peace of Christ, as umpire, rule in your hearts, your reward is sure. Let it act as umpire when wrong passions arise, and restrain them. Let not them rule, so that you should lose your prize."[47]

Paul then adds *to which also you were called in one body*. He is reminding them that they are called as a body to promote oneness in every way. He writes in Ephesians 4:1-4, "I, therefore, the prisoner of the Lord, beseech you to walk worthy of the calling with which you were called, with all lowliness and gentleness, with longsuffering, bearing with one another in love, endeavoring to keep the unity of the Spirit in the bond of peace. There is one body and one Spirit, just as you were called in one hope of your calling." The Gnostics were trying to steal the unity of the church at Colossae, as well as their peace. But again, Paul reminds the Colossian believers that they have been called to be one body and they are called to peace.

---

47 *Jamieson, Fausset, and Brown Commentary, Electronic Database. Copyright ©*
1997, 2003, 2005, 2006, by Biblesoft, Inc. All rights reserved.

2. *Paul then gives a second command and that is to be thankful; this is the second command for the new woman.* We are to be *thankful*, or grateful. The Greek tense here gives the idea of a continual obligation to be thankful. It's as though Paul is saying to us, "be constantly thankful ones." You might be wondering if there is a connection between peace and being thankful. I believe there is, because when we maintain a spirit of thankfulness, we almost always find that we are peaceful. Gratitude promotes peace, but an ungrateful person is often restless and contentious. Ingratitude is a mark of an unbeliever. Consider Romans 1:21, which says, "because, although they knew God, they did not glorify Him as God, nor were thankful, but became futile in their thoughts, and their foolish hearts were darkened." A lack of thankfulness is also characteristic of those in the last days, according to 2 Timothy 3:1-4: "But know this, that in the last days perilous times will come: For men will be lovers of themselves, lovers of money, boasters, proud, blasphemers, disobedient to parents, unthankful, unholy, unloving, unforgiving, slanderers, without self-control, brutal, despisers of good, traitors, headstrong, haughty, lovers of pleasure rather than lovers of God." Did you know that, as a daughter of God, being thankful is His will for your life? Consider 1 Thessalonians 5:18: "In everything give thanks; for this is the will of God in Christ Jesus for you." Not only are we to let the peace of God rule in our hearts, not only are we to be thankful, but Paul goes on in verse 16 to give us two more commands to obey. He says,

> Let the word of Christ dwell in you richly in all wisdom, teaching and admonishing one another in psalms and hymns and spiritual songs, singing with grace in your hearts to the Lord. (Colossians 3:16)

3. *Paul begins verse 16 by saying let the word of Christ dwell in you richly; this is the third command for the new woman (and man!).* The word *let* here is a different Greek word than the one in verse 15, which meant to rule. This word means to inhabit, and the word for *word* is logos, which means the entire body of truth. Paul is commanding the Colossians to let the Word of God inhabit them. Now, ladies, the Word of God can only dwell in us to the extent that

we know it. At the time Paul wrote this epistle, most of the Colossian believers did not have a copy of the written Word, and yet Paul tells them to let it dwell in them. *Dwell* is the same Greek word as let. The Word of God is to inhabit us, to be at home in us. Is the Word of Christ at home in you? Does it inhabit you? Does your blood bleed Bibline, as Charles Spurgeon said of John Bunyan? "Why, this man is a living Bible! Prick him anywhere; his blood is Bibline, the very essence of the Bible flows from him. He cannot speak without quoting a text, for his very soul is full of the Word of God."[48] Paul is clear that it should dwell in us *richly*, abundantly.

My friend, it was essential that the Word dwell richly in these believers, because they couldn't pick up a Bible and start reading it or studying it as you and I can. They were dependent on what was in their hearts and minds. Men and women of old had a special challenge to hide God's Word in their heart because personal copies of it were unheard of. Even as the New Testament church progressed, according to church history, many cherished God's Word much more than we do today. Tertullian devoted his days and nights to Bible reading, so much so that he even memorized much of its punctuation. Beza could repeat all of Paul's letters in Greek at the age of 80. Cramer could repeat the entire New Testament from memory. Theodosius the Younger could repeat any part of Scripture exactly. Frances Havergal, who wrote my favorite hymn, *Take My Life and Let It Be*, memorized the entire New Testament, the Psalms, and Isaiah, in her teenage years; in her later years, she memorized the Minor Prophets. When she died at the age of 43, she had 12,935 verses committed to memory.

One man I read about, who was converted at the age of 20, determined to memorize only one verse a day, and the result was that he knew over 1000 verses at the end of his first three years as a Christian. These saints of old are a model for us to follow. The early church did not know about a "Quiet Time" or "Daily Devotions" or "a chapter a day keeps the devil away." The Word was in them. It dwelt and

---

48 Charles Spurgeon. "May We Bleed Bibline!" *The Old Guys. https://theoldguys. org/2013/05/03/charles-spurgeon-may-we-bleed-bibline/.*

abode in them. I've heard my husband say that the concept of "Quiet Time" has done a great injustice to Christians by giving us the idea that by a few moments in the morning with God we have somehow done our duty for the day. We tack God on to our lives when he should be our life. We have the written Word; in fact, we have many copies of it and usually several translations. It is accessible in a moment online if we need it. And yet, unfortunately, even with all the advantages we have over the saints at Colossae, it does not dwell in us. Some Christians unfortunately are biblically illiterate and do not know where the simplest truths in Scripture are. "The family Bible is more often used to adorn coffee tables or press flowers than it is to feed souls and discipline lives."[49]

What about you? Do you read the Word? Not just a chapter a day, but great portions of it? Do you read from Genesis to Revelation? Do you study it and memorize it? The truths of God's Word should permeate our lives, should govern our thoughts, words, and deeds. We must read, study, memorize, and live it! We must pass it on to our children diligently, as Deuteronomy 6:6-9 and 11:18-20 tell us. In fact, the word diligently in the Hebrew means to repeat again and again. The Jews learned no differently than we do; they learned by repetition. When we stop to consider what the Psalmist says in the first Psalm—that the godly man (or woman) meditates day and night on the Word—we should do some serious self-examination. The word meditate means to murmur in a low tone of voice until whatever is being murmured—in this case, the Word of God— becomes implanted in our mind. That is what we call "Scripture memorization" in the 21st century.[50]

Now, some will use the excuse that they cannot understand the Bible and therefore don't read, study, or memorize it. And I will grant that some of it is difficult to understand. But I love what Mark Twain was reported to have said, and it should prick each of our hearts: "Most people are bothered by those passages of Scripture which

---

49 Charles W. Colson, *Loving God (Grand Rapids: Zondervan, 2011)*, 74.

50 For more information on this topic and how to memorize God's Word for a changed life, read *A Call to Scripture Memory, by Susan Heck (Bemidji: Focus Publishing, 2009).*

they cannot understand, but as for me, I have always noticed that the passages in Scripture which trouble me most are those which I *do* understand" (emphasis mine).

4. Paul adds a fourth command for us to follow in this verse. He puts in like this: *teaching and admonishing one another in psalms and hymns and spiritual songs, singing with grace in your hearts to the Lord. The fourth command is that we teach and admonish one another.* Recall from Colossians 1:28 that Paul and Timothy did this, and now Paul is commanding the Colossians to do the same. This isn't just for pastors, elders, and their wives, but for the whole body of Christ. We all should be involved in teaching and admonishing one another. Paul says in Romans 15:14, "Now I myself am confident concerning you, my brethren, that you also are full of goodness, filled with all knowledge, able also to admonish one another." The church at Colossae was to know the Word of God so well that they could teach and admonish one another, and so should the church of the 21st century. *Teaching* is simply instructing or imparting truth to others. *Admonishing* means to caution or reprove gently; to warn. By the way, before we go on, allow me to add a word here about how we receive admonishment: We need to remember, when we are the recipients of admonishment, to be gentle and humble as we receive it and to examine our hearts before God to see if what is being said is valid. It is the proud woman who defends herself without serious examination of her heart.

When Paul commands the Colossians to do this teaching and admonishing, he does so in a way that is perhaps foreign to us. He says to do this *with psalms and hymns and spiritual songs, singing with grace in your hearts to the Lord.* In biblical times, they would take the oral Word that they heard week after week and allow it to dwell richly in their hearts and minds. By doing this, they were then able to admonish and teach one another these truths in psalms and hymns and spiritual songs. They were dependent on listening to the Word, so if they did not listen, and then let it inhabit them, they could not sing it to each other. One historian, Tertullian, helps us to understand what would take place after the love feasts in the early church. He says, "After water for the hands and lights have been brought in, each is invited to sing to God in the presence of the others from what he knows of the holy Scriptures or from his own heart."[51] The early church was very different from the churches of our day, in that they were much less formal. Paul speaks of this in 1 Corinthians 14:26: "How is it then, brethren? Whenever you come together, each of you has a psalm, has a teaching, has a tongue, has a revelation, has an interpretation. Let all things be done for edification." One historian writes "that they would form choirs, one of men and one of women, and then they sing hymns to God composed of many measures and set to many melodies, sometimes chanting together, sometimes taking up the harmony, hands and feet keeping time in accompaniment."[52]

What exactly are *psalms and hymns and spiritual songs*? A *psalm* was originally a song accompanied by a stringed instrument. The psalms in our Bible, all 150 of them, were originally put to music. A *hymn* is a song of praise. Augustine said a hymn must be sung, it must be praise, and it must be directed to God. Hymns were songs of praise usually focused on Christ, whereas the psalms focused on God. It is supposed by some that Paul's writings have fragments of these hymns in some of his epistles (1 Corinthians 13; Ephesians 5:14; 1 Timothy 3:16; 2 Timothy 2:11-13). This explains how they could admonish one another with music, because the words set to these musical pieces were not devoid of meaning, as some of our modern worship songs are. I remember attending a Christian meeting years ago with my husband, and one of the songs we sang was *Let's Celebrate Jesus*—and those were the only lyrics in the song! And we sang it over and over and over again! The third type of music Paul mentions is *spiritual songs*, which were sacred poems giving personal testimony to what God has done. This singing was not to be done rotely, but as Paul says, *with grace in your hearts to the Lord.* They were to sing with gratitude, pleasure, thanksgiving

---

51 R. Kent Hughes, *Preaching the Word: Colossians and Philemon (Westchester: Cross-way Books, 1989), 112.*

52 David E. Garland, *The NIV Application Commentary: Colossians and Philemon (Grand Rapids: Zondervan, 1998).*

to the Lord. Our singing should be for the glory of God. As one man puts it well: "Music is the window of your soul."[53] I do believe our music is a reflection of what is in our hearts. It is to be sung sincerely and with humility of heart. It is to be sung in connection with the *grace* that God has given us that has made us what we are in Him. "When the Word of God dwells richly within you, you want to sing with gratitude in your hearts to God."[54] And it is not only the singing that is to be done unto the Lord, put Paul goes a step further in verse 17 and says:

> And whatever you do in word or deed, do all in the name of the Lord Jesus, giving thanks to God the Father through Him. (Colossians 3:17)

5. *The final command is that everything we do be done in the name of the Lord.* This would contrast with what the false teachers were teaching. Could they practice legalism, asceticism, and mysticism in the name of The Lord Jesus Christ? No way. Christ would not be pleased nor put His stamp of approval on their man-made lists of traditions and rules. Paul says that *all* we do, whether *in word or deed*, is to be done in His name. *Word* refers to what we say, and *deed* refers to what we do. That encompasses just about all of life, doesn't it? Our words are powerful, and we would do well to remind ourselves of Jesus' words in Matthew 12:36-37: "But I say to you that for every idle word men may speak, they will give account of it in the day of judgment. For by your words you will be justified, and by your words you will be condemned." That should give us all pause before speaking! Our deeds include everything we do—preaching, teaching, eating, exercising, driving, cleaning house, shopping, visiting, working, playing, everything! We are to speak and act *in the name of the Lord Jesus*, which means in the spirit of the Lord Jesus. This is a convicting verse here, because many of our words and deeds are not in the spirit of our Lord and Master. Here are some helpful questions I once came across that may help you to decide if a particular word or deed can be done in the name of the Lord Jesus:

---

53 R. Kent Hughes, *Preaching the Word, 112.*
54 Ibid.

1. What is the Christian thing to do or say here?

2. Can I do or say this without compromising my Christian confession?

3. Can I do or say it "in the name of the Lord Jesus," whose reputation is at stake in the conduct of His known followers?

4. Can I thank God the Father through Him for the opportunity of doing or saying this? Jim Elliott once wrote, "Wherever you are, be all there. Live to the hilt every situation you believe to be the will of God."[55] That is exactly what Paul is conveying here.

Paul concludes these thoughts with the phrase *giving thanks to God and the Father through Him.* Paul mentions *giving thanks* (expressing gratitude) again, just as he did in verse 15. Obviously, this is an important command because he repeats it twice in three verses! In fact, Paul mentions thanksgiving 41 times in his letters. In Colossians alone, he mentions it in 1:3; 1:12; 2:7; 3:15; 3:17; and 4:2. A true believer has a heart of thanksgiving. And you know, if we are doing things and saying things in the spirit of Christ, won't we be thankful? It only seems natural that thanksgiving will follow. When our sinful flesh creeps in, that's when being thankful is difficult. Can we be thankful at the same time we are using our mouths for evil? Can we be thankful when we are doing things that are sinful? We can't—and that is the idea here! If we could say and do everything in His name, then we could give thanks in all those things as well.

---

55 Goodreads.com, Jim Elliot, "Live to the Hilt…"

Summary

What are the five commands for the new woman to obey?

1. *Let the peace of God rule in your heart* (v 15): Does the peace of God rule in your heart, or do you resort to worldly means in your pursuit of peace? Have you made peace with God by being reconciled to Him through the death of His Son?

2. *Be Thankful* (v 16): Are you thankful in every situation and with every individual and situation that God has placed in your life? Can you give thanks in everything?

3. *Let the Word of Christ dwell in you richly* (v 16): Does it? Do you know the Word so well that when the evil one tempts you, you are able to resist his temptations? Will you be able to stand in the day of adversity because you know the Word so well? What are you currently reading in the Word? What are you studying? What portion of God's Word are you memorizing?

4. *Teach and Admonish Others* (v 16): Do you know the Word of God so well that you can pass it on to your children? Are you able to lovingly admonish those who need it from the Word of God? Is there someone you need to admonish, but you're putting it off? Do you sing with gratitude in your heart to the Lord, or has your singing become a dull and boring routine?

5. *All is to be done in the name of the Lord Jesus Christ* (v 17): Are the words you speak each day words that Christ would speak, or have you allowed your mouth to be a tool of the evil one? What about your deeds? Do you do each task to the glory of God? Are you motivated to speak and act in a Christ-like way because you love God and want to put Him on display?

What great nuggets of truth are here in these three verses! We who know the Lord are able to let His peace rule in our hearts, no matter what. We can also admonish each other in song by the Word that richly dwells in us. And we can use the life He gave us to say and do things that will be for Him and in Him, all the time giving thanks to His name.

There was a hymn written more than a century ago by Kate Wilkinson, and I wonder if she had this portion of Colossians in her mind when she wrote it. Since Paul tells us to teach and admonish each other in song, I thought this song would be a wonderful way to close our lesson. Consider the words. How wonderfully rich it would be to prayerfully sing these words to our Master!

> May the mind of Christ, my Savior,
> Live in me from day to day,
> By His love and pow'r controlling
> All I do and say.
>
> May the Word of God dwell richly
> In my heart from hour to hour,
> So that all may see I triumph
> Only through His pow'r.
>
> May the peace of God my Father
> Rule my life in everything,
> That I may be calm to comfort
> Sick and sorrowing.
>
> May the love of Jesus fill me
> As the waters fill the sea;
> Him exalting, self-abasing,
> This is victory.
>
> May I run the race before me,
> Strong and brave to face the foe,
> Looking only unto Jesus
> As I onward go.

May His beauty rest upon me,
As I seek the lost to win,
And may they forget the channel,
Seeing only Him.[56]

---

56 Words by Kate Wilkinson, 1913.

Questions to Consider

Colossians 3:15-17
Five Commands for the New Woman

1. (a) Read Colossians chapter three. What are the "one-anothers" that you notice? In other words, what should we be doing to one another and not doing to one another, according to this chapter? (b) How does this go along with what Jesus said in Matthew 7:12?

2. Memorize Colossians 3:17.

3. (a) According to Numbers 6:24-26; John 16:33; and 1 Peter 5:14, how does one acquire peace? (b) When one does not have peace, what does that indicate, according to James 3:14-18? (c) What is our responsibility in retaining that peace? See Isaiah 26:3 and Philippians 4:6-7. (d) How do you practically retain peace in your life?

4. (a) To whom is our singing to be directed? See Psalm 28:7 and 47:6-7. (b) Who is singing in the following verses: what are they singing; where or when are they singing; and why are they singing? Matthew 26:30; Acts 16:25; 1 Corinthians 14:15, 26; Ephesians 5:19; Hebrews 2:12; James 5:13. (c) What does this tell you about music and its importance in our lives?

5. (a) Paul says in Colossians 3:17 that whatever we do, we are to do it in the name of the Lord. What specifically does that mean, according to Matthew 28:19; Romans 14:8; 1 Corinthians 10:31; 2 Corinthians 5:15; and 1 Peter 4:11? (b) How can you apply these verses to your daily living? (c) Is there anything that you are currently saying or doing about which you cannot honestly say, "I am doing this in the name of my Lord"?

6. (a) What does Job say about God's Word in Job 23:12? (b) What does Jeremiah say about the Word of God in Jeremiah 15:16? (c) Also, *skim* Psalm 119 and list at least five attitudes the Psalmist had about God's Word. (d) Do these characterize your attitudes about God's Word?

7. Since your conversion, how has your life changed in the areas of inner peace, the Word of God, being thankful, admonishing others, and speaking and doing all to the glory of God?

8. (a) In what ways is it apparent to you that God's Word is dwelling in you? (b) How have you grown in your understanding of God's Word?

9. After looking over question 7, write a prayer of thanksgiving to God for the changes He has made in your life.

Chapter 17

Me Obey Him?

Colossians 3:18

In 1972, a book was written entitled *Me Obey Him?* Since I was only 16 at the time, I obviously didn't read it. But in 1995, several women I knew purchased this book and began reading it. At the same time, Elisabeth Elliott, who was still living at the time, was reading portions of it on her radio program. Many women in my church were listening to her and began to ask me questions about the book. Because of their questions and my curiosity, I purchased a copy and read it. My husband read it as well. I was so disturbed by what I read that I wrote a letter to Elisabeth Elliot, which eventually led to me writing a letter to the author of the book. My husband also got involved, writing a rather lengthy letter to the author as well. By way of introduction to this lesson, I want to share some excerpts from my letter to Mrs. Elliot. I assure you, there is a reason for me doing this—and it is not to teach you how to dictate a letter!

> Dear Elisabeth Elliott,
>
> For many years now I have read your books and newsletters. I have listened to you on the radio and have had the privilege of attending some of your conferences. God has blessed my life richly through you, and I consider you one of my "older women." Recently, on the radio, you read from a book entitled *Me Obey Him?* I was not able to hear most of it due to a busy time. My husband pastors a church here in Tulsa. Several women in our church, however, purchased that book because of your recommendation of it, read it, and began to ask questions. So, we read it. I was somewhat taken back by the extremes of this

book and was concerned that you would promote it. I believe firmly that the Bible teaches that women are to submit to their husbands as unto the Lord. And I teach and counsel women to do just that. However, I do not believe our Lord would ever ask us to murder, commit adultery, violate our conscience, have abortions, and never express an opinion unless we are asked. Mrs. Elizabeth Rice Handford (the author of the book) states, "God is not going to give anybody two conflicting commands so that it is impossible to obey both" to prove that a wife is to be submissive regardless it if conflicts with the moral law of God. Where is that in the Bible? [If I were writing this letter today, I would word that question in a more gracious way!] Many times, we are given two conflicting commands. For example, "Wives submit yourselves unto your husbands," and "Honor your father and mother," and yet we know that many times a wife must dishonor her father and mother in order to submit to her own husband. Another example is in Exodus 1:15-16, "The King (authority) spoke to the Hebrew midwives … when ye do the office of a midwife to the Hebrew women, and see them upon the stools, if it be a son, then ye shall kill them…." However, verse 17 says that the midwives feared God, and did not as the King commanded them. Those are conflicting commands. We are to obey God and we are to obey those in authority over us. It also says God blessed the midwives for their obedience. There are numerous other conflicting commands in the Word. Her command that wives should never express an opinion unless they are asked is totally contrary to Matthew 18, where it states that if a brother offends you, you go to him and tell him his fault between him and thee alone. And there is no exception clause (like "except your husband"). Does that mean that if you have a husband and wife who are both believers that a wife can never fulfill Matthew 18?

I could go on and on because there are numerous concerns that my husband and I had about this book. I would hope and pray that you might reread the book with an open heart before God and reconsider what she is saying. (She also takes many passages out of context to prove her points.) Her idea was good, and I agree with some of the book. I just honestly believe she goes too far and is leading many astray. If you choose to disagree, I will still read your books and newsletters and listen to you on the radio and hear you when you're in the area and consider you a God-given "older woman" in my life. I will not, however, be able to support your support of this book.

Sincerely and prayerfully,
Susan Heck.

Her response was short and sweet:

Dear Susan,

Thank you very much for your gracious letter which has only just reached my desk. You have certainly given me pause. I have trusted my friend Elizabeth Handford so implicitly that I did not challenge her on any point. I did wonder if there might be some "conflicting commands" and you have cited several which appear to be. I do not agree that wives should never express an opinion. That seems a bit extreme, doesn't it? I appreciated your mention of Matthew 18.

Sincerely,
Elisabeth Elliott Gren.

This generated several letters of correspondence between the author, myself, and my husband. Unfortunately, no questions were really answered to my satisfaction.

Perhaps you are wondering why I'm referring to that experience as my introduction to this lesson. The reason is that there are many false teachings regarding the subject of submission. If we have learned anything in our study of Colossians, I hope we have learned the danger of false teaching. Even Elisabeth Elliott said, "I trusted my friend so implicitly that I did not challenge her on any point." Do you see the danger of believing even what your friend says without checking it out biblically? What does the Bible have to say on this issue? Am I as a wife never to express an opinion, as some would have us believe? Do I have to disobey my Lord to obey my husband? What does the Bible say about this? And, in case you are wondering, I am not a women's libber or a feminist. Let me be clear: I do believe the Bible teaches submission, but I do not believe the Bible teaches what some call "doormat theology." We must be concerned with what the Bible has to say, not with what man (or woman, in this case) has to say. God's Word is very clear on this subject, and that is why I want to take one whole lesson on this verse alone. I do not think we will clear up all the issues after this one lesson, but perhaps I will at least challenge your thinking on it. Let's read this verse, which is so very vital for us as women, from Colossians 3:18.

Colossians 3:18

Wives, submit to your own husbands, as is fitting in the Lord.

In our last lesson, we learned of five commands for the new woman. They are: to let the peace of God rule in our hearts; to be thankful; to let the Word of Christ dwell in us richly; to teach and admonish others; and to do all things in the name of the Lord Jesus Christ. In this lesson, our outline will include:

> *To Whom Do We Submit?* (v 18a)
> *Why Do We Submit?* (v 18b)

Some Answers to Common Questions about Submission

To Whom Do We Submit?

Colossians 3:18a

Wives, submit to your own husbands, (Colossians 3:18a)

Let's begin by defining submission. The word *submit* means to put under, to place in an orderly fashion under. Such an orderly fashion could liken the husband to the role of president and the wife to the role of vice president, or the husband to a five start general and the wife to a four-star general. The Greek indicates that there is a willingness involved in this submission. The verb is in the middle voice. It is not in the active voice, which means that the husband cannot rightly use it to say, "You must submit to me." Some husbands like to use the "submission club" as if this is what the Greek means, but it doesn't. It is also not in the passive voice, which means the wife cannot rightly use it to say, "I am forced to submit to you." The middle voice represents the wife participating in the results of the action. The middle voice is used to show the necessity of the submission being voluntary. It is the wife's willing choice. This is not the same Greek word for obedience that we will see when we get to verse 20, where Paul commands children to obey their parents in the Lord. That is an absolute. But here in the case of the wife submitting, it is not. One of my objections with the book, *Me Obey Him?* was that it did not teach biblical submission but, rather, had the tone of doormat theology.

When I got married, I didn't have a clue about submission, even though my mother was a good role model of submission. I was an independent, young wife who was trying to be the president. I certainly didn't want anyone telling me what to do. My lack of obedience to the Lord and submission to my husband created some tension, to say the least. And, after God saved me 10 years into my marriage, I was forced to look at my sin in this area. To my own shame, I struggled at first with the whole concept. My husband used to say to me, "Susan, you are submitting outwardly, but your attitude is not one of submission." I was not submitting joyfully. By God's grace, He has changed me to the point where I now see submission as His will for me, and I see it as a liberty. To be clear, that is not to say that I never struggle with submission or that my flesh never creeps in.

Now, ladies, if you think your situation is bad, you need to thank God that you were born in this era. In the ancient world, and even today in some cultures, things were very different for women. Consider what one scholar has written about the life of a woman in biblical times: "Under Jewish law a woman was a thing: she was the possession of her husband, just as much as his house or his flocks or his material goods were. She had no legal right whatever. For instance, under Jewish law, a husband could divorce his wife for any cause, while a wife had no rights whatever in the initiation of divorce. In Greek society a respectable woman lived a life of entire seclusion. She never appeared on the streets alone, not even to go marketing. She lived in the women's apartments and did not join the men even for meals. It was demanded of her to live a life of complete servitude and chastity; but her husband could go out as much as he chose and could enter as many relationships outside marriage as he liked and incur no stigma. Both under Jewish and Greek laws and custom, all the privileges belonged to the husband, and all the duties to the wife."[57] (As you can see, we've come a long way!) To the Greeks, women were not considered equals to their husbands, or even companions. One Jewish philosopher, Philo, regarded women as selfish, jealous, and hypocritical, and said married men were no longer free men but slaves.[58] So, what Paul is commanding is very different than what was being commonly practiced. This is one area in which we can see clearly that Christ comes into one's life and changes all relationships, even those of one's family.

---

57 William Barclay, *The Letters to the Philippians, Colossians, and Thessalonians (Lou-isville: Westminster John Knox Press, 1975), 187.*
58 William Hendriksen, *New Testament Commentary: Exposition of Colossians and Philemon (Grand Rapids: Baker Book House, 1964), 169.*

So, whom do we submit? Notice what Paul says, he says to submit *to your own husbands*. We do not submit to another man's husband, but to our *own*. The one who, hopefully, is loving us the way Christ loved the church. The one whom we love, cherish and respect. The one with whom we hopefully have an intimate and close relationship. We submit to our own husbands.

Why Do We Submit?

Colossians 3:18b

as is fitting in the Lord. (Colossians 3:18b)

The second question we need to address is: Why do we submit? (or, put another way: How are we to submit?) Paul says we are to submit *as is fitting in the Lord*. The word *fitting* means proper. We are to submit in harmony with Christ's will. This is our obligation and duty. He is our *Lord*, as Paul makes clear, which means that He is our Master and Controller. We submit to our husbands because it is proper before the Lord and in harmony with His will for our lives. My husband has often said that a woman's submission is the main part of her sanctification. If you are not a submissive wife, I think it would be wise for you to carefully examine whether you are growing in your relationship to Christ.

Why is it that submission is so hard for so many women? It certainly is a challenge at times, and it will always be a challenge until we reach glory. Let's remind ourselves of why submission is a struggle. Consider Genesis 3:1-19:

> Now the serpent was more cunning than any beast of the field which the Lord God had made. And he said to the woman, "Has God indeed said, 'You shall not eat of every tree of the garden'?" And the woman said to the serpent, "We may eat the fruit of the trees of the garden; but of the fruit of the tree which is in the midst of the garden, God has said, 'You shall not eat it, nor shall you touch it, lest you die.'" Then the serpent said to the woman, "You will not surely die. For God knows that in

the day you eat of it your eyes will be opened, and you will be like God, knowing good and evil." So when the woman saw that the tree was good for food, that it was pleasant to the eyes, and a tree desirable to make one wise, she took of its fruit and ate. She also gave to her husband with her, and he ate. Then the eyes of both of them were opened, and they knew that they were naked; and they sewed fig leaves together and made themselves coverings.

And they heard the sound of the Lord God walking in the garden in the cool of the day, and Adam and his wife hid themselves from the presence of the Lord God among the trees of the garden. Then the Lord God called to Adam and said to him, "Where are you?" So he said, "I heard Your voice in the garden, and I was afraid because I was naked; and I hid myself." And He said, "Who told you that you were naked? Have you eaten from the tree of which I commanded you that you should not eat?" Then the man said, "The woman whom You gave to be with me, she gave me of the tree, and I ate." And the Lord God said to the woman, "What is this you have done?" The woman said, "The serpent deceived me, and I ate." So the Lord God said to the serpent: "Because you have done this, You are cursed more than all cattle, And more than every beast of the field; On your belly you shall go, And you shall eat dust All the days of your life. And I will put enmity Between you and the woman, and between your seed and her Seed; He shall bruise your head, and you shall bruise His heel." To the woman He said: "I will greatly multiply your sorrow and your conception; In pain you shall bring forth children; Your desire shall be for your husband, and he shall rule over you." Then to Adam He said, "Because you have heeded the voice of your wife, and have eaten from the tree of which I commanded you, saying, 'You shall not eat of it': Cursed is the ground for your sake; In toil you shall eat of it All the days of your life. Both thorns and thistles it shall bring forth for you, And you shall eat the herb of the field. In the sweat of your face you shall eat bread Till you return to the ground, For out of it you were taken; For dust you are, And to dust you shall return."

As we see from Genesis 3, sin came into the world and the result was judgment for everyone involved: the serpent, the man, and the woman. The woman's curse was two-fold, the first part being pain in childbearing. Whether or not you've experienced childbirth, it's likely that nothing more really needs to be said for us all to understand what this part of the curse means. The second part of the woman's curse is the one I am interested in for our lesson's sake: that our desire shall be for our husband, but that he shall rule over us. The word desire means turn or determination of the will. The determination of the wife's will that wants to rule her husband will be met by his rule over her. Part of the curse is the desire to rule or control your husband, but God says no, your husband will rule over you. We can thank our mother Eve for our life-long struggle of wanting to control our spouses! We really can't blame her, but we do need to realize that this will be an issue for us from time to time because of the curse. That isn't an excuse for the sin of not submitting to our husbands. My friend, we should be progressing toward Christ-likeness in this area. Our husbands should be able to say that we are more submissive today than we were a year ago.

I also want to be clear that submission does not imply that wives are inferior. Paul is clear in Galatians 3:26-29: "For you are all sons of God through faith in Christ Jesus. For as many of you as were baptized into Christ have put on Christ. There is neither Jew nor Greek, there is neither slave nor free, there is neither male nor female; for you are all one in Christ Jesus. And if you are Christ's, then you are Abraham's seed, and heirs according to the promise." In Christ, there is no male or female because we are all one, yet there are still those in positions of authority over us and we must yield to them: children to parents, children to teachers, employees to employers, citizens to governing authorities, and yes, wives to husbands. Even Jesus Himself submitted to His Father's will when He was here on earth, and yet He was not inferior to the Father because He and the Father are one. I trust you will answer the Questions to Consider at the end of this chapter and study the other main passages in the Word of God that deal with a wife's submission (Ephesians 5:22-33, Titus 2:3-5, and 1 Peter 3:1-7).

Some Answers to Common Questions about Submission

For the remainder of this lesson, I would like to give you some biblical answers to common questions I have received regarding the issue of submission.

1. *"What do I do if my husband asks me to sin?"* I have counseled women whose husbands wanted them to view pornography, lie to his employer, cheat on their income taxes, etc. We must keep in mind that submission to one's husband is not absolute. In Acts 5, we have a very telling passage, where the apostles were imprisoned for sharing the gospel and commanded by the governing authorities not to do it anymore. The apostles answered by saying that they were going to obey God rather than man. We know that God has commanded us to go into all the world and preach the gospel. The apostles were certainly not going to obey a governing authority over their Lord. We must also keep in mind that we are not to have loyalty to or love for any family member over God. Jesus says if you do you are not worthy of Him (Matthew 10:37). A wife need not submit to her husband when what he is asking her to do is contrary to God's Word. I know of some who have used Peter's words in 1 Peter 3, where it mentions how Sarah obeyed Abraham and called him lord, to try to prove that Sarah was commended for her lying in Genesis 12 and 20, when Abraham told her to lie and say she was his sister. You can search diligently in 1 Peter and find nothing in the text that will allow you to come up with such a ridiculous interpretation. That would be twisting the Scriptures for your own means. But we do need to be careful here, because some women will choose not to submit on issues that are really matters of preference and doing so is not commendable. Some things are not clearly revealed in Scripture; they are preferences, not commands. It is possible for us to use Acts 5:29 as an excuse to not submit. I would encourage you, if you are uncertain whether something your husband is asking you to do is sin or not, to seek out the counsel of an older godly woman or your pastor. I realize that some husbands are overbearing and unloving

and harsh, and that makes submission especially difficult for wives, but, nonetheless, we are commanded to submit.

2. *"Do I have to submit to my husband if he is not a believer?"* Those who ask this often use the excuse that an unredeemed man could not possibly make wise decisions. But the answer to this question is yes, you must submit even to a non-believer. In all the passages in the Word of God that deal with the wives' submission, there is not one exception clause. There is not one that says, "Wives, submit—unless you are married to an unbeliever." First Peter 3:1-7 is a helpful encouragement for wives who are married to unsaved husbands, because the wives Peter is addressing in 1 Peter were enduring harsh treatment and persecution from their unsaved husbands. Your husband is the one that God has placed in authority over you. I know many women who have unsaved husbands, and I sympathize with them deeply. You must remember that even an unsaved husband is God's tool for sanctifying you. However, the principle of not submitting to your husband if he has asked you to sin does apply to this situation. And the probability of an unsaved husband asking his wife to sin would be greater than that of a saved husband. But keep in mind that any refusal on your part to sin at your husband's request must be done with an attitude of respect and graciousness.

3. *"Can I never express an opinion?"* Yes, you can express an opinion. Husbands and wives should have a loving relationship in which both desire to listen to and share ideas. What we must avoid is nagging. Proverbs talks about this; Proverbs 19:13b says, "The contentions of a wife are a continual dripping." If you continually nag your husband, you will be like that dripping faucet that won't shut off. If you've ever had a dripping faucet in your home, you know just how annoying it can be. (If you don't believe me, consider turning on a faucet and letting it drip for an hour—then see what you think!) Proverbs also says that it's better for a husband to dwell in the corner of a rooftop than to dwell with a contentious wife. In fact, when I was studying this lesson, I realized for the first time this is mentioned twice in Proverbs (Proverbs 21:9 and Proverbs

25:24); so, ladies, listen up—this must be important! If you find your husband not coming home much, you might ask yourself if your behavior has anything to do with that. We are not our husbands' mothers, and we are not their Holy Spirit, either. We can appeal, and we can pray. In fact, praying would be the wise thing to do first. Often, when we begin by praying, we find that these issues we have with our mates lose their importance. I have learned in my marriage to wait before appealing to my husband on an issue. I try to weigh whether it is worth bringing up. Sometimes, I have found that if I just wait, things will work themselves out. Other times, I find that my heart is growing resentful or bitter, and so I must bring it up to keep from allowing a root of bitterness to defile myself and others. May I add here that good timing and proper tone of voice are essential to a godly appeal? This has not always been easy for me, but God has helped me to grow so much in this area that one time my husband thanked me not only for my rebuke, but for the way in which I did it. I was so grateful to the Lord! Esther is an excellent example in Scripture of a woman who appealed in a godly fashion.

A great book that will help you in all areas of your marriage is *The Excellent Wife*, by Martha Peace.[59] In it, Martha deals not only with the subject of submission but also with many topics that pertain to the wife's role, including communication, anger, impatience, loneliness, sorrow, idolatry, respect, love, intimacy, conflict, and others. In my opinion, it is the best book written on the subject apart from the Scripture. By way of closing, I would like to share her thoughts on how wives' attitudes toward their husbands reflect a lack of submission. Rather than giving them word for word, I have paraphrased them here.

1. *We annoy our husbands by doing things that bug them.* I didn't do this intentionally, but one day I learned that my husband does not like hard butter, and it annoyed him that I did not keep soft butter in the cupboard. You can go to my home right now and you will find soft butter in our cupboard.

---

59 Martha Peace, *The Excellent Wife (Bemidji: Focus Publishing, 1995).*

2. *We annoy our husbands by not disciplining our children as we should.* I've heard wives say they wait for their husbands to get home to spank or discipline their children. This is not a wise thing because it is just as much a mother's responsibility to discipline the children as it is a father's, if not more so, since the mother is with the children a great deal more.

3. *We annoy our husbands by being more loyal to others than we are to our husbands.* I see this more often than I would like to, and I guarantee you will do great damage to your marriage if this is your pattern.

4. *We annoy our husbands by arguing or pouting or giving them the cold shoulder when we do not get our own way.* In this, a wife may submit, but she lets her husband know that he will pay for it.

5. *We annoy our husbands by not staying within the limits of the family budget.* This one especially grieves me. I see women working outside the home with small children and sometimes the reason is that they refuse to live within their husbands' means. I know women who go out and purchase things they cannot afford and don't give it a second thought.

6. *We annoy our husbands by correcting, interrupting, talking for our husbands, or being too outspoken when others are around.* This is a problem for some wives. We do not need to be the first one to talk; instead, we need to let our husbands lead. Learn to be quiet and to cultivate a meek and quiet spirit.

7. *We annoy our husbands by attempting to manipulate them to get our own way.* A wife does this by deceit, tears, begging, nagging, complaining, anger, or intimidation. My friend, if this describes you, I beg you to stop sinning by being manipulative and to speak the truth in love. This type of behavior will drive your husband far away.

8. *We annoy our husbands by making important decisions without consulting him.* I know women who do this, and this is not wise. My husband and I do not make major decisions without first talking them through.

9. *We annoy our husbands by directly defying his wishes.* I was talking to a woman once and twice in the conversation she said, "I just told my husband no." I thought to myself, "That would happen once in my home!" To do so is willful rebellion, which is, in God's eyes, quite serious.

10. *We annoy our husbands by worrying about the decisions he makes and taking matters into our own hands.* We must remember we are not responsible for the decisions our husbands make; they are. They will stand before God someday, but we too will stand before God and give an answer for how we have—or have not—submitted.

11. *We annoy our husbands by not paying attention to what he says.* I'm sure this describes all wives at some point. Sometimes, we really aren't interested in our husbands' work, hobbies, stories, etc., and so what he has to say is just not all that important to us. Yet, we desire our husbands' undivided attention when we're talking to them about our day, don't we? We must remember to do unto them as we want done unto us.

Summary

Are you submitting to your own husband? If not, why not? Do you see this as God's will for your life, as in harmony with His will? If not, why not? My friend, if you are not a wife who is known to be submissive to her husband, then you need to confess it to the Lord and to your husband and purpose to do what is right. There is nothing more unattractive than a wife who is not submissive to her husband. She brings shame on her husband and her Lord. But a woman who is submissive and respectful toward her husband adorns the doctrine of God and makes it attractive.

Now, in case this concept is hard for you and your flesh is already rearing up against it, be encouraged, not that your flesh is rearing up, but because the command for you is to submit. The reason I say this is because, in my opinion, the husbands have been given the more difficult command to obey. And you will have to tune in for our next lesson to hear "the rest of the story."

Questions to Consider

Colossians 3:18
Me Obey Him?

1. (a) What do Ephesians 5:22-24, 33; Colossians 3:18; Titus 2:3-5; and 1 Peter 3:1-6 all have in common? (b) What are the similarities and the differences in these passages?

2. Memorize Colossians 3:18.

3. (a) According to Ephesians 5:22-24 and Titus 2:3-5, why are wives to be subject to their husbands? (b) Who is mentioned in 1 Peter 3:1-6 as a role model for us? (c) How did she show submission to her husband according to Genesis 12:1-9?

4. (a) Do you think Sarah should have done anything different in the stories mentioned in Genesis 12:10-20 and Genesis 20? If so, what? If not, why? (b) What was Sapphira's consequence for her submission to her husband, in Acts 5:1-11? What should she have done instead?

5. Why is the husband head over the wife, according to 1 Corinthians 11:1-16 and 1 Timothy 2:9-15?

6. (a) Read Esther chapter one. Who was not submissive to her husband? (b) What happened to her? (c) Who took her place, according to Esther 2:16-18? (d) From what you read in Esther 7:1-6, how was Queen Esther different from Queen Vashti? (e) What can you learn from these two queens?

7. How would you explain submission to a new Christian woman or to a newly married wife?

8. (a) Is submission difficult for you (to husband, to authorities, to church leadership)? Why or why not? (b) What benefits of submission have you learned that you can pass on to others by way of encouragement? (For the brave: Ask your husband if you are a submissive wife.)

9. How has God spoken to you this week through your study of His Word? Write down your thoughts in the form of a prayer request.

Chapter 18

Virtuous Living in the Home
Colossians 3:19-21

The Christian home should be a place where a lost world can look in and see Christ represented. But many who look into our homes react much like the seven-year-old girl who was told the story of Cinderella. When the end of the story declared, "And they lived happily ever after," she replied, "Oh no, they didn't! They got married!"

This little girl's response betrays a harsh reality: that the Christian family in America isn't all that different from the non-Christian family. The very things that plague non-Christian homes plague Christian homes as well—divorce rates are roughly the same; abuse is just as present; little-to-no discipline of children is practiced; conflict abounds; and the love of the world dominates. Christendom has, to a large extent, disgraced the name of Christ by failing to represent the type of marriage relationship Paul mentions in Ephesians 5, where he states that the husband-wife relationship should be a representation of Christ and the church.

In our last lesson, we began considering Paul's words to the Colossians concerning family relationships. We narrowed in on the admonishment for wives to be submissive to their own husbands. But Paul doesn't stop there; he also has a word for the husbands, a word for the children, and a word for the parents. In this lesson, we'll consider what it means to live virtuously in the home. Let's read what Paul writes in Colossians 3:18-21.

Colossians 3:18-21

Wives, submit to your own husbands, as is fitting in the Lord.
[19]Husbands, love your wives and do not be bitter toward them.
[20]Children, obey your parents in all things, for this is well
pleasing to the Lord. [21]Fathers, do not provoke your children,
lest they become discouraged.

Our outline for this lesson will include

The Responsibility of the Husband to the Wife (v 19)
The Responsibility of the Children to the Parents (v 20)
The Responsibility of the Parents to the Children (v 21)

The Responsibility of the Husband to the Wife

Colossians 3:19

Husbands, love your wives and do not be bitter toward them.
(Colossians 3:19)

Husbands are given a two-fold command in this verse. First,
husbands are to love their wives, and second, they are not to be bitter
toward their wives. Let's consider what it means when Paul tells the
husbands to *love your wives*. The word for *love* here is not phileo,
or tender affection—it is rare that husbands need to be commanded
to practice that—rather, the word here for love is agapao. This is not
a sexual love nor an emotional love but a love that willingly looks
out for and cares for the needs of its object. It is also here used in
the present imperative in the Greek, which means that husbands are
being commanded to keep on loving their wives in a continuous
action. Essentially, they are called to love us even when we are
not so lovely. Husbands are obligated to exercise compassionate
care for their wives, and wives are obligated to respond to that
care willingly. It is true that the responsibility for final decisions
rests with the husband, but the method of reaching those decisions
leaves ample room for mutual deliberation and gentle persuasion.
At times, the husband's conclusion may prevail; at other times,

the wife's conclusion may prevail. In Ephesians, the sister epistle to Colossians, Paul writes something similar. He says in Ephesians 5:25-29,

> Husbands, love your wives, just as Christ also loved the church and gave Himself for her, that He might sanctify and cleanse her with the washing of water by the word, that He might present her to Himself a glorious church, not having spot or wrinkle or any such thing, but that she should be holy and without blemish. So husbands ought to love their own wives as their own bodies; he who loves his wife loves himself. For no one ever hated his own flesh, but nourishes and cherishes it, just as the Lord does the church.

Husbands are to love their wives the way Christ loved the church and gave Himself for it. How did Christ show love to the church? He died for her, spilled His blood for her, and endured extreme pain and persecution for her. He left her instructions on how to live and follow Him. He protects her. He wants fellowship with her. He faithfully loves the church even though she is often unlovely and sinful and denies the very One she says she loves. The church's actions many times fail to show devotion to her Lord, and yet He does not become bitter toward His church. He continues to pour out His grace and mercy! Ladies, we must stop and realize what a death to self this commandment demands of our husbands! Quite frankly, many of us can be unlovely at times and have probably made this command difficult for our husbands to obey. It is absurd for a Christian husband to demand the submission of his wife if he does not radically love her; but it is likewise ridiculous for a wife who is not submissive to demand such love from her husband.

The second part of the two-fold command regarding how husbands are to relate to their wives is that they *not be bitter toward them.* Paul is saying to husbands, "Stop being bitter!" The word *bitter* refers to something that is bitter in taste. I've heard it said that "a husband should not call his wife honey and then act like vinegar." A husband should not be harsh or cross or resentful toward his wife. I must admit that when I first meditated on this command, I had a hard time understanding why Paul wrote this. The reason I struggled so is that in all my years of teaching and counseling women, I've met numerous bitter and resentful wives but few bitter husbands, at least among those I've had the opportunity to talk with. Yet, as I continued thinking on this command to husbands, I came to see several ways such bitterness could arise. A man can become bitter toward his wife when she nags him continually, as though she were her husband's mother or Holy Spirit. He can also become bitter when his wife is not submissive to him or when she treats him with disrespect. Bitterness can also result when a wife denies her husband the sexual intimacy he desires; this can be frustrating for the husband and provide a context in which he is tempted toward sexual sin. I've seen husbands become bitter toward their wives when their wives give their children or friends greater priority or preference than their husbands. Bitterness could even result from no fault of the wife but simply from a husband who views himself as superior to his wife and her as one who is beneath him. A husband is not to treat his wife as an object or as an inferior person. It's true: "Wherever bitterness is, there love is wanting. And where love is wanting in the married life, there is hell upon earth."[60]

In addition to these commands given to husbands and wives, Paul also gives a command to the children. We turn now from the responsibility of the husband toward the wife to the responsibility of the children toward their parents, in verse 20.

The Responsibility of the Children to the Parents

Colossians 3:20

> Children, obey your parents in all things, for this is well pleasing to the Lord. (Colossians 3:20)

Simply put, the responsibility of children is to *obey your parents*. The word *obey* comes from two Greek words which mean listen and under. Together, they mean that children are to listen under their

---

60 Adam Clarke. *Adam Clarke Commentary. Biblesoft, 2006.*

parents. Obedience begins with listening. Children cannot obey their parents if they do not listen to what their parents are asking them to do. In fact, several times in the book of Proverbs, Solomon wrote, "Listen, my son." Some of us have failed to train our children to listen to our instructions and that is the reason they do not obey. I had a child who would just "forget," and when they did so, they would be disciplined because they had not listened. In order to train your children to listen, ask them to repeat back to you what you have just told them to do. They shouldn't challenge your commands; they should simply obey the spoken word. I've been at countless gatherings where children are present and where parents will give a command to their child, only to have that child go about his or her business completely ignoring the parent, or worse, tell their parents, "No!" And these are Christian gatherings I'm referring to! It breaks my heart for both the parents and the children. It's exasperating to the parent, and it is damning to the child. Now, you might be saying to yourself, "Whoa, Susan that's a bit extreme!" It's not, when you consider what Proverbs 23:13-14 warns us: "Do not withhold correction from a child, for if you beat him with a rod, he will not die. You shall beat him with a rod and deliver his soul from hell." If we do not demand obedience from our children, what makes us think they will obey the Lord? They will look at all commands, whether at home or church or school or work, as optional because they have not been taught from their inception to obey authority. Some believers are careful to follow the Lord and His Word in countless ways, but fail to follow this one command.

The tense in which this command is given in the Greek indicates that it is to be ongoing; that is, this command for children to obey their parents is one of continuous obedience. This would indicate that the child is to obey, even when he or she doesn't feel like it, just as a wife is to submit even when she doesn't feel like it. And the reality is that a child will often pattern their behavior after what they see modeled in their parents. If children do not see loving submission by their mother toward their father, why should we expect that those children should act any differently toward their parents? In fact, I was in a home once where I saw this so clearly displayed by a daughter who was disobedient and disrespectful to her father. When she was confronted about her behavior, she responded, "Why not? Mommy does it." It was an awful indictment on that family!

We must remind our children that disobedience is intended to be severely punished, according to the Word of God. Deuteronomy 21:18-21 says,

> If a man has a stubborn and rebellious son who will not obey the voice of his father or the voice of his mother, and who, when they have chastened him, will not heed them, then his father and his mother shall take hold of him and bring him out to the elders of his city, to the gate of his city. And they shall say to the elders of his city, "This son of ours is stubborn and rebellious; he will not obey our voice; he is a glutton and a drunkard." Then all the men of his city shall stone him to death with stones; so you shall put away the evil from among you, and all Israel shall hear and fear.

When my children were growing up, I often reminded them of this passage because I wanted them to know how seriously God took their disobedience to me as their mother.

Now, ladies, when we train our children to obey, it does not mean we scream and yell at our kids 15 times and then swat them. Nor does it mean we give them time out. There should be punishment resulting from disobedience. If our heavenly Father loves us enough to discipline us, should we not love our own children enough to discipline them? Consider Hebrews 12:7-11:

> If you endure chastening, God deals with you as with sons; for what son is there whom a father does not chasten? But if you are without chastening, of which all have become partakers, then you are illegitimate and not sons. Furthermore, we have had human fathers who corrected us, and we paid them respect. Shall we not much more readily be in subjection to the Father of spirits and live? For they indeed for a few days chastened us as seemed best to them, but He for our profit, that we may be partakers of His holiness. Now no chastening seems to be joyful for the present, but painful; nevertheless, afterward it yields the

peaceable fruit of righteousness to those who have been trained by it.

If you and I do not discipline our children, it is really a sign that we do not love them. God loves us, and because He does, He disciplines us when we get out of line. It is painful, to be sure, but it ultimately yields righteousness, in the same way that a spanking is painful in the moment but eventually yields right behavior in a child. I must say I am concerned that parents in our age seem afraid to tell a child no and seem more interested in being a friend to their child than being a parent to their child. "Waves of lawlessness sweep over the world because children are not taught to obey."[61]

Now, I do believe that there is one exception to this command, and it would be the same as that given to the wife regarding the command to submit to her husband: If a parent were to ask a child to sin, I would not counsel that child to sin against the Lord by doing what his or her parent is asking them to do. Jesus makes clear in Luke 12:51-53 that some children will be forced to demonstrate greater loyalty to Christ than to their parents because of their choice to live righteously. He says, "Do you suppose that I came to give peace on earth? I tell you, not at all, but rather division. For from now on, five in one house will be divided: three against two, and two against three. Father will be divided against son and son against father, mother against daughter and daughter against mother, mother-in-law against her daughter-in-law and daughter-in-law against her mother-in-law." And in Luke 14:26, He says, "If anyone comes to Me and does not hate his father and mother, wife and children, brothers and sisters, yes, and his own life also, he cannot be My disciple." Understandably, a young child may not recognize that she has been asked to sin, but an older child might.

The motivation behind this command for children to obey their parents is simply this: their obedience *is well pleasing to the Lord*. The term *well pleasing* means it is acceptable and fully agreeable to the Lord. In chapter 1, verse 10, Paul prayed for the Colossians to

---

61 A.T. Robertson. *Robertson's Word Pictures in the New Testament. Biblesoft, 2006.*

walk worthy of the Lord with a view to pleasing Him; certainly, the obedience a child demonstrates toward his or her parents would be one way that Paul's prayer would be answered. We should remind ourselves and our children that this command comes with a promise. Exodus 20:12 commands, "Honor your father and your mother," and then gives this promised result: "that your days may be long upon the land which the Lord your God is giving you." This is one of the Ten Commandments. In Ephesians 6:1-3, Paul says, "Children, obey your parents in the Lord, for this is right. 'Honor your father and mother,' which is the first commandment with promise: 'that it may be well with you, and you may live long on the earth.'" Such is the promised blessing for the child who obeys his parents: that it will go well with him.

There is one more command to look at that will fulfill the virtuous Christian family, and it is found in verse 21. It is the responsibility of the parents to the children.

The Responsibility of the Parents to the Children

Colossians 3:21

> Fathers, do not provoke your children, lest they become discouraged. (Colossians 3:21)

In order for us to understand this commandment, we must realize that in the New Testament times things were very different in the father-child relationship than we'd expect them to be today. A father could do anything he wanted with his children. He could sell them; he could turn them into slaves; he could even take their lives. But for the Christian father, Christ comes and changes cultural trappings. As Christians, we must remember that we are to always follow Christ over culture.

Perhaps when you first looked at this command for fathers to not provoke their children, you breathed a sigh of relief and thought that mothers are "off the hook," so to speak, and free to provoke their children all they want. But that would be far from what the text teaches! The Greek word for *fathers* here actually means parents. So really, both mother and father are commanded not to provoke their children. I will say that the father, as head of the home, certainly bears more responsibility in this. What does Paul mean by not provoking our children? The word *provoke* means to nag as a habit. Essentially, Paul is saying, "Stop nagging your kids!" This provoking is done by agitating them and by issuing unreasonable demands. Some translations might say, "don't provoke your children to anger," but the words "to anger" are not in the original text. It literally reads: "Parents provoke not your children, lest they be discouraged." However, in Ephesians 6:4, Paul states, "And you, fathers, do not provoke your children to wrath, but bring them up in the training and admonition of the Lord." Instead of nagging, we are to nurture, which means training by chastening, and we are to admonish, which means training by words. We are really our own worst enemy when we constantly nag and yell at our kids, as it is physically and spiritually exhausting.

Paul gives an important reason why we should not provoke children. That reason, he says, is so they won't *become discouraged.* To be *discouraged* is to be spiritless, disheartened, dismayed, without courage or spirit. When we continually nag our children, it causes them to lose heart and become spiritless. I've seen this in the faces of many children, and I'm sure you have as well. "A broken-down spirit is fatal to youth."[62] Parents should create an atmosphere of love and confidence that will make obedience easy and natural.

Allow me to share with you some ways that we, as parents, often provoke or discourage our children. Now, you might be thinking to yourself, "Why don't you give me some ways that my husband should be loving me, and then I can go home and share that list with him?!" Well, I'll leave that up to the Lord. Besides, I'm commanded in Titus 2 to teach *you* how to love *your* husbands and children, not to teach your husbands how to love you. So, what are some of the ways that we parents can, and often do, discourage our children?

---

62 *Jamieson, Fausset, and Brown Commentary. Biblesoft, 2006.*

1. *Overprotection*. If you want a discouraged child, never let them have any freedoms; always be suspicious and overbearing and you can guarantee yourself a discouraged, and perhaps even rebellious, child. This does not mean we should not have rules and guidelines—I think we all know Scripture teaches us that—but those rules should not become so ridiculous that a child cannot even go to the bathroom without you being notified of it.

2. *Showing favoritism*. Parents who compare their children to one another will often show favoritism toward one child above the other. A specific child might receive special favors or treats or special time with mom and dad; the other does not. Some parents even compare their children with their peers and that is not a good idea either. They will feel unloved and terribly frustrated, as if they can never measure up to your expectations. Genesis 25:28 tells us of the favoritism shown by Isaac and Rebekah; Isaac loved Esau, Rebekah loved Jacob, and the results were disastrous.

3. *By depreciating their worth*. We communicate to our children that they are not important to us by not listening to them and by not taking time for them. Please understand that I am not saying that our children should be the center of all our attention all the time. I've seen that done too, and the results are equally awful; such parents end up worshiping the family. I am not endorsing a child-centered home, but I am saying that our children should be given at least some of our time.

4. *Setting unrealistic goals*. Many parents set goals for their children that are unattainable, and nothing their child does is enough or good enough. Some parents try to make their children into what they as parents want those children to be instead of seeking after what God has planned for their children's lives. The results of these misguided efforts can be disastrous, to the point that some children commit suicide.

5. *Lack of affection*. We can say that we love our children, but if we fail to tell them so or if we fail to demonstrate our affection for them,

how will they know it? Some of you are thinking to yourselves, as one woman once told me, "I'm just not a huggy person." Well, your child very well may be a "huggy" person and may be crying out for your affection. All of us need to be touched and loved. They tell us that physical affection is imperative for the well-being of all human beings. John Newton, the great preacher and hymn-writer of *Amazing Grace*, once said, "I know that my father loved me, but he did not seem to wish me to see it." Older women are taught in Titus 2 to teach the young women to love their children. And the Greek word for love in that passage is phileo, which means to show tender affection.

6. *Not providing for their needs.* Children need clothes and food. They need privacy and a place to play. They need to be children. When we do not provide for our children's needs in these ways, we show a lack of respect and concern for their welfare. Perhaps also we need to consider that we reap what we sow. When we're old and potentially living in a nursing home, will we want to be treated by our children with the same level of respect we're showing them now?

7. *Lack of standards and boundaries for the child.* Simply leave your child to his or her desires, and disaster will set in. Proverbs 29:15 states that "The rod and rebuke give wisdom, but a child left to himself brings shame to his mother." Standards and boundaries give a child a sense of love and security. I am grateful for parents who believed in discipline and practiced it! Don't be afraid to have guidelines and rules for your children, and don't be afraid to correct them when they disobey the guidelines and rules you've set for them.

8. *Criticism.* Someone once wisely said, "If a child lives with criticism, he learns to condemn." He will not only condemn others but himself as well. He will distrust others. As moms, we should have a positive influence on our children and not always be criticizing them for their actions. There was a brief period of time in the life of one of my children when, quite frankly, this was a struggle for me. The lady who was discipling me at the time gave me the important and

transformative assignment of praising that child instead of always being critical—needless to say, it was a good exercise for me!

9. *Neglect.* We need to be involved in our children's lives. In the Scriptures, David and Absalom are good examples of this need. David was indifferent toward Absalom, and that indifference led to rebellion and civil war and, eventually, Absalom's death. Now, I don't mean that you must be enslaved to your child's every whim. Some people are so involved in their kid's lives, pushing them to participate in every activity, that it becomes ridiculous. In fact, I remember working on a cross-stitch project when I was a young mother, that said, "If a woman's place is in the home, why am I always in the car?" In my opinion, we do an injustice to our children and to our families when we tote them around to every kind of sporting event and social activity. When our children were growing up, we allowed one extra-curricular activity at a time, like soccer or gymnastics.

10. *Excessive discipline.* This is the parent who uses verbal or emotional or physical abuse in their efforts to discipline their children. Some parents will say things to their children that they would never say to anyone else. And many of us have heard them do so in the grocery store, restaurants, airports, and other places. Some parents spank their kids to the point of abuse. One man, in writing to his friend regarding how he perceived that friend to be too harsh in the treatment of his son, said this: "I was reminded by this example of excessive severity to write to you, as one friend to another, lest you on some occasion treat your son too harshly and strict. Remember that he is a boy, and that you were once a boy, and perform your duty as a father, always remembering that you are a human being and the father of a human being."[63]

11. *Hypocrisy.* Children become very frustrated and discouraged when we set standards for them that we are unwilling to live out ourselves. We tell our children not to lie, and then they hear us

---

63 Charles Talbert, *Paideia Commentaries on the New Testament: Ephesians and Colossians (Grand Rapids: Baker Academic, 2007), 233.*

exaggerate or tell a "white lie," both of which are lies. We stress the importance of being in God's house, and yet we allow the littlest thing to keep us from it. Double standards are very frustrating to children! In fact, I was talking to a young woman once who was extremely bitter toward one of her parents and much of it stemmed from the hypocrisy she saw in her own home growing up. God-words without God-actions is hypocrisy.

Summary

What is *the responsibility of the husband to the wife*? (v 19) To love her and to not be bitter toward her. What is *the responsibility of the children to the parents*? (v 20) To obey them. What is *the responsibility of the parents to the children*? (v 21) To not provoke them to anger.

This certainly is a beautiful picture Paul has painted for us in Colossians: husbands loving their wives, wives graciously submitting to their husbands, children obeying their parents, and parents not irritating their children. Sounds blissful, doesn't it? Is it a picture of your home this past week? Our homes should reflect Christ, and if they don't, there is a problem. Charles Spurgeon well said that what we are at home is what we are. I cannot admonish your husband or your children, but I can admonish you as a woman. If your family does not see Christ in you at home, then you should be concerned. If you are not doing your God-given part to be the wife and mother He has called you to be, then you should be concerned. If you are not graciously submitting to your husband, then you should be concerned. (My husband often said that a woman's submission to her husband is the biggest part of her sanctification.) If you are not disciplining your children as God commands, you should be concerned. If you are provoking and discouraging your children, you should be concerned.

As we close out this lesson, I would like for us to pray a prayer that is actually a hymn about the Christian home. May this be the desire of all of our hearts:

O give us homes built firm upon the Saviour,
Where Christ is Head, and Counsellor and Guide;
Where ev'ry child is taught His love and favor
And gives his heart to Christ, the crucified:
How sweet to know that tho' his footsteps waver
His faithful Lord is walking by his side!

O give us homes with godly fathers, mothers,
Who always place their hope and trust in Him;
Whose tender patience turmoil never bothers,
Whose calm and courage trouble cannot dim;
A home where each finds joy in serving others,
And love still shines, tho' days be dark and grim.

O give us homes where Christ is Lord and Master,
The Bible read, the precious hymns still sung;
Where prayer comes first in peace or in disaster,
And praise is natural speech to ev'ry tongue;
Where mountains move before a faith that's vaster,
And Christ sufficient is for old and young.

O Lord, our God, our homes are Thine forever!
We trust to Thee their problems, toil, and care;
Their bonds of love no enemy can sever
If Thou art always Lord and Master there:
Be Thou the center of our least endeavor:
Be Thou our Guest, our hearts and homes to share.[64]

---

64 Barbara B. Hart, 1965.

Questions to Consider

Colossians 3:19-21

Virtuous Living in the Home

1. (a) Read Ephesians 5:25-33; Colossians 3:18-19; and 1 Peter 3:7. In these verses, how are husbands commanded to love their wives? (b) What do these verses tell you about why husbands are to love their wives?

2. Memorize Colossians 3:21.

3. (a) Read Luke 2:41-52. In this passage, who was subject to his parents? (b) How could you use this passage to teach a child the importance of obeying his or her parents?

4. (a) According to the following Proverbs, why is it essential that children be obedient to their parents? Proverbs 1:8-9; 4:1-4; 6:20-23; 22:15; 23:13-14; 23:24; 29:15; 30:17.

5. (a) What was the Lord's attitude toward children? See Matthew 19:13-15; Mark 10:13-16; and Luke 18:15-17. (b) What did Jesus say would happen to one who offends a child, according to Matthew 18:1-6? (c) How is it possible to have Christ's attitude toward children and also discipline them as His Word commands?

6. (a) When you read the commands in Colossians 3:18-21, what families or individuals in Scripture come to mind as good role models for us to follow? (Example: Hosea's love for his adulterous wife, in Hosea 3:1-3.) (b) What examples come to mind as bad role models? (Example: Absalom's rebellion against his father David, in 2 Samuel 15.) (c) What can you learn from these examples?

7. (a) Why do you think husbands are commanded to not be bitter (KJV) toward their wives? (b) What are some ways wives provoke their husbands?

277

8. (a) How have you trained or did you train your children to obey you? (b) Share some things you have learned about obedience and discipline that could be of help to others.

9. Has God spoken to you through this lesson? How can we pray for you? Write your prayer request down to share with others.

Chapter 19

Working as Unto the Lord!

Colossians 3:22-4:1

The principal cause of boredom is the hatred of work. People are trained from childhood to hate it. Parents often feel guilty about making children do anything but the merest gestures toward work. Perhaps the children are required to make their beds and, in a feeble and half-hearted fashion, tidy up their rooms once a month or so. But take full responsibility to clear the table, load the dishwasher, scrub the pots, wipe the counters? ... Is work a necessary evil, even a curse? A Christian who spent many years in Soviet work camps, learning to know work at its most brutal, its most degrading and dehumanizing, testified that he took pride in it, did the best he could, worked to the limit of strength each day. Why? Because he saw it as a gift from God, coming to him from the hand of God, the very will of God for him.[65]

In essence, the words of Elisabeth Elliot above are an echo of Paul's words to the slaves in the church at Colossae. He says:

Colossians 3:22-4:1

Bondservants, obey in all things your masters according to the flesh, not with eyeservice, as men-pleasers, but in sincerity of heart, fearing God. [23]And whatever you do, do it heartily, as to the Lord and not to men, [24]knowing that from the Lord you will receive the reward of the inheritance; for you serve the Lord Christ. [25]But he who does wrong will be repaid for what he has done, and there is no partiality. 4:1Masters, give your bondservants what is just and fair, knowing that you also have a Master in heaven.

In our last lesson, we saw that the responsibility of the husband to the wife is to love her and not be bitter toward her. We saw that the

---

65 Elisabeth Elliot, *Keep a Quiet Heart* (Ann Arbor: Servant Publications, 1995), 100-*101.*

responsibility of the children to the parents is to obey them. And we saw that the responsibility of the parents to their children is to not provoke their children lest they become discouraged. In this lesson, we'll look at two more household relationships and consider their application for us today:

The Responsibility of the Servant to the Master (3:22-25)
The Responsibility of the Master to the Servant (4:1)

In the Questions to Consider, you are asked to consider why so much more space was given to the relationship between slaves and masters in comparison to the space given to family relationships. Wherever you find in Scripture that a good deal of space is devoted to a particular subject, it means that subject is important. One possible reason for Paul inserting these admonitions here in this letter concerns a man named Onesimus, who was a slave at the time of Paul's writing and who was coming along with Tychicus to Colossae to deliver this letter. In Colossians 4:7-9, Paul writes, "Tychicus, a beloved brother, faithful minister, and fellow servant in the Lord, will tell you all the news about me. I am sending him to you for this very purpose, that he may know your circumstances and comfort your hearts, with Onesimus, a faithful and beloved brother, who is one of you. They will make known to you all things which are happening here." The Epistles to the Colossians and Philemon were written at the same time by the apostle Paul while he was in prison in AD 60. In his epistle to Philemon, Paul writes about returning Onesimus, the slave, to his master Philemon to be received by him as a Christian brother. Onesimus had wronged Philemon by robbing him. In fact, Onesimus' name means profitable, an irony given that he had been unprofitable to his master by robbing him and then running away from him. Onesimus had fled from his master to Rome where he met the apostle Paul. But, as we would expect, Paul had witnessed to Onesimus, with the delightful result that Onesimus had become a Christian. In his letter to Philemon, Paul asks that Onesimus be received and not rejected. Onesimus had likely become something of a spiritual son to Paul, and so Paul urges Philemon to treat Onesimus with kindness and forgiveness. Philemon, verses 15-19, says:

> For perhaps he departed for a while for this purpose, that you
> might receive him forever, no longer as a slave but more than a
> slave—a beloved brother, especially to me but how much more
> to you, both in the flesh and in the Lord. If then you count me as
> a partner, receive him as you would me. But if he has wronged
> you or owes anything, put that on my account.

After Onesimus' conversion, he and Paul evidently developed a deep relationship and Paul wanted Onesimus to remain with him. This could not happen, though, until Onesimus had made things right with his master. So, Paul convinced Onesimus to return to Philemon and sent along a letter (the Epistle to Philemon) with Onesimus encouraging Philemon to treat Onesimus as a brother rather than a slave. In that letter, Paul implied that freeing Onesimus was Philemon's Christian responsibility. This seems to be the most probable reason why so much space is given in the Epistle to the Colossians to the master-slave relationship—Onesimus was heavily on Paul's mind. The responsibilities of Christian slaves and Christian masters were of great importance in the era in which Paul was writing, and, as we'll see, Christ changes even the slave and master relationship! With these things in mind, let's look more closely at what the responsibility of the slave is to his or her master.

The Responsibility of the Servant to the Master

Colossians 3:22-25

> Bondservants, obey in all things your masters according to the
> flesh, not with eyeservice, as men-pleasers, but in sincerity of
> heart, fearing God. (Colossians 3:22)

Before we begin explaining these verses, we must first understand something of the culture at the time Paul wrote to the Colossians. It has been estimated that a third of the population of the Roman Empire at this time was made up of slaves. Some have even estimated that is was up to half the population, which means there could have been up to 60 million slaves. Practically every kind of work imaginable was performed by slaves, even vocations like teaching and practicing medicine. The life of a slave wasn't necessarily a happy one. Most were considered morally incapable of choosing to do good, being controlled by their passions. Some masters would toss out old slaves to die, in the same way they would throw out broken tools. If a slave ran away, he was branded on the forehead with the letter F for "fugitive" and sometimes even put to death without a trial.

With this historical and cultural context in mind, Paul commands the slaves in the Colossian church to obey their masters. The word for *obey* in this verse is the same as in verse 20, where children are commanded to obey their parents. It means to listen under. The slave must listen to the command that is given by his master and then he must obey it. And notice who Paul says these slaves are to obey. He says they are to obey their *masters according to the flesh*, that is, the ones who are their earthly masters. A *master* is one who is in supreme authority over another.

Notice also that this obedience is to be *in all things*, just as it would be for children. Slaves are to obey the spoken word just as a child is to obey the spoken word. The only exception for the slave would be the same as for the child and the wife, and that concerns being asked to do something contrary to God's will. We see an example of this in Acts 5:29, where the apostles said to the religious leaders that they would obey God over man. We also have another example of this in Exodus 1:15-21, where the Hebrew midwives were commanded by the king of Egypt to kill all male babies born to the Hebrew women. There, it says the midwives feared God and did not do as the King of Egypt commanded them, and God blessed the midwives for their obedience. While most of us do not work in an environment of slavery, this principle regarding when we should and should not obey our employers does apply in our workplaces. Simply put, when your boss asks you do to something ungodly, you don't do it. It might be lying on a report you have to write; lying to customers; perhaps even out of town travel or lunches with members of the opposite sex, which could lead to sexual temptation. I knew a man who was forbidden to share the gospel at work. Now, to be clear, I don't think we should use work time to share the gospel; during a break or lunch hour, however, it should not be an issue, and certainly we must live out the gospel before our co-workers. But never should our loyalty to any earthly master cause us to sin against our Heavenly Master.

There are numerous other Scriptures that deal with slaves' responsibilities, and especially, their attitudes. First Timothy 6:1-2 tells slaves, "Let as many bondservants as are under the yoke count their own masters worthy of all honor, so that the name of God and His doctrine may not be blasphemed. And those who have believing masters, let them not despise them because they are brethren, but rather serve them because those who are benefited are believers and beloved. Teach and exhort these things." Titus 2:9-10 states, "Exhort bondservants to be obedient to their own masters, to be well pleasing in all things, not answering back, not pilfering, but showing all good fidelity, that they may adorn the doctrine of God our Savior in all things." Even Peter, who writes to slaves who were living in terrible times, says in 1 Peter 2:18-19, "Servants, be submissive to your masters with all fear, not only to the good and gentle, but also to the harsh. For this is commendable, if because of conscience toward God one endures grief, suffering wrongfully."

What does Paul say here in Colossians regarding the required attitude of servants as they obey? He says they are to do their work *not with eyeservice, as men-pleasers*. The word *eyeservice* means doing your work only when the boss is looking. One man defines the meaning in this way; he says it is "service performed under the master's eye, service which is most zealous when the eye of the master or overseer is upon them."[66] This they do, Paul says, to be *men-pleasers*, which means to court men. This is seen in the one who sweeps the floor but brushes the dirt under the rug when the boss isn't looking, or in the person who takes a break and doesn't return to work until the boss returns. In the biblical world, slaves usually had but one motive for

---

66 W. Robertson, *The Expositors Greek New Testament (London: Hodder and Stoughton, 1903)*, 542.

working and that was to avoid punishment. Because of that, they would only work hard when the master was watching. But Paul is saying that for the Christian slave this should not be the case; their motivation for working should be that their Heavenly Master's eye is upon them.

This principle applies equally to those of us who are under the authority of an employer. Perhaps your motive, if you're employed outside the home, is to earn a raise or to receive the praise of men. Perhaps your motive, if you work as a homemaker, is to receive the praise of your husband or to look better than the wives and mothers around you. But Paul says this should not be! Our motive should be to please the Lord. Galatians 1:10 states, "For do I now persuade men, or God? Or do I seek to please men? For if I still pleased men, I would not be a bondservant of Christ." And in 1 Thessalonians 2:4, Paul says, "But as we have been approved by God to be entrusted with the gospel, even so we speak, not as pleasing men, but God who tests our hearts."

Slaves are not to obey for the purpose of being men-pleasers, but they are to obey *in sincerity of heart, fearing God.* The idea behind the phrase *sincerity of heart* is that of an undivided mind, a singleness of heart. In it, there is no self-seeking, like wanting to receive a promotion or even a pat on the back; one's only motive for working should be fear and reverence for God. The servant Paul speaks of here should be like the one Jesus mentions in Luke 17:10, who simply did what he ought to have done. Such a servant would obey with a sincere heart whether the work is pleasant or unpleasant, dull or challenging, menial or interesting. Such obedience to one's master should not only be when the master is looking but also when they're not looking. Ultimately, obedience to one's master should be performed out of reverence for the Lord. Pagan slaves served their masters because they were bound by fear; Christian slaves were to serve their masters because they feared God! Now, there's no promise here, as some of you can attest, that simply trying to live up to this verse as an employee will mean that all will go well for you. But that shouldn't matter for a slave—or for an employee—who is trying to please the Heavenly Master. As believers, our work ethic ought to be the best; we should have the best attitudes, we should be the most dependable, and have the utmost integrity. No matter what it is we are called to do as employees, as Paul now tells us, it should be as unto the Lord.

> And whatever you do, do it heartily, as to the Lord and not to men (Colossians 3:23)

This is very similar to what we saw in 3:17. The word *heartily* comes from two Greek words which together mean from the heart and soul and carry the idea of completion, along with the idea of doing that work with a good disposition. In other words, put your whole heart and soul into it; work hard at it. To work heartily involves both the right mental attitude and the putting of one's whole physical body into that work. And, lest we forget, Paul makes it clear again that this work is *to the Lord and not to men.* As one commentator put it, "Throw your whole soul into the work as if your one employer were the Lord."[67] Why are we to do things unto the Lord, and not unto men? Paul answers that question in verse 24.

> knowing that from the Lord you will receive the reward of the inheritance; for you serve the Lord Christ. (Colossians 3:24)

The word *knowing* points us to the motive for working heartily. It means in the Greek, "because you have come to know." Paul says we do our work heartily because we have come to know that because we are Christians we are working for the Lord and not for man. No matter what the job may be, the Christian slave has come to know that, ultimately, his work is for the Lord. Such knowledge would have been a special encouragement to Christian slaves because slaves didn't receive any kind of earthly inheritance. As Christians, though, they would be privileged to receive an eternal inheritance, and that *reward of the inheritance* would be heaven to come! Slaves had nothing on earth that they could call their own unless their masters chose to set them free, but in heaven they had a portion of

---

67 R.C.H. Lenski, *Commentary on the New Testament: Colossians, 1-2 Thessalonians, 1-2 Timothy, Titus, Philemon* (Peabody: Hendrickson Publishers, 1998), 184.

the lot that we saw back in Paul's prayer in Colossians 1:12-14. In Roman society, many slaves were set free if their masters willed, because of the good they had done and the love they had shown their masters. But Paul is saying here, "Don't be good slaves because you think you might be set free someday for your good work; rather, be good slaves because you have come to know that you will receive a reward from the Lord!" Ladies, this should be a sobering reminder to all of us as we do our daily tasks, that there is coming a time when we will all stand before the judgment seat of Christ and receive rewards for the things that we have done, whether they be good or bad. Paul says in 2 Corinthians 5:10, "For we must all appear before the judgment seat of Christ, that each one may receive the things done in the body, according to what he has done, whether good or bad." We must keep in mind that the rewards we receive will be according to the Lord's decision and not according to the whims of any man or woman.

Paul goes on to remind the slaves of something we all need to be reminded of, that we *serve the Lord Christ*. My friend, we are here to *serve*, and we are servants of *the Lord*. Even our Lord says in Matthew 20:28, "the Son of man came not to be ministered unto, but to minister, and to give his life a ransom for many." He also said in John 5:30, "I can of Myself do nothing. As I hear, I judge; and My judgment is righteous, because I do not seek My own will but the will of the Father who sent Me." The Christian employee must remember, no matter what work they are doing, that they serve the Lord, and that the work they do is a privilege and an honor. What an encouragement it would have been to slaves who were undergoing harsh treatment to remember that as children of the Lord they were serving the Lord and from Him they would one day receive an eternal reward that would far outweigh any difficulties they were currently enduring. I would encourage you to examine your own work and be willing to ask yourself why you do the things you do. Is it for the Lord, for others, or for your own glory?

In verse 25, Paul goes on to soberly remind the slaves in Colossae of a truth that we too need to be reminded of. He says,

> But he who does wrong will be repaid for what he has done, and
> there is no partiality. (Colossians 3:25)

Paul is clear that anyone who *does wrong*, both slave and master, *will be repaid for what he has done*. It has been suggested that there may have been unrest among the slaves at Colossae and that is why this admonition is included here. Paul reminds the slaves if you do wrong, you will receive for the wrong which you have done. But also remember that masters will also. This is both an encouragement and a sobering reminder. Again, remember 2 Corinthians 5:10, "For we must all appear before the judgment seat of Christ, that each one may receive the things done in the body, according to what he has done, whether good or bad."

When Paul tells the believers at Colossae that they will be *repaid* for the wrong they have done, he is saying that they will receive back for whatever wrong they have done. Just as we will receive rewards for the good we have done, we will also receive loss of rewards for the bad we have done. So many employees look forward to payday, but as believers we would be wise to remember there will be a "payday" for all of us on judgment day, whether we are employees or employers. We all then will receive just rewards for what is due us. Paul reminds us in Galatians 6:7, "Do not be deceived, God is not mocked; for whatever a man sows, that he will also reap."

Paul reminds the slaves as he ends his admonition to them, that with God *there is no partiality*, or no "respect of persons," as your translation might say. The world *respect* comes from the word face. In other words, God doesn't judge us based on our outward appearance; He shows no partiality. Paul clearly wrote of this in Colossians 3:11, "Where there is neither Greek nor Jew, circumcised nor uncircumcised, barbarian, Scythian, slave nor free, but Christ is all and in all." Christ is not a respecter of persons when it comes to one's salvation—He chooses from all races and all stations in life— nor does He show partiality when it comes to judgment. It doesn't matter what your face looks like, because physical appearance makes no difference to God. Some people think they can get away with things because of their good looks, but with God that is impossible. He makes His decisions based not on one's facial features but on the inner motives of the heart. In 1 Samuel 16, when God told Samuel that one of Jesse's sons was going to be king, we read that Samuel looked on Eliab, one of the sons and thought to himself, "Surely, *this* is the one." "But the Lord said to Samuel, 'Do not look at his appearance or at his physical stature, because I have refused him. For the Lord does not see as man sees; for man looks at the outward appearance, but the Lord looks at the heart'" (1 Samuel 16:7). We must keep in mind that it will not matter on the Day of Judgment who we are; all people, all races, all religious leaders (even your favorite preacher) will receive for the wrong they have done. Paul writes in 1 Corinthians 3:12-15:

> Now if anyone builds on this foundation with gold, silver, precious stones, wood, hay, straw, each one's work will become clear; for the Day will declare it, because it will be revealed by fire; and the fire will test each one's work, of what sort it is. If anyone's work which he has built on it endures, he will receive a reward. If anyone's work is burned, he will suffer loss; but he himself will be saved, yet so as through fire.

What is the responsibility of the slave to the master? The slave's responsibility is to obey in all things, not just when his or her master is watching, knowing that the Lord is always watching. The slave is to do her work as unto the Lord and not unto men, knowing that it is God who will one day reward her work, whether it is good or whether it is bad.

Before we close out this lesson, there is an admonition given to another classification of people, and that is to masters. They are not off the hook just because they are in a position of authority. This is certainly an unfortunate chapter division, because Paul is still writing about slave and master relationships. In my opinion, those who inserted the verse and chapter divisions would have been wise to begin chapter four with verse 2. Nevertheless, let's consider the responsibility of the master to the servant in verse 1 of chapter 4.

The Responsibility of the Master to the Servant

Colossians 4:1

Masters, give your bondservants what is just and fair, knowing
that you also have a Master in heaven. (Colossians 4:1)

The master or employer who is a Christian should hold to a
different set of work ethics than the employer who is not. Yet, if
all employers followed this command, there would certainly be
fewer employee strikes. What servant would have trouble obeying
a master like that? This is similar to the principle we brought out
when we were studying the husband-wife relationship. What wife
would have trouble submitting to a husband who loved her the way
Christ loved the church? Masters must remember that they have a
Master too! Just as servants are accountable to a master, so masters
are accountable to God. If they truly understood this, they would not
treat their slaves unjustly.

Paul writes to the masters: *give your bondservants what is just and
fair*. The word *give* means to offer from one's own resources or by
one's own power. Masters are to offer what is *just*, which means that
which is right, and they are to offer what is *fair*, which means equal
or what is alike in condition or proportion. The master should give
to the servant from his own resources that which the servant has
earned and what is fair. The condition of slaves among the Greeks
and Romans was difficult indeed, especially because they could not
appeal in a court of law; they could not expect justice. But Paul
warns the masters that they should act toward their slaves according
to both justice and fairness because God their Master has required
this of them, and He will be the final judge. What would justice and
fairness require? It would require that slaves be given proper food
and clothing, that they be given proper rest and not be overworked.
This is certainly a principle that all masters throughout all ages
should heed; they should not treat their servants as if God has made
them inferior.

Paul gives to the masters a motivator for obeying this command; he says they should know that they also, just like their slaves, *have a Master in heaven*. Is He not just? Is He not equal? We know that He is; we have already seen in Colossians 3:25 that He is not partial in judgment. Those who do wrong will receive for the wrong which they have done, and that will include masters who have been harsh to their servants. James has a very sober warning for those who refuse to do what is right to those they employ. Consider his words in James 5:1-6,

> Come now, you rich, weep and howl for your miseries that are coming upon you! Your riches are corrupted, and your garments are moth-eaten. Your gold and silver are corroded, and their corrosion will be a witness against you and will eat your flesh like fire. You have heaped up treasure in the last days. Indeed the wages of the laborers who mowed your fields, which you kept back by fraud, cry out; and the cries of the reapers have reached the ears of the Lord of Sabaoth. You have lived on the earth in pleasure and luxury; you have fattened your hearts as in a day of slaughter. You have condemned, you have murdered the just; he does not resist you.

What is the responsibility of masters to their servants? They are to give what is right and just to their servants. Their motive in obeying this command is to be the knowledge that they have a Master who is just and right and will reward or punish according to their obedience.

Summary

I am well aware that in our country we do not have institutional slavery, though some of you might feel like you are a slave. Some of you might feel as if you are a slave to your children; a slave to your husband; a slave to the dishes; a slave to the laundry; a slave to housework; a slave to errands; a slave to your phone; a slave to your pet; or perhaps a slave to something I haven't mentioned. Whatever your work might be, do you do it as unto the Lord? Is your attitude pleasing to Him? Do you do your work as if He were standing right there with you? Or do you do your work half-heartedly? Are you lazy in your housework? Are you less than diligent in your parenting? Do you have ever before your mind that you will receive a reward or loss of reward for those things you have done in the body, whether good or bad?

For those of you who are employers—or even moms—do you treat those who are under your authority with harshness, expecting things out of them that you would not expect of yourself? Do those under you have proper food, clothing, rest, and pay (if you are an employer)? Do you have before your mind's eye that you will give an account one day before your heavenly Master for how you have treated those who are under your authority? Elisabeth Elliot closes her thoughts on work with this:

> Wouldn't it make an astounding difference, not only in the quality of work we do (in office, schoolroom, factory, kitchen, or backyard), but also in our satisfaction, even our joy, if we recognized God's gracious gift in every single task, from making a bed or bathing a baby to drawing a blueprint or selling a computer? If our children saw us doing "heartily as unto the Lord" all the work we do they would learn true happiness. Instead of feeling that they must be allowed to do what they like, they would learn to like what they do.[68]

---

68 Elisabeth Elliot, *Keep a Quiet Heart (Ann Arbor: Servant Publications, 1995)*, 100-101.

Questions to Consider
Colossians 3:22-4:1
Working as Unto the Lord!

1. (a) Read Colossians 3:22 – 4:1 along with Ephesians 6:5-9. What admonitions does Paul give that are the same in both of these passages? (b) What differences do you notice?

2. Memorize Colossians 3:23.

3. (a) In looking at the work of the virtuous woman in Proverbs 31:10-31, would you say she did her work as unto the Lord or unto men? (b) What were her attitudes in her work? (c) In what ways was she diligent? (d) How does this relate to what Paul says in Colossians 3:22-4:1?

4. (a) Make two columns on the back of your paper, one marked "Diligent," the other marked "Lazy." (b) Read the following Proverbs and contrast the diligent with the lazy. Proverbs 10:4-5; 12:24; 12:27; 13:4; 15:19; 18:9; 19:24; 20:4; 21:25-26; 22:13; 22:29; 24:30-34; 26:13-16; and 27:23-27. (c) Write a summary sentence of what you have learned. (d) According to what Paul and Peter say in Colossians 3:22-25; 1 Timothy 6:1-2; Titus 2:9-10; and 1 Peter 2:18-19, what should be the attitudes of those who work?

5. (a) In the parable mentioned in Matthew 25:14-30, which servants did their work as unto the Lord and which servants did not? (b) What was the result for each? (c) How does this parable fit with what Paul is saying in Colossians 3:22 – 4:1?

6. Why do you think Paul devotes the amount of space he does in this letter (number of verses in his letter to the Colossians) to the role of slaves and masters in comparison to the amount of space he devotes to other family relationships? For possible answers, read Colossians 4:7-9 and the book of Philemon.

7. (a) When you work, whatever it may be, do you do it as unto the Lord? (b) Is your work done with your whole heart and with thoroughness and completeness? (c) How are you training your children to do work with a right attitude?

8. (a) How could you use the verses you have studied in Colossians to encourage someone who is struggling in their job (husband, friend, child, etc.)? (b) Do you think when one is not enjoying their work that they should quit? Why or why not?

9. What area of work is hard for you? Attitude? The actual work? Completion? Thoroughness? Etc? Please write your need in the form of a prayer request.

Chapter 20

Three Essentials in Evangelism

Colossians 4:2-6

Recent statistics indicate that only 2% of churchgoers actively share their faith with others. That is a sad indictment on the Christian world! Thankfully, there are faithful believers who have endeavored to see that number grow, and who have poured their efforts into equipping the saints in evangelism. Among them, D. James Kennedy, who founded the organization *Evangelism Explosion*, which trains men and women to actively share their faith. Kirk Cameron, Ray Comfort, and Todd Friel developed a video series entitled *Way of the Master*, which equips and motivates Christians to start evangelizing. Grace Community Church in Sun Valley, California created the *Discipleship Evangelism* program to do the same. In addition to these programs, a number of individuals have written books in an effort to motivate Christians to share the gospel. One of my favorites is *Tell the Truth*, by Will Metzger. E. K. Bailey, pastor of a church in Dallas, said he wanted to see our entire nation evangelized by the turn of the millennium and encouraged numerous pastors to join him in prayer evangelism. His desire was for Christ to be shared with every person in our nation by the year 2000. Well, the year 2000 has come and gone and still our world is very lost; many have never heard the gospel.

Did you know that our Lord has this same burden? His last words before leaving Earth to go to heaven were, "Go into all the world and preach the gospel to every creature" (Mark 16:15). And we know from 2 Peter 3:9 that "The Lord is not slack concerning His promise, as some count slackness, but is longsuffering toward us, not willing that any should perish but that all should come to repentance." Yet, the fact remains that even with all the programs and all the helps available, most professing believers are not doing their part to share the gospel. In his book, *Tell the Truth*, Will Metzger writes that many of us never witness because we never start. We simply never open our mouths. We do not take the initiative to begin a conversation that will lead toward spiritual things. Common excuses are: "I don't have time," "It's the pastor's job to share the gospel," "I'm afraid of what others will think of me," "I don't know how to share the gospel," "I might lose my job," "my family will reject me," "God is sovereign in salvation, so why share the gospel?" But whatever excuses we might come up with, it is hard to get away from the command of the Great Commission. We are to pray, we are to go, and we are to speak. And it is these three responsibilities that we will clearly see in this lesson from Colossians. Let's read what Paul wrote in Colossians 4:2-6.

Colossians 4:2-6

Continue earnestly in prayer, being vigilant in it with thanksgiving; ³meanwhile praying also for us, that God would open to us a door for the word, to speak the mystery of Christ, for which I am also in chains, ⁴that I may make it manifest, as I ought to speak. ⁵Walk in wisdom toward those who are outside, redeeming the time. ⁶Let your speech always be with grace, seasoned with salt, that you may know how you ought to answer each one.

In this lesson, we will see how Paul shifts his focus to how all classes of people, slaves and masters, wives and husbands, children and parents, are to pray for the lost, reach the lost, and speak to the lost. These responsibilities will form the basis for this lesson's outline:

How to Pray for the Lost (vv 2-4)
How to Reach the Lost (v 5)
How to Speak to the Lost (v 6)

How to Pray for the Lost

Colossians 4:2-4

Continue earnestly in prayer, being vigilant in it with thanksgiving (Colossians 4:2)

Paul begins by admonishing his readers to *continue earnestly in prayer*. The idea is that we are to be constantly diligent in prayer. We should cling ever so close to prayer, and we should persevere in it. Paul repeats this idea in 1 Thessalonians 5:17, where he says that we are to "pray without ceasing." In Romans 12:12, he writes that we are to be "continuing steadfastly in prayer." And in Ephesians 6:18, he puts it this way: "praying always with all prayer and supplication in the Spirit, being watchful to this end with all perseverance and supplication for all the saints." We should be in a constant attitude of prayer. In fact, the way this admonition is worded indicates that Paul is assuming his readers are already praying. And this admonition is for all the classifications of people he has just addressed in the previous verses; without prayer, neither wives, nor husbands, children, parents, servants, or masters could fulfil the duties which God requires of them.

This praying, Paul says, is to be done with *vigilance*. Essentially, he is saying that we must stay awake and alert when we pray. We are never to neglect it or grow careless in it. These requirements also include the idea of staying alert for specific needs for ourselves and others. I often hear women say that they have a difficult time staying alert in prayer; thankfully, there are many things we can do to alleviate this difficulty. We can pray out loud; we can use Scripture to pray; we can avoid being rote in our prayers by praying for a variety of people and needs; we can pray different requests each time we pray for the needs of a specific person; we can sing our prayers; we can use the written prayers of others. But we cannot avoid prayer because prayer is to our spiritual life what breathing is to our physical life—without it we will die! Matthew 26 records for us the sad account of Jesus taking three of his closest friends, Peter, James, and John, with Him to pray prior to His crucifixion. They fell asleep and failed to stay awake with Him during this dark hour. After praying once, He found them sleeping and said to them in verses 40-41, "What! Could you not watch with Me one hour? Watch and pray, lest you enter into temptation. The spirit indeed is willing, but the flesh is weak." But, after praying two more times, He found them sleeping yet again. Matthew records for us Jesus' response, in verses 45-46: "Then He came to His disciples and said to them, 'Are you still sleeping and resting? Behold, the hour is at hand, and the Son of Man is being betrayed into the hands of sinners. Rise, let us be going. See, My betrayer is at hand.'" Peter must have often remembered how he failed his Lord in His final hours. Perhaps it was the lesson learned in that failure which prompted Peter to write in 1 Peter 4:7, "But the end of all things is at hand; therefore be serious and watchful in your prayers."

There is an attitude which ought to accompany our praying and watching, and that attitude is *thanksgiving*. In other words, we are to express gratitude to the Lord in our prayers. Paul mentions this same principle in Philippians 4:6-7: "Be anxious for nothing, but in everything by prayer and supplication, with thanksgiving, let your requests be made known to God; and the peace of God, which surpasses all understanding, will guard your hearts and minds through Christ Jesus." As we continue diligently in prayer, there should be an attitude of thanksgiving—even if God doesn't answer our prayers to our liking! Given the context here, Paul is conveying the idea that as we pray and watch for opportunities to share with the lost, we are to do so with an attitude of gratitude for having been given the opportunity to share. To think that God would use any of us to proclaim His gospel is amazing!

After Paul gives this admonition to pray, he then gives a prayer request for himself and Timothy, and it pertains to the gospel and sharing with those who are lost. How do we pray for the lost? Listen to what Paul says:

> meanwhile praying also for us, that God would open to us a door for the word, to speak the mystery of Christ, for which I am also in chains (Colossians 4:3)

I find it very refreshing that the apostle Paul wasn't too prideful to ask for prayer. I've met some Christians who pretend that everything is always fine with them, and they don't need a thing. Oh, my friend, we need to be in prayer for one another—and so much more as the day approaches! We need to humble ourselves and confess our sins and admit our needs to God and to each other! Now, the prayer request Paul gives here is somewhat different than some of our prayer requests, just as his prayer for the church at Colossae earlier in the letter was different than some of our prayers for our churches. Instead of asking the Colossians to pray that he would be released from the prison doors, Paul asks them to pray that a door would be opened to share the gospel. It's interesting that Paul asks *that God would open to us a door for the word*. It is God who opens and shuts doors of opportunities for us to share the gospel. Sometimes we open the door prematurely and abort the process, and sometimes we close the doors that God has opened. That is why we need to be in prayer continually about these things, heeding the Spirit's prompting. It appears from the way Paul words this prayer request that there were some obstacles standing in the way of this door being opened. Naturally, he'd want those obstacles removed, so he asks for a door of admission to be opened so that he would have that opportunity to preach the gospel. There are no hints of self or selfish motive in his prayer request. In fact, this isn't the only time Paul desired to share his faith while in prison; in his letter to the Philippians, he spoke of this same desire (see Philippians 1:12-18 and 4:22). And we know that God answered his prayer then, because he tells us that even some in Caesar's household had become followers of Christ. Paul describes this gospel as *the mystery of Christ*, a concept he also wrote of in Colossians 1:26-27 and 2:2. When we studied those verses, we learned that the term *mystery* refers to a truth which was once hidden but is now revealed. And it is this mystery which Paul longs to make known.

Before we go on, allow me to ask you a couple questions. Do you ever have a burden for someone's soul, like a family member or friend? Of course, you do! When you have that burden for them, do you ask God to open a door of opportunity to share with them and then take it when He opens it? Too many times, I've seen God open a door for me, but then I've shut it by my lack of boldness. I've also failed to ask God to open doors of opportunity when I knew I was going to be around lost people. We can learn much from the apostle Paul; he was so passionate and so bold about the gospel that he ended up in prison for it. He makes that clear when he says *for which I am also in chains*. He was closely watched and guarded by a Roman guard, handcuffed to a Roman soldier 24 hours a day. Even as he's writing this letter, he's in prison for sharing the gospel, and yet he's still concerned about getting the gospel out. Amazing! In 2 Timothy 2:8-10, he writes, "Remember that Jesus Christ, of the seed of David, was raised from the dead according to my gospel, for which I suffer trouble as an evildoer, even to the point of chains; but the word of God is not chained. Therefore I endure all things for the sake of the elect, that they also may obtain the salvation which is in Christ Jesus with eternal glory." Even though Paul was often chained for the gospel, the gospel itself was never chained. Ladies, this is a rebuke to our comfortable Christianity! We are often fearful of sharing the gospel because we fear being ridiculed, not being liked, or messing up in our sharing. But what if we faced imprisonment for sharing our faith? How many of us would wimp out then? And if we did land in prison for the gospel, would we have a burning in our soul to get the gospel out or just to get ourselves out? Paul had a burning in his soul to share his faith; do you and I? We should ask God to give us that burning desire to share with the lost. This is the great commission that Jesus left us in Matthew 28:18-20—and it is a command, not an option. Paul elaborates on his prayer request in verse 4.

> that I may make it manifest, as I ought to speak.
> (Colossians 4:4)

Paul says that he wants to make the gospel *manifest*, which means that he wants to make it known. He then uses an interesting phrase; he says *as I ought to speak*. Paul is asking his Colossian friends to pray not only for a door to be open for the gospel, but that he would present the gospel clearly. A good message presented in a bad way can do a lot of damage. And Paul knows that, so he asks for a clear message and a bold message. He was not ashamed of the gospel, as he wrote in Romans 1:16. He knew it was the power of God for salvation. In fact, in 1 Corinthians 9:16, he even writes, "woe is me if I do not preach the gospel." I fear our woe is if we don't get our family vacation this year, or the raise we're hoping for, or the special attention we want from our husbands. Oh, that we had this same passion and boldness and desire to share the gospel! We should know how to share our faith in a clear and precise way. How do we pray for the lost? We pray for God to open doors of opportunity, and we pray that we will present the gospel clearly. In verse 5, Paul turns from how to pray for the lost to how to reach the lost.

How to Reach the Lost

Colossians 4:5

> Walk in wisdom toward those who are outside, redeeming the time.

Paul tells us that if we want to win the lost with the gospel message, we must live out the gospel. To *walk in wisdom* means to order our behavior in a wise way. Walking in wisdom involves properly evaluating circumstances as well as making godly decisions. A wise person is one who knows how to regulate his relationships with God and others and with his circumstances. "Behave wisely towards outsiders, always bearing in mind that though few men read the sacred scrolls all men read you."[69] One of Paul's prayers for the church at Colossae was that they would walk worthy, and this admonition to walk in wisdom is certainly one way to walk worthy (see Colossians 1:10). He describes those without Christ as being *outside*. He's not talking about those who are outside his prison walls. Rather, he's referring to those who are without the gospel, who are estranged from the gospel. Paul speaks of the importance of walking in a worthy manner in 1 Thessalonians 4:12. There, he says, "That you may walk properly toward those who are outside, and that you may lack nothing." When writing about the qualifications of a deacon in 1 Timothy 3:7, Paul is clear that this is imperative for them. He writes, "Moreover he must have a good testimony among those who are outside, lest he fall into reproach and the snare of the devil." My friend, we must be careful about how we as believers

---

69 William Hendriksen, *New Testament Commentary: Exposition of Colossians and Philemon* (Grand Rapids: Baker Book House, 1964), 182.

conduct ourselves toward those who are outside, lest we blaspheme the name of God and ruin any chances we might have of effectively sharing the gospel with them. And we have a bigger challenge in our day because so many so-called "Christians" have already been a laughingstock to the unbelieving world. We need to reclaim our testimony by walking in wisdom.

Paul goes on to say that we also must be *redeeming the time* with the lost. This means that we must buy up any opportunity we have to rescue the lost, to rescue those who are perishing. We must rescue or recover our time; we must not waste the precious time God gives us. We must use it for important purposes like the gospel. Believers are to buy up time like determined bargain hunters. We've all seen those determined bargain hunters at garage sales—they're serious and intent! That's how we should be when we're around the lost; redeem that time! This was illustrated to me the very week I was writing this lesson, as I sat at lunch with several ladies, one of whom is a determined evangelist. She would not let that lunch go without endeavoring to share with our waitress. In fact, I don't think I've ever been out with her where she didn't try to buy up the time with a lost person. That is what Paul is saying: Be intent on redeeming the time. The *time* is the season or occasion God has given us. Time is precious and we shouldn't wasting it on the trivial drippings of this world while people are dying and going to hell. "Do not just sit there and wait for opportunity to fall into your lap but go after it. Yes, buy it!"70 Paul writes similar words in Ephesians 5:15-16: "See then that you walk circumspectly, not as fools but as wise, redeeming the time, because the days are evil."

Several years ago, I failed in buying up an opportunity, and I've not forgotten it. I was pumping gas in my car and had to go in for some reason, and the guy at the cash register said something like, "Looks like you're happy. What's the key?" In my mind, I was thinking that I really should get home and cook dinner for Doug. But what a copout! As if my husband would have been upset because I was 15 minutes late because I'd been sharing the gospel! I missed that open

---

70 Ibid, 183.

door and sure didn't buy it up. Sadly, I've learned that those types of opportunities rarely recover themselves.

So, how are we to reach the lost? We are to reach them by conducting ourselves in wisdom, by buying up the opportunities we have with them. We have seen how we are to pray for the lost, how we are to reach the lost, and now Paul tells us how we are to speak to the lost, in verse 6.

How to Speak to the Lost

Colossians 4:6

> Let your speech always be with grace, seasoned with salt, that you may know how you ought to answer each one. (Colossians 4:6)

What does it mean that our *speech* should *always be with grace*? It means that our speech toward the unbeliever should always be gracious and joyful. I've often heard my husband use the word "winsome" to describe it. We should be winsome toward unbelievers. And not only should our speech be gracious, but it should also be seasoned with salt. The church at Colossae would have understand this well because not far from their city there was a salt lake. This phrase, *seasoned with salt*, is in the present tense in the Greek; it conveys the idea that our speech has been seasoned with salt and should continue to be seasoned with salt. *Seasoned* means to prepare with stimulating condiments, and *salt* enhances flavor. Our speech should be thought provoking and worthwhile and not a waste of time. It should be attractive and have spiritual charm if I may use that term. I have met some Christians and so have you who, quite frankly, if I were an unbeliever, I would not be attracted to because of their speech alone. Their tone of voice is far from gracious. Harshness, anger, sarcasm, and impatience are not becoming to a believer. Sour faces and negative speech are not attractive to a lost world. We must remember what our Lord said in Matthew 5:13: we are the salt of the earth. I'm afraid some of us have lost our saltiness when our speech is more like pepper than salt. Some examples of unsalted speech toward an unbeliever would be: "Are you saved?!" "Did you know you're going to hell?!" "Don't you know there's only one way to heaven?!" These are not salty approaches, my friend; they're more like a hot pepper approach. Instead of these, you could say things like, "I notice you seemed to be struggling with something; may I help?" Or "You know, my life has been given such meaning since I came to know Christ." Or "What is your religious background? Who do you believe Jesus is?"

Salt has a two-fold purpose. It gives flavor and it preserves from corruption. As we have said, as far as flavor goes, our speech should be joyful, even witty, for this is what salty speech meant in classical Greek. Rather than boring, it should be stimulating. It doesn't always have to be religious, but whatever the topic it should be properly seasoned. It should be witty, amusing, clever, and, yes, even humorous. As a preservative, our speech should preserve unbelievers from corruption. Ephesians 4:29 says, "Let no corrupt word proceed out of your mouth, but what is good for necessary edification, that it may impart grace to the hearers." One man has said, "Foolish remarks, ungracious, surly, cutting retorts, and saltless talk that is vapid and from which the hearer's mind turns away because it is not worth considering, never do the Christian cause any good." [71]

Why should our speech be seasoned with salt? So that we may know how you ought to answer to each one. *Each* person is to be answered appropriately to his question, whether his question is sincere or insincere, whether it's a dumb question or a smart question. Peter says something similar in 1 Peter 3:15: "But sanctify the Lord God in your hearts, and always be ready to give a defense to everyone who asks you a reason for the hope that is in you, with meekness and fear." My friend, we need to know the gospel and the Word of God so that we are ready when someone should ask us about our faith. What if Phillip had not known how to answer the Ethiopian eunuch in Acts 8? What if Phillip had said, "Sorry, gotta go home

71 R.C.H. Lenski, *Commentary on the New Testament: Colossians, 1-2 Thessalonians, 1-2 Timothy, Titus, and Philemon* (Peabody: Hendrickson Publishing Company, 1998), 194.

and look up the answer to your question"? It would have been a lost opportunity.

Summary

How do we pray for the lost? We pray that doors of opportunity would be opened and that we would present a clear message. *How do we reach the lost?* By conducting ourselves with wisdom and by buying up opportunities with the lost. *How do we speak to the lost?* We speak with gracious and seasoned words.

If you do not know how to share the gospel, I would encourage you to pursue those avenues I listed in the Questions to Consider. My friend, time is fleeting, and we must evangelize the lost while there is still time. In fact, there are six "musts" that we must do, according to this text.

1. *We must pray.* Do you pray for opportunities to share the gospel? When was the last time you prayed for an opportunity to share the gospel? How often do you pray for the lost?

2. *We must buy up the time.* There must be a sense of urgency. Do you have a sense of urgency with those you know who are lost? Too often, we excuse ourselves by thinking we will share with that lost person another day. Wouldn't it be wonderful if we were as urgent about the gospel as we are about paying our bills on time; or securing a mate, a home, and a family; or getting that email or tweet sent; or getting our taxes done; or meeting some deadline at work? If we were as urgent about sharing the gospel as we are about other things, we might see some wonderful results.

3. *We must walk wisely.* Would your next-door neighbor tell me that your life is conducted differently than those who are outside the faith? Do others see you as different from the world?

4. *We must be gracious.* We must not go to the extreme and be so gracious that we never open our mouths to share the gospel. Some

people are so afraid of offending the unbeliever that they never open their mouths. We must open our mouths, but when we do, our words should be gracious and kind.

5. *We must be lively.* (Seasoned with salt) Our gospel presentation should not be dull and boring; it should be lively and exciting. The gospel of Jesus Christ is truly an amazing and exciting story. This does not mean that we leave out hard truths like repentance and the Lordship of Christ, because even these things are exciting. When we consider that we have been granted forgiveness of sins and we now have a new Master who leads us into paths of righteousness, we're reminded that these things truly are exciting stuff!

6. *We must be well-grounded.* (Know how to answer every man) We shouldn't have a canned gospel, but we must be able to answer questions that are asked of us concerning the gospel and the truths of Scripture. Questions like: "What makes Christianity different from other religions?" "How can I know I have eternal life?" and "How do you know Jesus was the Son of God?" This doesn't mean that we have to have the Bible mastered, but it does mean that we should be pursuing the Scriptures with the intent of knowing them thoroughly. We cannot afford to not buy up the opportunities to share our faith. I fear that many of us will stand ashamed on that day for not having redeemed the time as we should have.

Will you pray? Will you go? Will you speak?

Years ago, a song was written that I think would be good for us to meditate upon as we end this lesson.

> Lord, lay some soul upon my heart,
> And love that soul through me;
> And may I bravely do my part
> To win that soul for thee.
> Some soul for Thee,
> Some soul for Thee,

This is my earnest plea;
Help me each day,
On life's highway,
To win some soul for Thee.
Lord, lead me to some soul in sin,
And grant that I may be
Endued with power and love to win
That soul, dear Lord, for Thee.
To win that soul for Thee, my Lord,
Will be my constant prayer;
That when I've won Thy full reward
I'll with that dear one share.[72]

---

72 Bayless Benjamin McKinney, 1886-1952.

Questions to Consider

Colossians 4:2-6
Three Essentials in Evangelism

1. Read Colossians 4 and list all the commands that you find.

2. Memorize Colossians 4:6.

3. (a) Paul says we are to walk in wisdom toward those that are outside (Colossians 4:5). What does that mean, in light of what Jesus said in Matthew 7:6 and 10:16? (b) According to James 3:13-18, what does true wisdom look like? (c) Would you say the wisdom James describes is the same wisdom that unbelievers observe in you?

4. (a) What do you think is the main point of Jesus' parable in Luke 18:1-8? (b) How does this coincide with what Paul says in Colossians 4:2? (c) Would you say that you are persistent in prayer? (d) What keeps you from persevering in it?

5. (a) What other prayer requests does Paul ask for from other churches? See Romans 15:30-32; 2 Corinthians 1:11; Ephesians 6:18-20; Philippians 1:18-20; 1 Thessalonians 5:25; 2 Thessalonians 3:1-2; Philemon 22; and Hebrews 13:18-19. (b) In what ways do these requests challenge you? (c) If you could ask for three prayer requests, what would they be?

6. Make two columns on a sheet of paper, one labeled "Question" and the other labeled "Answer." (a) For each of the following passages, list the question and then how Paul or Jesus answered it: Matthew 16:1-4; 21:23-27; Luke 20:20-26; 20:27-40; John 14:5-6; Acts 8:26-40; Acts 17:16-34. (b) How do these questions and answers seem to relate to Colossians 4:6? (c) If these questions would have been posed to you, would you have been able to answer them?

7. (a) When was the last time you shared the gospel? (b) Will you pray this week that God will give you an open door to share the gospel as Paul did? Come prepared to share if that door was opened and what happened.

8. (a) If someone came to you today and asked you of the "hope within you," would you be ready to share with them? Are you prepared to do so now? What are some ways you can or have prepared? (The following passages are good ones to consider: Acts 20:17-27; Romans 3:19-28; 1 Corinthians 15:1-8; Ephesians 2:8-10; and Titus 3:4-7.) (These are good tools that are helpful for being equipped in effective evangelism: *Discipleship Evangelism*; *Evangelism Explosion*; *Way of the Master*; *Tell the Truth*, by Will Metzger; and *The Master Plan of Evangelism*, by Robert Coleman.)

9. Come with a prayer request either for someone who is lost, or a prayer for yourself as you endeavor to share the gospel.

Chapter 21

Paul's Partners in Ministry (Part 1)

Colossians 4:7-11

As you've read through the New Testament, have you ever wondered how the apostle Paul did all the things he did? Have you ever wondered where he got the time and energy to start all those churches, travel on all those missionary journeys, and write all those letters? And that doesn't even include the other things he endured: imprisonment; sufferings; beatings; stonings; three shipwrecks; hunger and thirst and nakedness; and caring for all the churches (see 2 Corinthians 11). So many times, I've read about all that the apostle Paul did and wondered to myself, "How did he do all of this?!" Even in our day, we look at certain men and women who seem to accomplish such great things for the kingdom and we wonder how they do all they do. We know, of course, that no one can do anything apart from the help of the Lord, but we often forget that there are also many hardworking men and women behind the scenes of these so-called "great men and women." Most of the time these helpers receive little recognition; nonetheless, the work of the Lord would not go on as it does without them.

Before the apostle Paul closes out his letter to the church at Colossae, he makes sure to give honor where honor is due by recognizing the faithful men who have helped him in ministry. Without these partners in ministry, the work would not have succeeded as it did, and Paul knew that. He mentions eight different individuals who have been a help to him. And these aren't just names; they're real people with real character qualities that God divinely gave them for His glory, and to be partners in ministry with the apostle Paul. We will consider the first five individuals in this lesson and the last three in our next lesson. Let's read verses 7-11 and make note of these five men.

Colossians 4:7-11

Tychicus, a beloved brother, faithful minister, and fellow servant in the Lord, will tell you all the news about me. [8]I am sending him to you for this very purpose, that he may know your circumstances and comfort your hearts, [9]with Onesimus, a faithful and beloved brother, who is one of you. They will make known to you all things which are happening here. [10]Aristarchus my fellow prisoner greets you, with Mark the cousin of Barnabas (about whom you received instructions: if he comes to you, welcome him), [11]and Jesus who is called Justus. These are my only fellow workers for the kingdom of God who are of the circumcision; they have proved to be a comfort to me.

In our last lesson, we considered our three-fold responsibility to the lost. When we consider the transition between our responsibility toward the lost and recognizing faithful partners in ministry, it's a simple connection. Proclaiming the gospel is great; it is especially great to have partners who come alongside you in this effort. Even Jesus sent out the 70 in twos, according to Luke 10:1. Paul was blessed to have wonderful co-laborers in the gospel, and what help and joy they were to him! Let's look at the first of these helpers in verse 7.

Tychicus

Colossians 4:7-8

Tychicus, a beloved brother, faithful minister, and fellow servant in the Lord, will tell you all the news about me (Colossians 4:7)

The first partner-in-ministry Paul mentions is *Tychicus*, and his name means fortunate. Tychicus was a Gentile convert from the providence of Asia, whom Paul took along with him to Jerusalem (see Acts 20). It's likely that Tychicus had witnessed the great riot against Paul in Ephesus, mentioned in Acts 19 and 20, and was probably with Paul at the time of his arrest and imprisonment in Jerusalem and Caesarea. We also know that Tychicus was present with Paul in his first imprisonment in Rome, because it was during that imprisonment that Paul wrote his letter to the Colossians, which Tychicus was responsible for delivering to the Colossians, along with Onesimus.

As we consider this helper of Paul's, we see three things he wants his readers to know about Tychicus. First, he is *a beloved brother*. This means he is dear to Paul and he is a Christian. We saw the word *beloved* when we were in chapter three, verse 12; it is a word that means loved now and forever. Second, Paul mentions that Tychicus was a *faithful minister*. In other words, he is a trustworthy table-waiter. Paul makes mention of this same idea in his letters to Timothy (2 Timothy 4:12) and Titus (Titus 3:12); both verses suggest that Tychicus was willing to be sent by Paul when needed. Faithfulness is a must for all of God's children. Paul writes of this in 2 Timothy 2:1-3: "You therefore, my son, be strong in the grace that is in Christ Jesus. And the things that you have heard from me among many witnesses, commit these to faithful men who will be able to teach others also. You therefore must endure hardship as a good soldier of Jesus Christ." Paul wanted faithful partners in ministry and so should we. When I look for women to help in ministry, faithfulness is one of the top characteristics I look for. We know God considers faithfulness important, and one day I trust we all will hear those words, "Well done, good and faithful servant." Someone once said, "The greatest ability in the world is dependability."[73] Because Tychicus evidenced this character quality, Paul could trust him to carry this letter and others (Ephesians and Philemon) to the intended churches. The third thing Paul says about Tychicus is that he is a *fellow servant in the Lord*, which means he is a co-slave in the Lord. My friend, all of us are slaves—and I know that is not a popular term in the 21st century! But the truth is, when you and I embraced Christ as Lord and Savior, we signed up to be slaves to a heavenly Master. We are not the captains of our own ships, though some of us sure think we are!

Paul adds that Tychicus *will tell you all the news about me*. He will let you know how it's going with me here in prison. I mean,

---

73 Unknown.

think about it, if your pastor was in prison for the gospel, wouldn't you want to know how he was faring? We have modern ways of learning of someone's welfare in our culture, but in Paul's day the only method would have been by a messenger, and in this case that messenger was Tychicus. What a role model for all of us! Paul goes on to give some more great qualities about this man in verse 8:

> I am sending him to you for this very purpose, that he may know your circumstances and comfort your hearts, (Colossians 4:8)

Paul writes that he is sending Tychicus to the Colossians for a *purpose*. His willingness to travel to Colossae from Rome shows not only this man's faithfulness but also his servant's attitude. My friend, traveling in those days was no picnic! You couldn't catch the next flight on Southwest Airlines and have free snacks! Traveling was difficult, and it was dangerous. He talks about his travels like this:

> Three times I was beaten with rods; once I was stoned; three times I was shipwrecked; a night and a day I have been in the deep; in journeys often, in perils of waters, in perils of robbers, in perils of my own countrymen, in perils of the Gentiles, in perils in the city, in perils in the wilderness, in perils in the sea, in perils among false brethren; in weariness and toil, in sleeplessness often, in hunger and thirst, in fastings often, in cold and nakedness—besides the other things, what comes upon me daily: my deep concern for all the churches (2 Corinthians 11:25-28).

How would you like to go on a journey with Paul? Tychicus would not only have experienced some of these same dangers, but he would have been away from family and friends for quite a long time. He would have traveled much on foot and even on water, just like Paul. We see Tychicus' servant heart as he made the long journey from Colossae to Rome with this letter in hand, and my friend, it was no short distance, as it was over 1000 miles. And this is not the only letter he delivered. He delivered this letter to the Colossians, the letter to the church at Ephesus (see Ephesians 6:21), the letter to Philemon (see verses 9-10 of Philemon in conjunction with Colossians 4:7-9), and a letter to the church at Laodicea (see Colossians 4:16). No wonder Paul speaks so highly of him! And it is probably this servant's heart that prompts Paul to mention him first.

Paul mentions a few reasons why he sent Tychicus. First, he indicates that he wants to know their *circumstances*. Paul could not be there to see the Colossians himself, as he was providentially hindered, so he sent Tychicus. Here, we see that Paul is concerned about their welfare even though he is the one in prison. He wasn't focused on his own needs, but on the needs of others. Second, Paul sent Tychicus to be a *comfort* to the Colossians. Paul had already mentioned in Colossians 2:2 his desire to comfort the Colossians' hearts. He was agonizing over them and wanted them to be comforted, which means to be consoled. We know the dear Holy Spirit is our comforter, but God also uses human individuals to comfort others. The very morning I sat down to write this lesson, I had just gotten off the phone with my daughter, who had recently moved to Houston. Hurricane Harvey had devastated their church building, as well as the homes of many in their church. Cindi was burdened and overwhelmed and I wanted to comfort her, but she was so far away. I felt helpless, much like I think Paul must have felt for the church at Colossae. Tychicus was sent to encourage them and to see how they were doing. I'm certain that Paul would have been anxiously waiting to hear back from Tychicus to see how the church was doing. One of the ways that Tychicus would be a comfort would be in the bringing of this letter from Paul. Remember, they were in danger of being led astray by the Gnostics, the false teachers. And Paul sends them this letter of warning, but also a letter of great comfort, as he shares his own prayer requests for them. In it, he details of the dangers of Gnosticism, how the Colossian believers need to put off sin and put on righteousness, and how they should act in family relationships and in work ethics. These are four small chapters, but they are rich with comfort and hope. This letter would have been of great comfort to a church that was struggling.

Tychicus was a very important friend to Paul and a great help to him in the ministry. What a blessing he was to Paul! The Lord used Tychicus as part of His divine plan for the apostle Paul's ministry. My friend, the behind-the-scenes, small things are actually great things when they are done for the kingdom of our Lord and His glory! We all work together with the gifts and talents God has given us for the edification of the saints and the glory of God! And an example of that is that Tychicus did not travel alone; Paul sent a companion with him, a runaway slave. This is the second partner-in-ministry Paul mentions.

Onesimus

Colossians 4:9

> with Onesimus, a faithful and beloved brother, who is one of you. They will make known to you all things which are happening here. (Colossians 4:9)

Onesimus is someone we considered a few lessons back when we were studying about the master-slave relationship. His name means profitable, which means that he is helpful and wholly reliable. If you recall, he is only mentioned here and in the letter to Philemon. Onesimus was a slave who belonged to Philemon and had apparently run away from Philemon at some point. Such an offense was punishable by death, according to Roman law. But Onesimus had apparently met the apostle Paul and become a believer. So, along with Tychicus and this letter to the Colossians, Paul sent Onesimus back to Philemon, apparently so that the two could reconcile. The epistle to the church at Colossae and the epistle to Philemon were written at the same time. Paul wrote to Philemon a touching letter encouraging him to receive Onesimus, not as a servant but as a brother. Paul even took it a step further, offering to repay anything that Onesimus owed to Philemon. This slave, who was once unprofitable, is now profitable. Isn't that encouraging?!

Paul also calls Onesimus *a faithful and beloved brother*. These are the same two qualities Paul mentioned in verse 7 regarding

Tychicus. Paul does not, however, call Onesimus a fellow servant, perhaps because he had not yet been in the faith long enough to have become active in the ministry. But Paul does say this: that Onesimus *is one of you*. He was one of them in the sense that he too had become a recipient of God's grace; he had become a Christian. But some scholars think this could refer to the fact that Onesimus was from Colossae, so he was one of them in the sense that he had come from Colossae. Both interpretations are true: Onesimus was a Colossian, and he was a Christian—a Colossian Christian! One man helpfully encourages us here: "Let your imagination picture the scene when Tychicus brought Onesimus back to Colossae, when the remarkable news spread, when Philemon had his slave back with a special letter from Paul."[74] Can you imagine the scene? Is this Onesimus? It would be quite the opposite of Naomi in the book of Ruth, who went out full and came home empty. Those who knew her asked, "Is this Naomi?" Onesimus, however, had run away empty but was coming back full—full of the Holy Spirit! Too often, we are guilty of reading the Bible without stopping to put ourselves in the shoes of the writer, the initial readers, and the characters involved. What blessings we miss out on! (That is one of the blessings of memorizing God's Word! It forces one to think and ponder each word, each phrase, each verse.)

Paul adds that *they*, Tychicus and Onesimus together, *will make known to you all things which are happening here*. It's likely that the Colossians were concerned about Paul's welfare; Tychicus and Onesimus would fill them in on how Paul was doing. Remember, there were no cell phones, no email, no faxes, and no internet in those days. Paul and his companions would have relied upon faithful, risk-taking brothers in the Lord to deliver news of their well-being. In addition to these two faithful men, Paul goes on to mention two more of his co-laborers in verse 10.

---

74 R.C.H. Lenski, *Commentary on the New Testament: Colossians, 1-2 Thessalonians, 1-2 Timothy, Titus, and Philemon (Peabody: Hendrickson Publishing Company, 1998), 197.*

Aristarchus and Mark

Colossians 4:10

Aristarchus my fellow prisoner greets you, with Mark the cousin of Barnabas (about whom you received instructions: if he comes to you, welcome him), (Colossians 4:10)

The third helper Paul mentions is *Aristarchus*, and his name means best ruler. According to Acts 20:4 and 27:2, he was a native of Thessalonica. He was also one of Paul's companions who was seized by the rioting mob in Ephesus, in Acts 19:29. According to Acts 21 and 27, he accompanied Paul as Paul sailed to Jerusalem and later back to Rome. It must have been a great comfort to Paul to have with him a companion like Aristarchus on long journeys at sea, especially when a dangerous storm arose and nearly wiped them all out.

Paul mentions something about Aristarchus that he did not say of Onesimus or Tychicus; Paul calls Aristarchus *my fellow prisoner*. He is a co-captive with Paul. Interestingly, Tychicus is called a co-slave and Aristarchus a co-captive. There are two predominant opinions as to why Paul refers to Aristarchus this way. The first is that Aristarchus had likely been imprisoned along with Paul for preaching the gospel just as Paul had. In this case, Aristarchus would be considered a fellow prisoner in the sense that he was literally in prison with Paul. But others think that Paul means to convey the idea that Aristarchus is "my fellow war captive," that Aristarchus shared in the special hardship that was familiar to Paul's spiritual warfare. The Christian life truly is a war, and Paul had special challenges with hardships and persecution—and Aristarchus shared in those challenges with Paul. In Paul's letter to the Philippians, he speaks of wanting to share in Christ's sufferings; it could be that Aristarchus shared that same longing. At the end of Paul's letter to Philemon, he refers to Aristarchus as his fellow worker, so we know that Aristarchus was a help to Paul in the ministry. Beyond these things, however, it is hard to find much information about Aristarchus. Either of these views is plausible, so again, take whatever view you wish. Aristarchus does send greetings, though. He *greets* the Colossians or wishes them well. The verb here really means to draw one to oneself, to embrace. It is a word used in many New Testament letters. In our vernacular today, we might say, "Give so and so a hug for me," or "Tell them hello from me."

There is another man Paul mentions in this verse, and that is *Mark*. Who is he? Mark is the author of the second gospel account, the Gospel of Mark. He is also the one mentioned in Acts 15:38, over whom Paul and Barnabas had a significant quarrel. In that account, we learn that Paul did not think it was a good idea to take Mark along with them because Mark had departed from them at Pamphylia. We do not know why Mark departed from Paul and Barnabas then, but it's possible that the hardships of the missionary work had something to do with it. When we read in Paul's writings of his sufferings, it's easy to see how those hardships might be enough to scare some away. Because Mark had previously deserted Paul and Barnabas, Paul refused to take him along this time and instead took Silas. But now, some 12-14 years later, Paul is writing this epistle to the Colossians and sending greetings from Mark. While we do not know for sure what happened, it is clear that something significant did happen sometime between the events of Acts 15 and the writing of 2 Timothy 4:11, where Paul instructs Timothy to bring Mark with him because Paul considered Mark to be profitable for the ministry. Evidently, Paul had reconciled with Mark by that point, even recommending him to other churches. Ladies, this is an excellent example of a truly forgiving Christian spirit; one that I wish we would see more of in our day. Holding grudges and harboring an unforgiving spirit is the opposite of the spirit of Christ.

Paul also mentions that Mark is *the cousin of Barnabas*. This is an interesting statement, as well, because we already know that it was Barnabas who contended with Paul over Mark and Acts 15:39 indicates that the contention was so sharp that Paul and Barnabas departed from each other. Barnabas was also the one who introduced Paul to the church in Jerusalem. Consider what we learn of him and his character from Acts 11:22-26: "Then news of these things came to the ears of the church in Jerusalem, and they sent out Barnabas to go as far as Antioch. When he came and had seen the grace of God, he was glad, and encouraged them all that with purpose of heart they should continue with the Lord. For he was a good man, full of the Holy Spirit and of faith. And a great many people were added to the Lord. Then Barnabas departed for Tarsus to seek Saul. And when he had found him, he brought him to Antioch. So it was that for a whole year they assembled with the church and taught a great many people. And the disciples were first called Christians in Antioch." It is said that Barnabas converted to Christianity at an early age and that the reason Paul mentions Barnabas is because mentioning him would seem to convey some element of approval for Mark. Barnabas must have been familiar to the saints at Colossae. It's possible that they may have had some sort of prejudice against Mark, and the mention of Barnabas' name may have eased their minds.

Receiving Mark is the subject of what Paul says next. He says *if he comes to you, welcome him*. But before Paul says that, he says *about whom you received instructions*. What these instructions were and who issued them, we do not know. Nevertheless, the Colossians were to have accepted both these instructions and Mark himself. This means that they were to provide for him a place to stay and food to eat—what an incredible change of attitude and heart from the apostle Paul! There is no malice on the part of Paul. And there must have been significant spiritual growth on the part of Mark for Paul to make such comments regarding him. More than likely, the Colossian believers had known of the dispute between Paul and Mark (bad news spreads fast!) and would have been hesitant about receiving Mark. But Paul affirms his confidence in Mark. I find great encouragement here, as well as a warning. The encouragement I see is that people change and grow in the Lord; we are not what we used to be, and we are not today what we will be in the future, and we can praise God for that reality. But I also find a warning here for us: when we give a bad report regarding an individual and at some point, that person repents, we need to be just as quick as Paul to reinstate their character as we were to malign their character.

Too often, we are quick to verbalize another's faults, but we're not nearly as quick to verbalize when God has transformed their lives into greater conformity to His Son.

Paul has told us of Tychicus and Onesimus, of Aristarchus and Mark. Now, Paul tells us of one more of his friends whom we want to consider, and that is Jesus, or Justus.

Jesus, Called Justus

Colossians 4:11

> and Jesus who is called Justus. These are my only fellow workers for the kingdom of God who are of the circumcision; they have proved to be a comfort to me. (Colossians 4:11)

Jesus, we know, is the name of our Lord, but it was also a common name among the Jews. Paul mentions here *Jesus who is called Justus*. *Justus* means righteous or just. The reference here to a man named Jesus, but who is called Justus, might be an indicator that Justus had changed his name in honor of the name of his Redeemer. Or it could indicate that Jesus was this man's Jewish name and Justus was his Roman or Latin name. We really don't know, especially given that there is no other mention of him in Scripture, except what is mentioned here.

Paul ends this verse by saying that *these are my only fellow workers for the kingdom of God*. Notice that the work these men do is for *the kingdom of God*. They worked for things above, not things of the earth. They set their minds on things above and not on things of the earth, as Paul wrote about in chapter three. And not only are they *fellow workers for the kingdom*, but they are *of the circumcision*, which means they are Jews by birth or by conversion. These three men, Aristarchus, Mark, and Justus are of the circumcision, are Jewish believers. And Paul says *they have proved to be a comfort to me*. The words *these ... only* are emphatic in the Greek, which indicates that only these men were a comfort, a solace, and a relief to Paul. The word *comfort* is a medical term; it means that they had been good medicine for Paul. In writing this letter, Paul desires to be a comfort to the church at Colossae, and these men are a comfort to him. Have you ever had friends like that? Sometimes, we can feel down or lonely, and a good friend proves to be better than any medicine we might want to take. Proverbs 27:9 says, "Ointment and perfume delight the heart, and the sweetness of a man's friend gives delight by hearty counsel." Paul says these three were of great comfort; they were the exception.

You might be wondering, "Does this mean that the other men were not a comfort to Paul?" One man says of this: "It must not escape our attention that Paul's statement with reference to these three men as the only Jewish Christian fellow-workers who had been a comfort to him implies deep disappointment with other people of his own race. Paul was aware of his estrangement from his own people."[75] Second Timothy 4:16 gives us a glimpse into Paul's disappointment with some of his friends: "At my first defense no one stood with me, but all forsook me. May it not be charged against them." This is quite a statement Paul makes here. Though he seems greatly disappointed, he also desires that God would forgive them. In my flesh, I'd probably be hoping that God would pay them back for the wrong they'd done to me, but not Paul! His was the attitude of a genuine friend—one who loves, thinks the best, and forgives! The attitude of the apostle Paul is the attitude of a true friend. There were many in Paul's day who envied him; some even wanted to add misery to his misery, at times. But not these men; they were a comfort to Paul. Even in 2 Corinthians 11:26, he writes about "perils among false brethren." I know some individuals who think ministry is fame and glamour, but I can assure you that is false thinking! The burdens are many, and often those in ministry feel like many are against them; it can truly be overwhelming at times. I remember sharing once with some missionaries we were hosting how much my husband and I loved the pastorate. And they were surprised! They had stayed in many a pastor's home and most of those pastors had shared that they truly did not like the ministry and wanted out of it.

---

75 William Hendriksen, *Colossians, and Philemon* (Grand Rapids, Michigan: Baker Book House, 1964), 190.

Summary

Who are the first five of Paul's partners-in-ministry listed in this epistle?

The first is *Tychicus*, beloved, faithful, and a fellow servant of Christ. Could someone honestly give these descriptions of you? Are you known as one who is loved among the brethren? Are you faithful to your ministries and to the local body? Are you willing to serve in whatever the Lord would ask you to do?

Paul's second partner is *Onesimus*, also faithful and beloved.

The third of Paul's partners is *Aristarchus*, fellow prisoner for the cause of Christ. Are you, like Aristarchus, willing to suffer anything for the sake of Christ? Do you wage war against the enemy?

Paul's fourth partner is *Mark*, a changed man. Do you find it hard to welcome those who once had a bad reputation? Do you objectively consider the changes that God has made in people's lives? What changes have you made toward Christlikeness this past year? Wouldn't it bring you great joy if others recognized those changes in you and refused to hold your former ways against you?

The fifth partner-in-ministry Paul mentions is *Jesus who was called Justus*. With Aristarchus and Mark, Justus was a comfort to Paul. Who is a comfort to you? To whom are you a comfort? In what ways do you comfort others in their afflictions, and in what ways have you been comforted in your afflictions?

Paul had a wide range of friends and companions in the ministry: a runaway slave, a Christian brother with whom he'd had a pretty good argument, and several others who seemed to be loyal from day one. Yet, no matter what their past included, as of the writing of this letter to the Colossians, these men were a great help to Paul, and he wanted others to know it. Who are the people that have helped you along the way to bring you to where you are today? Of course, it is ultimately the Lord who completes His work in each of us, but at the same time He uses men and women in our lives to be a part of that sanctifying process. Have you thanked those people? Perhaps it is your parents, your husband, your children, your pastor, or your friends. Why not give them a call or write them a note to let them know how very much you appreciate their service to you.

Also consider these questions: Are you helping others to succeed? Are you willing to be an errand boy in service to others as Tychicus and Onesimus were? Are you loyal to others in the ministry, like Tychicus and Aristarchus? Are you dependable? Do you look for ways to help others in their ministries? It is my prayer that every one of us would be as Justus, Aristarchus, and Mark, a comfort to others and faithful workers in the task of expanding the kingdom of God. Let us carefully consider these five men and how they served Paul. Let's learn from them how we too might better bear each other's burdens.

Questions to Consider

Colossians 4:7-11

Paul's Partners in Ministry (Part 1)

1. Read Colossians 4 and list all the individuals Paul mentions and what facts or characteristics you notice about them.

2. Memorize Colossians 4:7.

3. Tychicus is mentioned four other times in Scripture. Look up the following passages and make note of what you learn about him: Acts 20:1-5; Ephesians 6:21-22; 2 Timothy 4:12; and Titus 3:12.

4. (a) Aristarchus is also mentioned four times in Scripture. Look up the following passages and make note of what you find regarding him! Acts 19:29; Acts 20:1-5; Acts 27:1-4; and Philemon 23-24. (b) Based on the verses you looked up from questions 3 and 4, does it appear that Tychicus and Aristarchus were ever together?

5. (a) Mark is mentioned five times in Scripture. Look up the following passages to see what you discover about Mark: Acts 12:12, 25; Acts 15:36-41; 2 Timothy 4:11; 1 Peter 5:13; and Philemon 24. (b) What do you think happened between the events of Acts 15 and the writing of 2 Timothy 4?

6. (a) Read the book of Philemon. Write down any observations you see regarding Onesimus. (b) Why do you think Paul is sending him to Colossae with Tychicus? See Colossians 4:7-9.

7. (a) What are the characteristics of a true friend, according to the following proverbs? Proverbs 17:9; 17:17; 18:24; 27:6; 27:10; and 27:17. (b) Are you blessed to have friends like this? (c) Are you this type of friend to others?

8. (a) If you were to describe your closest friend in three ways, what would you say? (b) With what words would *you* like to be described? (c) Do you think your friends would describe you as faithful, comforting, and self-sacrificing?

9. (a) Has there been a time recently when a friend comforted you? How did their comfort bless you? (b) Has there been a time recently when you knew a friend sacrificed on your behalf? What did you learn from their sacrifice?

10. Come with a prayer of thanksgiving to God for your friends *and* a petition to God for yourself concerning how you might be a better friend to someone else.

Chapter 22

Paul's Partners in Ministry (Part 2)
Colossians 4:12-14

Moses, Noah, Elijah, David, Solomon, Paul, Abraham, Timothy, John, and Joseph. Have you heard of these biblical characters? I would venture to say that most Christians have not only heard of these people but could give details pertaining to their lives. These are important men mentioned in the Word of God who exhibited great faith.

Eratus, Eubulus, Pudens, Linus, Claudia, Herodion, Appelles, Aristobulus, Persis, and Rufus. Have you heard of these biblical characters? I would venture to say that most Christians have not heard of them and could give few, if any, details about their lives. These men are also mentioned in the Word of God, just as the men in the first group, but most of us would have to admit that we don't have the foggiest idea who they are. Are these men any less important in God's eyes and in His service? Did they serve the Lord with any less zeal than those previously mentioned? The men in this second list are what we might call "hidden heroes of the faith." Too often, we come upon their names in Scripture and simply gloss over them because we deem them as unessential. But if we would stop and look a little bit closer, we would find wonderful little nuggets of encouragement as we examine their lives.

In our last lesson, we considered five of Paul's partners in ministry: Tychicus, Onesimus, Aristarchus, Mark, and Jesus who is called Justus. Five partners of the apostle Paul. Tychicus was beloved, faithful, and a fellow servant. Onesimus was also faithful and a beloved brother. Aristarchus was a fellow prisoner for the cause of Christ. Mark was a changed man; one whom Paul encouraged the church to welcome. Jesus who was called Justus was a comfort to Paul. Three of these men were of Jewish birth: Aristarchus, Mark, and Jesus who is called Justus. In this lesson, we will look at three of Paul's companions who were of Gentile birth, Epaphras, Luke and Demas. What did they contribute to the work of the Lord, and how were they of help to the apostle Paul? Let's read verses 12-14 and discover the answers to these questions.

Colossians 4:12-14

> Epaphras, who is one of you, a bondservant of Christ, greets you, always laboring fervently for you in prayers, that you may stand perfect and complete in all the will of God. ¹³For I bear him witness that he has a great zeal for you, and those who are in Laodicea, and those in Hierapolis. ¹⁴Luke the beloved physician and Demas greet you.

Let's take a closer look at another of Paul's partners in ministry who was of Gentile descent. His name is Epaphras.

Epaphras

Colossians 4:12-13

> Epaphras, who is one of you, a bondservant of Christ, greets you, always laboring fervently for you in prayers, that you may stand perfect and complete in all the will of God (Colossians 4:12)

Epaphras was the founder of the church at Colossae. If you recall from earlier lessons, Epaphras traveled more than 1000 miles from Colossae to Rome to inform the apostle Paul of the dangerous heresy of Gnosticism that had been creeping into the church. We studied this man when we considered Colossians 1:7-8: "as you also learned from Epaphras, our dear fellow servant, who is a faithful minister of Christ on your behalf, who also declared to us your love in the Spirit." Paul speaks well of Epaphras in these two verses in Colossians 1, specifically mentioning two things about him. First, that he was a *dear fellow servant*. This indicates that Paul and Timothy had a strong friendship with Epaphras. Second, Paul mentions that

Epaphras was also a *faithful minister*. He was worthy to be trusted as a minister or servant. The word *minister* comes from a Greek word which means "in the dust laboring" or "running through dust." Epaphras wasn't a lazy guy; he labored hard, running through the dust. In fact, there's a good chance that he literally ran through dust when you consider that he traveled 1000 miles by foot to reach the apostle Paul.

What else can we learn about this man from what Paul says about him in verses 12 and 13 of chapter 4? First, Paul writes that he *is one of you*. This means he was a native of Colossae. You'll recall that Paul also said this about Onesimus in verse 9. Second, Paul calls Epaphras *a bondservant of Christ*. In chapter 1, verse 7, Paul had not only called him a servant, but a dear fellow servant. A *bondservant*, or slave, is one who is bought with a price and owned by his master. To be a slave of Christ means that all of one's possessions, dreams, goals, energy, and time belong completely to Christ. How did Epaphras manifest that he was a bondservant of Christ? We have mentioned several ways already, but as Paul continues to write about Epaphras, a number of other qualities will become apparent that make his slavery to Christ even more clearly visible.

Before Paul mentions these other qualities, he lets the Colossians know that Epaphras *greets* them. Paul also mentions to the Colossians that Epaphras is a man who is *always laboring fervently for you in prayers*. He is a man of prayer. I am quite convinced that Epaphras had a pastor's heart and was missing his congregation, and he too might have been wondering how they were getting along. Being that he was 1000 miles away, we might even expect him to be tempted to worry about them. But it would seem, from this text, that he didn't worry, because Paul says Epaphras is a man of prayer and that he prays *fervently* for his congregation, which means that he prays red-hot prayers for them. And notice that Paul says Epaphras is *always* praying for them, that he always has them on his mind. In fact, this is laborious prayer; Paul says Epaphras is continually *laboring* in prayer for them. The word *labor* means to work to the point of exhaustion, and it has the idea of contending in the gymnastic games. It's the same Greek word for agonize, which speaks of the grueling competition endured by the athletes of the Olympic Games. Paul writes of this in 1 Corinthians 9:24-25, "Do you not know that those who run in a race all run, but one receives the prize? Run in such a way that you may obtain it. And everyone who competes for the prize is temperate in all things. Now they do it to obtain a perishable crown, but we for an imperishable crown." Epaphras was not a well-known man, yet he wrestled in prayer just like his Lord did in the garden of Gethsemane, just like Elijah did on Mount Carmel, and just like Jacob did when he wrestled with God. We would do well to remember what James 5:16 tells us: "Confess your trespasses to one another, and pray for one another, that you may be healed. The effective, fervent prayer of a righteous man avails much." The prayers of a righteous man—a righteous woman—avail much! In fact, right after this verse in James 5, James reminds us of the example of Elijah on Mount Carmel, wrestling in prayer for rain. Have you ever agonized and wrestled in prayer like Elijah, Jesus, or Jacob? These men labored fervently in prayer! E.M. Bounds, who wrote several books on prayer and typically prayed several hours a day, wrote that

> There is neither encouragement nor room in Bible religion for feeble desires, listless efforts, lazy attitudes; all must be strenuous, urgent, ardent. Inflamed desires, impassioned, unwearied insistence delight heaven. God would have His children incorrigibly in earnest and persistently bold in their efforts. Heaven is too busy to listen to half-hearted prayers to respond to pop-calls. Our whole being must be in our praying.[76]

Some of us use the excuse of not having enough time to pray, but perhaps the truth is that we do not make the time. Oswald Smith says, "Oh, how few find time for prayer! There is time for everything else, time to sleep and time to eat, time to read the newspaper and the novel, time to visit friends, time for everything else under the sun, but no time for prayer, the most important of all things, the one great essential!"[77] Another wise man has said, "You can tell how

76 E.M. Bounds, *Purpose in Prayer (New York: Fleming H. Revell Company, 1920)*, 59.
77 Oswald J. Smith. "Oswald J. Smith Quotes about Prayer." *AZQuotes. http://www. azquotes.com/author/26117-Oswald_J_Smith/tag/prayer*

popular a church is by who comes on Sunday morning. You can tell how popular the pastor or evangelist is by who comes on Sunday night. But you can tell how popular Jesus is by who comes to the prayer meeting!"[78] Think of Susannah Wesley who, despite having nineteen children, found time to shut herself in her room for a full hour each day so she could be alone with God. My friends, it is not so much a case of finding time as it is of making time. We can make time if we desire to, because we always make time to do what we really want to do. Prayer can indeed change things, but for many of us prayer is not a priority. As mothers and grandmothers, especially, we should be spending time on our knees in prayer for our families.

When Paul tells us that Epaphras is a man of red-hot prayer, Paul doesn't leave it at that; he tells us what is included in these red-hot prayers. Paul tells the Colossians that Epaphras prays specifically that *you may stand perfect and complete in the all the will of God.* The word *stand* means to hold up, to stay put. The concept of standing is an important theme which is common throughout Scripture as describing those who belong to Christ. Paul admonishes the carnal church at Corinth in 1 Corinthians 16:13, "Watch, stand fast in the faith, be brave, be strong." Paul tells the church at Ephesus the importance of standing, mentioning it several times in Ephesians 6:10-14:

> Finally, my brethren, be strong in the Lord and in the power of His might. Put on the whole armor of God, that you may be able to stand against the wiles of the devil. For we do not wrestle against flesh and blood, but against principalities, against powers, against the rulers of the darkness of this age, against spiritual hosts of wickedness in the heavenly places. Therefore take up the whole armor of God, that you may be able to withstand in the evil day, and having done all, to stand. Stand therefore, having girded your waist with truth, having put on the breastplate of righteousness.

Even to the church that was dear to Paul's heart, the church he longed for and loved, the church at Philippi, Paul encourages them to stand. Consider Philippians 4:1: "Therefore, my beloved and longed-for

---

78 Jim Cymbala, *Fresh Wind, Fresh Fire (Grand Rapids: Zondervan, 2010)*, 24.

brethren, my joy and crown, so stand fast in the Lord, beloved." To the church at Thessalonica, Paul writes in 2 Thessalonians 2:15, "Therefore, brethren, stand fast and hold the traditions which you were taught, whether by word or our epistle." And in 1 Thessalonians 3:8, Paul writes, "For now we live, if you stand fast in the Lord." We would do well to remember this command to stand fast, and we would do well to pray fervently that we and those we know will stand fast. So many do not hold on because they do not stand fast! We need men and women who will stand fast in the truth and in the faith in a day when many are not.

Paul goes on to write that not only is Epaphras praying that the Colossians would stand but that they would stand *perfect and complete in all the will of God. Perfect* would mean to be spiritually mature, or full grown. This does not mean that we will be sinless because that won't happen till glory. Rather, it has the idea of a horse that has grown to full maturity. In addition to this, Epaphras also prays that the Colossians will be *complete*, which means to bear or bring to the full, to carry through to the end. Epaphras desired the same thing Paul and Timothy desired for the church at Colossae. Recall the words of Colossians 1:28-29: "Him we preach, warning every man and teaching every man in all wisdom, that we may present every man perfect in Christ Jesus. To this end I also labor, striving according to His working which works in me mightily." These three men, Paul, Timothy, and Epaphras, wanted the church at Colossae to carry their faith to the end, to avoid falling into dangerous heresy. And all three of these men labored to the point of exhaustion on the Colossians' behalf.

Paul adds that this standing perfect and complete is *in all the will of God*. This means it is willed by God; it is God's design and plan for the Colossians from the beginning. This would be in stark contrast to the Gnostics, whose will the Colossians were being encouraged to follow. Remember the warning of Colossians 2:8? "Beware lest anyone cheat you through philosophy and empty deceit, according to the tradition of men, according to the basic principles of the world, and not according to Christ." But Epaphras prays fervently that his

Colossian brothers and sisters in Christ will follow the will of God and not be swayed by Gnostic thinking. If they followed this dangerous heresy, they would not stand firm at all but would fall; they would lack spiritual maturity and risk the danger of becoming apostate. Paul goes on to tell us a little more about Epaphras in verse 13.

> For I bear him witness that he has a great zeal for you, and those who are in Laodicea, and those in Hierapolis. (Colossians 4:13)

Paul says *I bear him witness*, which means I can testify for I have heard him speak his heart to me. It's as though Paul is saying: "This is indeed true! I've seen it and heard it because I've heard him pray for you! This man has a zeal for you, and I am a witness to it!" To say that Epaphras has *zeal* for the Colossians means he has an abundant pain for them. This was a zeal that left him fatigued as he labored outwardly and inwardly on their behalf. This zeal isn't only for those at Colossae, though, but also for those in neighboring areas. Paul specifically mentions *those who are in Laodicea* and *those in Hierapolis. Laodicea* was located about 11 miles northwest of Colossae, and *Hierapolis* about 11 miles northeast of Laodicea. Paul, too, had a great concern for these cities, mentioning them in Colossians 2:1. "For I want you to know what a great conflict I have for you and those in Laodicea, and for as many as have not seen my face in the flesh." We learned when we studied that portion of Colossians that because these cities were so close geographically to the church there at Colossae, they would have been exposed to the same heretical teachings. Those of us who live in the Tulsa, Oklahoma area, where I live, are likewise surrounded by the heretical teachings of the word of faith and prosperity gospel. We could be seriously affected by these erroneous teachings if we do not stand fast in the Lord. Epaphras was a man who had a great heart for the needs and concerns of others; it is said that he may have founded these other two churches as well, in Laodicea and Hierapolis. Without a doubt, the Gnostic heresy had targeted all three of these churches and Epaphras was greatly concerned for them. But Epaphras isn't the only one who wished to send his greetings. Paul mentions two more men in verse 14, two more of his partners in ministry.

Luke and Demas

Colossians 4:14

Luke the beloved physician and Demas greet you.
(Colossians 4:14)

The third Gentile Paul mentions is *Luke*, who also sends greetings to the Colossians. We know from this verse that Luke is *the beloved physician*. The word *physician* is the Greek word <u>iatros</u>, which means a healer. But its meaning isn't restricted only to being a physician; it could also be used of someone who served as a surgeon or someone who distributed medication. We really don't know much about Luke's background. According to church history, it has been speculated that he was Titus's brother, and that Luke knew Paul when he was a student at Tarsus. It has been suggested that Luke may have looked after Paul's health, much like a personal physician; it has also been suggested that Paul's recurring illnesses on his first missionary journey may have prompted him to take Luke along on his second missionary journey.

> Without Luke's help as a physician, as a companion and friend, Paul could never have carried his heavy load in the Christian ministry, and without Luke's pen, the same grave that covered Paul's body would also have covered his name. In my mind, the most important event in all the history of time took place on that day when a poor, sick, discouraged Jew went into the office of Luke, the Greek physician—with the single exception of that Friday afternoon when Jesus hung from the cross on Calvary.[79]

In addition to these things, we also know that Luke is the author of two New Testament books, the Gospel of Luke and the Acts of the Apostles. He was, as I mentioned, Paul's companion on his second missionary journey. Toward the end of Paul's third missionary journey, Luke seems to have joined Paul again, according to Acts 20, and then reappears again on Paul's long and dangerous sea-journey to Rome, according to Acts 27. We can surmise from these

---

79 John A. Scott, *Luke: Greek Physician and Historian* (Evanston: Northwestern University, 1930), no page number available.

things that Luke was not only a doctor but also an evangelist. I find it refreshing and encouraging that Dr. Luke didn't allow his profession of ministering to the sick to hinder his higher and divine calling of ministering the gospel to the lost. In my husband's first pastorate, we had a doctor who attended our church and served as an elder. Anytime I had to go see him for physical problems, he would always check on my spiritual walk with the Lord. He didn't allow his vocation to keep him from the most needful task at hand, the spiritual welfare of others. Luke's life is a lesson for each of us: our profession in this world should never keep us from professing the name of Christ to those with whom we come into contact in our work.

There is one more man Paul mentions who would like to send his greetings, Paul's third Gentile helper: Demas. Demas was a partner of Paul who would later desert him. "Demas fell in love with the present world and with that tragic statement disappeared from sacred history."80 What a sad contrast between Luke the beloved and Demas the deserter! One man said way back in the 1800s: "The absence of any honorable or endearing mention here may be owing to the commencement of this apostasy, or some unfavorable indication in his character."81 Paul speaks of Demas in 2 Timothy 4:10-11, saying, "Demas has forsaken me, having loved this present world, and has departed for Thessalonica—Crescens for Galatia, Titus for Dalmatia. Only Luke is with me. Get Mark and bring him with you, for he is useful to me for ministry." Seven years after Paul wrote his epistle to the Colossians, he says *Demas has forsaken me … only Luke is with me.* Demas loved the world, and it may have been that he was affected by the Gnostic heresy. Jesus was forsaken by Judas, and Paul was forsaken by Demas. These men once served alongside Jesus and Paul in the ministry; these men also abandoned the faith. We should not be discouraged as we work for the Lord when the people who have worked beside us come to hate us, forsake us, and even abandon the faith. Many great men and women of God, even

---

80 William Hendriksen, *New Testament Commentary (Grand Rapids: Baker Book House, 1964), 193.*
81 Henry Alford, *The New Testament for English Readers (London: Gilbert and Rivington Printers, 1865), 472.*

our Lord, have been abandoned in the work of the ministry. But despite the pain those experiences bring, we have the Lord, and He is enough.

Summary

In these past two lessons, we have looked at eight men who were a help to the apostle Paul, men who were his companions in the work of the Lord. As we close out these lessons focusing in on Paul's partners in ministry, we can glean at least one principle from each one of them.

Tychicus: a man with a servant's heart. Tychicus was willing to travel more than 1000 miles to deliver letters. He was willing to travel with a runaway slave. He was willing to encounter the difficulties and dangers of travel on Paul's behalf. Do you have a heart like Tychicus? Is yours a servant's heart, willing to do any menial task, without complaining?

Onesimus: a man with a sinful past. Onesimus is a reminder to us of God's grace in our own lives, that He would reach down to save us, who were dead in our trespasses and sins. Are you grateful to God for rescuing you from your slavery to sin and setting you free?

Aristarchus: a man with a sympathetic heart. Aristarchus was a fellow prisoner with Paul. He accompanied Paul on his journey and was seized by a rioting mob. Would you go the extra mile for a friend? Would you suffer the same persecution with them if God called you to, or would your shrink at the very thought?

Mark: a man with a second chance. Early on, it looked as though Mark would never make it in the ministry; he appeared as if he was going nowhere. Paul even refused to take him along on one of his missionary journeys. But something happened in Mark's life that changed him, and he grew up spiritually—so much so that Paul later said of him that he was useful in the ministry. Mark encourages me that next year I will be different than I am today. Next year, I will be more like my Lord than I am today. The tasks that you wouldn't think of entrusting me with today, perhaps you would then. Do you give the Marks in your life any second chances? Are there Christians you have written off as too immature? Have you visited with them lately and examined the changes in their lives? Will you give them a second chance?

Jesus, or Justus: a man with a strong commitment. Justus was a Jew and was willing to leave his people to identify with Paul. He was willing to make a strong commitment on behalf of Christ. To do so would have probably meant being ostracized by his family. Are you willing to make the kind of stand for Christ that might cause division in your earthly relationships? Are you willing to love God more than you love your own family members?

Epaphras: a man with a single passion. Epaphras was the founder of the church at Colossae. He journeyed to Rome from Colossae to bring Paul the news of the Gnostic heresy that had crept into his church. He had a deep concern for those caught up in false teaching; his prayers were red-hot for them. Is God calling you to be an Epaphras for our day? Will you be the one who will intercede for those caught up in false teaching? Will you be the one who will be zealous for Christ's sake?

Luke: a man with a specialized talent. Luke was Paul's personal physician and beloved friend. Luke used his talent to serve God, much like a medical missionary would in our day. I imagine he could have made far more money staying in his hometown and running his own private practice. Instead, he received the joy and delight of being the apostle Paul's personal physician. Is God calling you to use your talents and gifts for the benefit of someone else? Is He calling you to make less money but more fruit for the kingdom? Is He calling you to use your gifts as an open door for sharing the gospel? It might be your musical talent or a craft you are exceptional at doing, perhaps cooking or gardening or your skills in hospitality.

Demas: a man with a sad future. Oh, how I pray that none of us will be like Demas, forsaking Christ and the saints because of love for the world. But it happens to many, and more than likely it will happen to some of us. Do you feel a tug of war going on inside you, one tug for righteousness and the things of God, and another tug for unrighteousness and the things of this world? Do not give in to Satan, my friend! Stand fast in the Lord and in the power of His might!

Eight men, all with different strengths and weaknesses, yet all at one time a blessing to the apostle Paul. They were heroes, perhaps hidden, but heroes, nonetheless. They were of great service to the apostle Paul and to Christ's Heavenly Kingdom. I leave you with the challenge of John Wesley, who penned so wisely:

> Do all the good you can, by all the means you can, in all the ways you can, in all the places you can, at all the times you can, to all the people you can, as long as ever you can.82

---

82 John Wesley, *The New Encyclopedia of Christian Quotations (Grand Rapids: Baker Books, 2000), 942.*

Questions to Consider
Colossians 4:12-14
Paul's Partner's in Ministry (Part 2)

1. (a) Read Colossians chapter four and make note of all the cities Paul mentions. Locate these cities on a map. (b) How far is Laodicea from Colossae? How far is Hierapolis from Colossae?

2. Memorize Colossians 4:12.

3. (a) What does Paul say about Epaphras in Colossians 1:7-8 and Philemon 1:23?

4. (a) What facts do you already know about Luke? (b) What other facts can you glean about Luke from the following passages? (Note: Luke wrote the book of Acts; the references to "we" and "us" in these Acts passages include him.) Acts 16:10-17; 20:6-16; 2 Timothy 4:11; Philemon 1:24.

5. What do you learn about Demas from 2 Timothy 4:10 and Philemon 24?

6. Look up the following passages and answer the following questions: (a) Who is wrestling in prayer? (b) For what are they praying? (c) What was the result of their praying? (d) What do you learn about praying fervently? Genesis 32:24-32; 1 Kings 18:41-46; and Luke 22:39-46.

7. (a) In looking over the men and the qualities Paul mentions about them in chapter four of Colossians, which of these men would you most like to emulate, and why? (b) What is the biggest help to you personally in your service to Christ?

8. (a) Would you describe your prayers for others as fervent? (b) What do you think are some ways that we can become more earnest in our prayers?

9. Looking back at question seven, write a prayer request asking God to cultivate those character qualities in you.

Chapter 23

The Four Finals in Paul's Closing Remarks

Colossians 4:15-18

We have come to the end of our journey through Paul's epistle to the Colossians. Perhaps some of you feel like children often do when the pastor gets up to speak—that the end is the best part of the sermon because it means it's over! I'm going to trust that is not how you feel, but if you do, then you can rejoice because the end is indeed here.

As I considered the ending of this study of Colossians, I began to think about endings, particularly endings in the Bible. So many stories in the Bible have good endings, and, of course, there are also Bible stories that do not have such good endings. The story of Ruth has a great ending: she marries righteous Boaz, bears a son named Obed, and ends up in the genealogy of our Lord Jesus Christ. Esther, too, has a beautiful Bible story with an encouraging ending: she becomes queen and is used by God to save her people. But, as we've already said, not all the stories in the Bible have good endings. I think of Jonah: a guy who rebels against God, gets swallowed by a whale, repents, and then gets vomited out by that whale. He gets a second chance to obey the Lord, and this time he does, but then he pouts and gets angry when God doesn't zap the city of Nineveh—not such a great ending. One of the saddest endings of any story in the Bible, to me, is in Acts 5, when Ananias and Sapphira, husband and wife, agree together to lie and they're both struck dead by God—that is a terrible and sobering ending!

We've come to the end, not of a Bible story, but of a Bible letter, the letter to the church at Colossae written by the apostle Paul while he was in prison. Does it have a happy or a sad ending? Let's read the last few verses to answer that question.

Colossians 4:15-18

> Greet the brethren who are in Laodicea, and Nymphas and the church that is in his house.[16]Now when this epistle is read among you, see that it is read also in the church of the Laodiceans, and that you likewise read the epistle from Laodicea. [17]And say to Archippus, "Take heed to the ministry which you have received in the Lord, that you may fulfill it."[18]This salutation by my own hand—Paul. Remember my chains. Grace be with you. Amen.

As I considered Paul's final words to the church at Colossae, I noticed that he ended with four final things. Those four final things will form our outline for this last lesson:

> *Paul's Final Greeting* (v 15)
> *Paul's Final Admonition* (v 16)
> *Paul's Final Warning* (v 17)
> *Paul's Final Prayer Request* (v 18)

Paul's Final Greeting

Colossians 4:15

> Greet the brethren who are in Laodicea, and Nymphas and the church that is in his house. (Colossians 4:15)

Though Paul had never been to *Laodicea*, his love and concern for them compelled him to *greet the brethren*, or the church, there. This is what he does, and he does so though an individual named *Nymphas*. The name Nymphas comes from two Greek words meaning a young married woman and a sacrifice. The personal pronoun is in the feminine gender, which indicates that Nymphas is actually a woman. The reason that a female is mentioned here instead of a male is probably because she was either a single woman or a widow. If she were married, she would have been under her husband's legal authority and name, and because of that it is likely that Paul would have mentioned her husband's name and not hers. Evidently, Nymphas used her home as a place of meeting for the church. I've been there and done that many times! And I can identify with her and with the challenges and the blessings of having church in one's house! Nymphas was probably a wealthy woman as well, since in most cases only larger homes would be able to accommodate a gathering of believers for worship. Many early churches met in homes, since there were no official church buildings in which to meet. Christians would usually meet inside the home, in a courtyard, or on the roof of someone's house, if it was a large enough house to accommodate a group. This is both an encouragement and a challenge for you single ladies out there. Just because you are widowed, divorced, or have never been married does not mean that your service to God is any less important than those who are married. In fact, Paul says in 1 Corinthians 7:34 that you actually have an advantage over the woman who is married. Listen to what he writes there: "There is a difference between a wife and a virgin. The unmarried woman cares about the things of the Lord, that she may be holy both in body and in spirit. But she who is married cares about the things of the world—how she may please her husband." For those of you who are not married, you have the advantage of being able to give your total time and energy to your Lord, and using your home to be hospitable is certainly an excellent way to honor and glorify Him. And we all should be using our homes as a means of being hospitable, whether we are single or married! Paul now moves from his final greeting to his final admonition in verse 16.

Paul's Final Admonition

Colossians 4:16

> Now when this epistle is read among you, see that it is read also in the church of the Laodiceans, and that you likewise read the epistle from Laodicea. (Colossians 4:16)

Paul admonishes the Colossian believers to make sure that *this epistle is read* not only to their own church in Colossae but *also in the church of the Laodiceans*. And he adds that the Colossians are to *read the epistle from Laodicea.* An *epistle* is a written message or a letter, which is what these four chapters are that we've been studying! This is the third time Paul has mentioned *Laodicea* in this letter. We saw the city mentioned back in 2:1 and in 4:13, and now we see it here again. In chapter two, Paul mentioned that he was in great distress over the Laodiceans; in chapter four, he mentioned that Ephaphras was also concerned for the Laodiceans, being fervent in his prayers for them. So why did Paul want the epistle to the Colossians read to the church of the Laodiceans? More than likely, Paul wanted it read to them because they too were in danger of getting caught up in Gnostic heresy, and it may have infiltrated the church there, as well. Laodicea was geographically close to Colossae, and the saints in Colossae who were getting caught up in the nonsense of Gnosticism could have been influencing their brethren at Laodicea. When you look over the Questions to Consider that accompany this lesson, you will note that the church at Laodicea received a very sobering warning in Revelation 3. Perhaps the Holy Spirit who inspired Paul to write Colossians also prompted him to be concerned that this church was also in trouble. In Revelation 3, the Laodicean church is the only church that Christ does not commend for anything, yet He commends each of the other six churches He addresses. In His address to the Laodiceans, Jesus describes them as wretched, miserable, poor, blind, and naked. They had become nauseating to God because they had become lukewarm, so much so that God told them He wanted to spew them out of His mouth! And the believers in Laodicea would have known exactly what God meant, because their water supply came from Hierapolis, a few miles north, and was piped down to them. By the time it reached their city it was lukewarm. Sadly, one man writes that, "The threatening expressed in Revelation 3:10 has been fulfilled, and Laodicea is but a name. In the midst of one of the finest plains of Asia Minor, it is entirely without habitant."[83]

It might sound odd to us that these epistles were to be read aloud to these churches, but this was the practice in the early church. The

---

83 Albert Barnes, *Barnes' Notes on the New Testament (Grand Rapids: Baker Book House, 1983), 287.*

church would gather together, and the pastor would read Paul's letter to those who were assembled. Unfortunately, in our fast-paced, sound-bite, gotta-have-it-now society, we haven't trained ourselves to listen to the Word of God being read for long periods of time. Yet, even in 1 Thessalonians 5:27, Paul writes, "I charge you by the Lord that this epistle be read to all the holy brethren." We must remember that believers in the early church did not have personal copies of the written Word and, therefore, were dependent on it being read to them. That would probably present a challenge for many of us; we get restless when just a few verses are read. But if you didn't have a copy of the written Word, you would be much more intent on listening, especially if that was your only means of Bible intake. They probably hung on every word, trying to meditate on it and hide it in their hearts and minds.

Paul not only wants the epistle to the Colossians read aloud, but he also writes that he wants the Colossians to read the epistle from Laodicea. Now you might be wondering what *the epistle from Laodicea* is. I really don't know what it is, but I will tell you the six possibilities I've come across. It could be:

1. A letter written by the Laodiceans.

2. A letter written by Paul while he was in the city of Laodicea, which may have been Galatians, 1 Timothy, or 1 or 2 Thessalonians.

3. A letter written by Paul to Philemon.

4. The letter to the Laodiceans which today is known as the "Apocryphal Epistle to the Laodiceans."

5. The epistle of Paul to the Ephesians. (This one gets the most votes by the scholars, because most of Paul's letters were circulatory, that is, after they were read in one place, they would be taken to another church in another location and be read there. It is supposed that the letter to

the Ephesians was at the Laodicean church and when the church at Colossae received it, it was read to them).

6. It was a genuine letter of Paul addressed to the Laodiceans, but which is now lost. I certainly wouldn't make an issue of which of these possibilities is correct, nor do I think we should make an issue of it. But we can make an issue of the fact that Paul's final admonition to the Colossian church is for them to be sure that both epistles, the epistle addressed to the Colossians and the epistle from Laodicea, are read in both of these churches.

We now consider Paul's final warning in verse 17. Paul already warned the church about the danger of Gnosticism in chapter two, and he warned them about sin in chapter three; here, in chapter four, he singles out one individual to warn. This man is named Archippus.

Paul's Final Warning

Colossians 4:17

> And say to Archippus, "Take heed to the ministry which you have received in the Lord, that you may fulfill it." (Colossians 4:17)

Paul tells the church at Colossae to *say to Archippus* that he should give heed to his ministry. Now, who is *Archippus*, and why does Paul warn him? Archippus is mentioned here and in Philemon 1:2, where Paul writes: "to the beloved Apphia, Archippus our fellow soldier, and to the church in your house." The only things Paul mentions in his epistle to Philemon are that Archippus is a fellow soldier, he had a wife named Apphia, and together they had a church meeting in their house. Archippus means "horse-ruler," for those of you who like meanings to names. He was a member of the family of Philemon and was probably Philemon's son. He evidently lived in Colossae, and the church gathered in his home for worship.

Why does Paul admonish him to *take heed to the ministry* and to *fulfill it*? It has been suggested that Paul admonishes Archippus because he was ministering at the church at Colossae, possibly in Epaphras' absence, and needed to be faithful while Epaphras was away. Another suggestion, however, is that Archippus pastored the church at Laodicea, that was just mentioned in verse 16, and needed to be admonished to hang in there and not give up. A lukewarm church can be very difficult to minister to, and it would take a strong man to endure such a task. When we consider Christ's warning to the Laodiceans in Revelation, we can understand why Archippus would need this admonition.

You might also be wondering why Paul doesn't write Archippus a personal letter to warn him. Why does Paul do it publicly? Aren't we supposed to go to our brother in private when we have something against him? It has been suggested that Archippus was young, like Timothy, and may have needed the admonishment. Remember, Paul admonished Timothy publicly in a similar way, in 2 Timothy 4:5, which says, "But you be watchful in all things, endure afflictions, do the work of an evangelist, fulfill your ministry." And in 1 Timothy 5:20, we read that elders who sin before all are to be rebuked before all, so that others will fear. A public admonishment would allow the church to support Paul's concern and make sure there was some accountability both for the church and for Archippus. This would secure accountability for Archippus and for the whole church because they would all hear this being read. Granted, such an admonition may have produced a little personal embarrassment and humiliation. I personally would be embarrassed if my pastor read a letter by a respected minister, which said, "Tell Susan to shape up or ship out." (My paraphrase, of course!) Now, I want to be clear that these are all suggestions, and the Word of God is not clear about the meaning of this admonition, so we must be careful we don't attempt to turn our opinion of it into fact. I am certain Paul had a good reason for including it, and if we are really curious, we can find out when we get to glory.

Paul does admonish Archippus, however, and this is certain. The first part of the admonishment is for him *to take heed to the ministry. Take heed* means to regard something, to take a look at it. And notice that the ministry he is to take a good look at is one that he *received in the Lord.* It originated in the Lord; it was divinely given and should be treated as such. My friend, when the Lord gives us a ministry, we should give it high consideration and it should not be taken lightly. It is from the Lord God, who gifts His children for His glory. Every task God gives us should be taken with sincerity and with faithfulness. It is a grief to me to see women who have wonderful gifts use them haphazardly, and because of that do not have a reputation of being dependable.

Paul not only admonishes Archippus to take heed to his ministry but also admonishes him to *fulfill it,* which means to complete it. Ministry is a life-long job. Not long ago, someone asked my husband when he was going to retire, and he responded by saying that pastors don't retire. God's children use their God-given gifts until God takes them home! It's a life-time job. It appears that Archippus may not have been completing or fulfilling his work, and Paul would have been concerned for him, as well as for the church who would suffer under such weak leadership. The New English Bible renders this verse like this: "God called you into his service—oh, do not fail him." Perhaps Paul suspected that Archippus might forsake the ministry in the same way Demas would soon forsake the Lord. Also, remember that the church was getting caught up in heresy, and with pastor Epaphras away they needed a strong man to carry on the work of the Lord who would be unwavering in the Christian doctrines. Weak leadership makes for a weak and vulnerable church.

Archippus isn't the only one Paul admonishes in this way. Consider what Paul tells Timothy in 1 Timothy 4:14-16: "Do not neglect the gift that is in you, which was given to you by prophecy with the laying on of the hands of the eldership. Meditate on these things; give yourself entirely to them, that your progress may be evident to all. Take heed to yourself and to the doctrine. Continue in them, for in doing this you will save both yourself and those who hear you." And in 2 Timothy 1:6, Paul writes to Timothy, "Therefore I remind you to stir up the gift of God which is in you through the laying on of my hands." In 2 Timothy 4:5, again he warns Timothy, "But you be watchful in all things, endure afflictions, do the work of an evangelist, fulfill your ministry." In Acts 20:28, Paul even warns the elders at Ephesus, "Therefore take heed to yourselves and to all the flock, among which the Holy Spirit has made you overseers, to shepherd the church of God which He purchased with His own blood." In that address to the Ephesian elders, Paul makes it crystal clear that after his departure some of those elders would defect from the faith. Ladies, we must heed this admonishment in our own lives: to fulfill what God has called us to do and to do it with excellence. Paul has already admonished us that whatever we do we are to do it heartily, as unto the Lord (Colossians 3:23). When God calls you to a task, He expects you to fulfill it and not to do a half-hearted job. One of the things I have noticed in ministry, and it can be discouraging, is that people start out a task with a lot of gusto, but few complete it with the same enthusiasm. I have also noticed this over many years of being involved in women's Bible studies; the class always starts out with a certain number of ladies who are quite enthusiastic, but we always end with fewer ladies with less enthusiasm. And I've noticed that it doesn't matter what the study is about or who's teaching it. But Galatians 6:9 says, "And let us not grow weary while doing good, for in due season we shall reap if we do not lose heart." And 1 Corinthians 15:58 encourages those who are perhaps tempted to drop out of any ministry they're involved in: "Therefore, my beloved brethren, be steadfast, immovable, always abounding in the work of the Lord, knowing that your labor is not in vain in the Lord."

We can learn two principles here from Paul's words to Archippus: First, we should take heed to the ministry God has given us, not taking it lightly; and, second, we must complete it. Now, as Paul closes this wonderful epistle, we come to Paul's final prayer request in verse 18. If you will recall, he has already asked them to pray for him in chapter 4, verses 3 and 4.

Paul's Final Prayer Request

Colossians 4:18

This salutation by my own hand—Paul. Remember my chains.
Grace be with you. Amen. (Colossians 4:18)

Paul writes that *this salutation* is *by my own hand*. It was Paul's custom to dictate his letters. We have an example of this in Romans 16:22, where we read, "I, Tertius, who wrote this epistle, greet you in the Lord." Paul would dictate his letters to an amanuensis and then sign them himself so that his readers would know that the letter they were receiving was truly from Paul. His use of an amanuensis is most likely related to an eye disease. When God saved Paul on the Damascus Road, he was blinded for three days, and some scholars think that experience left him with some kind of permanent eye problem. There are a few other places in Paul's letters where Paul indicates this pattern of using dictation for the body of his letters and then signing them himself. In 1 Corinthians 16:21, he writes, "The salutation with my own hand—Paul's." And in 2 Thessalonians 3:17, he says, "The salutation of Paul with my own hand, which is a sign in every epistle; so I write." It appears, though, that he wrote Philemon with his own hands, as he writes in Philemon 1:19, "I, Paul, am writing with my own hand. I will repay—not to mention to you that you owe me even your own self besides." And Galatians was clearly written by Paul himself, because he writes in Galatians 6:11, "See with what large letters I have written to you with my own hand!"

Finally, Paul leaves the Colossians with his final prayer request, asking them to *remember my chains*. He's already mentioned his imprisonment in Colossians 4:3 and 4:10. I don't think Paul mentions this one last time so that they will feel sorry for him, but rather, so that they would remember to pray for him, and to remind them that it was for the sake of the gospel that he was in prison. Think about that: Paul isn't too proud to ask his friends to remember him in prayer. We need to remember that the apostle Paul was chained to a guard in prison 24 hours a day, and yet his heart was still burdened for this church and for so many others. We must make sure we don't become calloused toward those who are suffering for the cause of Christ; we are to weep with those who weep. In fact, Paul takes this a step further in Hebrews 13:3 when he says, "Remember the prisoners as if chained with them—those who are mistreated—since you yourselves are in the body also." We are to have compassion for these believers, putting ourselves in their shoes, so to speak. As 1 Corinthians 12:26 says, when one member suffers, we also suffer. Perhaps you don't know anyone who is in prison for the sake of the gospel, but you do have brothers and sisters in foreign countries who are being persecuted and even killed for their faith in Christ Jesus. We need to remember them and pray for them.

We would do well to remind ourselves of the very sobering message of Matthew 25:31-46.

> When the Son of Man comes in His glory, and all the holy angels with Him, then He will sit on the throne of His glory. All the nations will be gathered before Him, and He will separate them one from another, as a shepherd divides his sheep from the goats. And He will set the sheep on His right hand, but the goats on the left. Then the King will say to those on His right hand, "Come, you blessed of My Father, inherit the kingdom prepared for you from the foundation of the world: for I was hungry and you gave Me food; I was thirsty and you gave Me drink; I was a stranger and you took Me in; I was naked and you clothed Me; I was sick and you visited Me; I was in prison and you came to Me." Then the righteous will answer Him, saying, "Lord, when did we see You hungry and feed You, or thirsty and give You drink? When did we see You a stranger and take You in, or naked and clothe You? Or when did we see You sick, or in prison, and come to You?" And the King will answer and say to them, "Assuredly, I say to you, inasmuch as you did it to one of the least of these My brethren, you did it to Me." Then He will also say to those on the left hand, "Depart from Me, you cursed, into the everlasting fire prepared for the devil and his angels: for I was hungry and you gave Me no food; I was thirsty and you gave Me no drink; I was a stranger and you did not take Me in, naked and you did not clothe Me, sick and in prison and you did not visit Me." Then they also will answer Him, saying, "Lord,

when did we see You hungry or thirsty or a stranger or naked or sick or in prison, and did not minister to You?" Then He will answer them, saying, "Assuredly, I say to you, inasmuch as you did not do it to one of the least of these, you did not do it to Me." And these will go away into everlasting punishment, but the righteous into eternal life.

Jesus will judge his true children by whether they have demonstrated compassion toward those who are in prison, those who need food and water and clothing, and those who are sick.

Paul ends his letter with the way he ends all his letters: *Grace be with you. Amen.* He also ends this letter the same way he began it in Colossians 1:2, with the words *grace be with you,* God's unmerited favor be with you. Perhaps Paul ends all his letters this way as a reminder that except for God's grace none of us would be redeemed; salvation is and will always be of God and God alone. Perhaps it was Paul's intent to remind the Colossians—and us—not to fall into heresy. What does *Amen* mean? It means surely, so be it. And so, we end our journey through this little epistle.

Summary

Now that you've had some time to think about it, do you think the epistle to the Colossians has a good ending or a bad ending? I personally love the ending; Paul has a greeting, an admonition, a warning, and a prayer request. He ends on a spiritual note, making sure his final words are for the glory of God and a fulfillment of his calling. Paul's ending is an example to us in how to end well with an emphasis on the spiritual. Paul ended well, he wanted the church at Colossae to end well, and I would love for you to end well.

With that in mind, recall from our first lesson how I mentioned to you that we would be taking a journey together through this short epistle. Our journey has now ended, just as Paul's letter has ended. It is my earnest desire that your journey has ended well and that it was a journey worth your time and effort. Take a brief mental journey with me now by asking yourself some questions to see if you have also ended well.

As you consider chapter one: Do you now have a richer prayer life as a result of looking more closely at Paul's prayer? From gazing at Christ's preeminence, do you now have a greater appreciation and admiration for who He is?

From chapter two: Are you holding onto any form of legalism, mysticism, asceticism, or any forms of tradition? Do you now have a deeper understanding of Gnosticism and the danger it poses, not only in our lives personally, but also in our churches today? Are you in earnest prayer over the false teaching that is going on and are you speaking boldly to those you know who are caught up in it?

From what you learned in chapter three: Have you grown such that your affections are set more on the things above and less on things of this earth? Are you endeavoring to put off all sin and to put on each characteristic of Christlikeness? If you have a husband, are you practicing and enjoying submission to him? Are you disciplining your children in love and not provoking them? (And of course, I hope your husband is loving you the way Christ loves His church!)

From chapter four: Are you speaking more boldly to others about Christ and equipping yourself to be more effective in sharing the gospel? And last but not least, are you learning how to be a better friend and helper to others in ministry, and ministering more effectively yourself?

Did you end your journey well? That is a question only you and the Lord can answer. Only God knows the real change that has taken place in your life this year as the result of our brief journey together. But my prayer is that you have inched one more step toward Christ's likeness and that you will keep traveling upward and onward until you reach your final journey home! Then and finally then, you and I will be with our Master forever, and we will need nothing else!

Questions to Consider

Colossians 4:15-18
The Four Finals in Paul's Closing Remarks

1. (a) Read each chapter of Colossians and write down at least one truth you have learned *or* one change you have made from *each* chapter. (b) Look back at question 7 from lesson one to see how God answered your prayer for change.

2. Memorize Colossians 4:18.

3. In Colossians 4:15, Paul mentions Nymphas having church in her house. According to the following passages, who else had church in their house, and (if it is mentioned) what were they doing in church? Acts 12:12; 16:40; 28:30-31; Romans 16:3-5; 1 Corinthians 16:19; and Philemon 1:2.

4. (a) How many times does Paul mention the church at Laodicea in his letter to the Colossians? Write down each verse reference. (b) From Revelation 3:14-19, what else to you learn about this church?

5. Look at the ending of all of Paul's letters: Romans, 1 and 2 Corinthians, Galatians, Ephesians, Philippians, Colossians, 1 and 2 Thessalonians, 1 and 2 Timothy, Titus, Philemon, and Hebrews (if you think Paul wrote it). What do they all have in common? (You should find at least two commonalities.)

6. In Colossians 4:17, Paul admonishes Archippus to complete the work that God has given him to do. Looking at Numbers 20:7-13; 1 Samuel 15; John 17:4; and 2 Timothy 4:6-8, answer the following questions: (a) Who completed what God had given them to do, and who did not? (b) What were the blessings for those who completed what God had given them to do? (c) What was the result for those who did not complete what God had given them to do? (d) What do you learn about the importance of completing what God has called you to do?

7. (a) Do you know what your spiritual gifts are? (b) Are you sharpening them and using them for the glory of God?

8. (a) What ministries are you involved in? (b) Do you take those ministries seriously and are you faithful to them?

9. As we end our study in Colossians, what is the desire of your heart? Write it down as a prayer request to share.

About the Author

Susan Heck has been involved in Women's Ministries for over 30 years. This includes teaching Bible Studies, counseling, and leading Ladies with the Master women's ministry at Grace Community Church in Tulsa, Oklahoma. (www.gccoftulsa.net)

Susan is a certified counselor with the Association of Certified Biblical Counselors (ACBC, formerly NANC). She is the author of "With The Master" Bible Study Series for women. Previously published books in that series are,

*   With the Master Shepherding the Sheep:
    A Ladies' Bible Study of the 1 Timothy

*   With the Master on the Mount:
    A Ladies' Bible Study of the Sermon on the Mount

*   With the Master in the School of Tested Faith:
    A Ladies' Bible Study of the Epistle of James

*   With the Master in Heavenly Places:
    A Ladies' Bible Study on Ephesians

*   With the Master on our Knees:
    A Ladies' Bible Study on Prayer

*   With the Master in Fullness of Joy:
    A Ladies' Bible Study on the Book of Phillipians

*   With the Master Before the Mirror of God's Word:
    A Ladies' Bible Study on First John

She is also the author of five published booklets:
*   Putting Off Life Dominating Sins
*   A Call to Scripture Memory
*   A Call to Discipleship
*   Assurance: Twenty Tests for God's Children
*   The Liberating Gospel: A Call to Salvation

Susan's teaching ministry is an outgrowth of her memorization work on the Bible. She has personally memorized 23 books of the New Testament word-for-word (The Gospel of Matthew, The Gospel of John, Romans, Second Corinthians, Galatians, Ephesians, Philippians, Colossians, First and Second Thessalonians, First and Second Timothy, Titus, Philemon, Hebrews, James, First and Second Peter, and First, Second, and Third John, Jude, Revelation), one book of the Old Testament (Jonah), and several other portions of Scripture.

Susan has two grown children and seven grandchildren. Both children and their spouses are in full-time ministry. Because of the enthusiasm of ladies who attended Susan's Bible studies, she has been invited to speak to ladies' groups both nationally and internationally. (www.withthemaster.org)